CHILDREN'S

S0-ATS-384

MAY 3 1 2001

Is It Really
Mommie Dearest?

Daughter-Mother Narratives in Young Adult Fiction

Hilary S. Crew

The Scarecrow Press, Inc.
Lanham, Maryland, and London
2000

SCARECROW PRESS, INC.

Published in the United States of America
by Scarecrow Press, Inc.
4720 Boston Way, Lanham, Maryland 20706
http://www.scarecrowpress.com

4 Pleydell Gardens, Folkestone
Kent CT20 2DN, England

Copyright © 2000 by Hilary S. Crew

Based on a dissertation submitted to the Graduate-School-New Brunswick
Rutgers, The State University of New Jersey, in partial fulfillment of the
requirements for the degree of Doctor of Philosophy, Communication,
Information, and Library Studies, written under the direction of Professor Kay
E. Vandergrift.

All rights reserved. No part of this publication may be reproduced,
stored in a retrieval system, or transmitted in any form or by any
means, electronic, mechanical, photocopying, recording, or otherwise,
without the prior permission of the publisher.

British Library Cataloguing in Publication Information Available

Library of Congress Cataloging-in-Publication Data

Crew, Hilary S., 1942–
    Is it really Mommie Dearest? : daughter-mother narratives in young adult
fiction / Hilary S. Crew.
        p.   cm.
    Includes bibliographical references and index.
    ISBN 0-8108-3692-0 (cloth : alk. paper)
    1. Young adult fiction, American—History and criticism.   2. Mothers and
daughters in literature.   3. Domestic fiction, American—History and
criticism.   4. Teenage girls in literature.   5. Motherhood in literature.
    I. Title.
PS374.M547 C74   2000
813.009'352042—dc21   99-048315

⊚™ The paper used in this publication meets the minimum requirements of
American National Standard for Information Sciences—Permanence of
Paper for Printed Library Materials, ANSI/NISO Z39.48–1992.
Manufactured in the United States of America.

To the memory of my mother
and the years we shared together as mother and daugher
— and to Brianna.

Contents

v

Acknowledgments

I especially thank Dr. Kay E. Vandergrift, School of Information, Communication and Library Studies, Rutgers University, for her guidance and support, and for sharing with me her love and knowledge for and about young people and their literature. Special thanks must go to another academic mother, Jane Anne Hannigan, who was always ready to talk "daughters and mothers" and who, with Kay, introduced me to the joy of research and writing. I thank Dr. Lea Stewart and Dr. Stan Deetz for their insightful comments and encouragement. I thank, too, the many friends who have helped and supported me. I thank Anne Meany, director of Bernards Township Library, and Bonnie Kunzel, teen specialist at Princeton Public Library, for suggesting young adult books and books about mothers and daughters that I might include. I thank the staffs of Bernardsville Public Library and Bernards Township Library who have been so helpful in locating and obtaining books for me through interlibrary loan. A special thank you is due to Maud Thiebaud for reading the manuscript and for her helpful comments. I thank Erin Kleindorfer for her translation of *Rapunzel* by Fredrich Schulz.

I am grateful to my family—my husband, Michael; my daughter, Sarah; and my son, Nicholas—for their forebearance and support while I was writing and conducting the research for this book. I also thank my sister, Jocelyn, who has unfailingly cheered me on in our weekly telephone calls across the Atlantic. I have written about daughters and mothers; as a daughter and mother—and now also as a grandmother—I know that I have been blessed in my personal life.

The author gratefully acknowledges permission to quote from:

Amazing Gracie by A. E. Cannon, © 1991 by A. E. Cannon. Used by permission Doubleday, a division of Bantam Doubleday Dell Publishing

Group, Inc. *Author! Author!* by Susan Terris. Copyright © 1990 by Susan Terris. Reprinted by permission of Farrar, Straus & Giroux, Inc. *Camilla* by Madeleine L'Engle. Copyright © 1965 by Crosswicks Ltd. Used by permission of Dell Publishing, a division of Random House, Inc. Excerpts from *Cattail Moon* by Jean Thesman. Copyright © 1994 by Jean Thesman. Reprinted by permission of Houghton Mifflin Company. All rights reserved. *Claudia, Where Are You?* © 1969 by Hila Colman. Used by permission of William Morrow, division of Lothrop, Lee & Shepard Books. *Crazy Quilt* by Jocelyn Riley. © 1984 by Jocelyn Riley. Used with permission of William Morrow, division of Lothrop, Lee & Shepard Books. *The Dear One* by Jacqueline Woodson. Copyright © 1991 by Jacqueline Woodson. Used by permission of Dell Publishing, a division of Random House, Inc. *The Dream of Water* by Kyoko Mori, © 1995 by Kyoko Mori. Reprinted by permission of Henry Holt & Co., Inc. Excerpts from *Echoes of the White Giraffe*. Copyright © 1993 by Sook Nyul Choi. Reprinted by permission of Houghton Mifflin Company. *Exercises of the Heart* by Jan Greenberg. Copyright © 1986 by Jan Greenberg. Reprinted by permission of Farrar, Straus & Giroux, Inc. *Find a Stranger, Say Goodbye* by Lois Lowry. Copyright © 1978 by Lois Lowry. Reprinted by permission of Houghton Mifflin Company. All rights reserved. *A Formal Feeling* by Zibby Oneal. Copyright © 1982 by Zibby Oneal. Used by permission of Viking Penguin, a division of Penguin Putnam Inc. *H., My Name Is Henley* by Colby Rodowsky. Copyright © 1982 by Colby Rodowsky. Reprinted by permission of Farrar, Straus & Giroux, Inc. *Hangin' Out with Cici* by Francine Pascal. Copyright © 1977 by Francine Pascal. Used by permission of Viking Penguin, a division of Penguin Putnam Inc. *Hannah In Between* by Colby Rodowsky. Copyright © 1994 by Colby Rodowsky. Reprinted by permission of Farrar, Straus & Giroux, Inc. *Haveli* by Suzanne Staples, © 1993 by Suzanne Staples. Reprinted by permission of Random House, Inc. *I Hadn't Meant To Tell You This* by Jacqueline Woodson. Copyright © 1994 by Jacqueline Woodson. Used by permission of Random House Children's Books, a division of Random House, Inc. *Julie's Daughter* by Colby Rodowsky. Copyright © 1985 by Colby Rodowsky. Reprinted by permission of Farrar, Straus & Giroux, Inc. *Leave Me Alone, Ma!* by Carol Snyder. Copyright © 1987 by Carol Snyder. Used by permission of Bantam Books, a division of Random House, Inc. *Just Like a Friend* by Marilyn Sachs. Copyright © 1989 by Marilyn Sachs. Used by permission of Dutton Children's Books, a division of Penguin Putnam Inc. *Like Sisters on the Homefront* by Rita Williams-Garcia, © 1995 by Rita Williams-Garcia. Used by permission of Lodestar Books, an affiliate of Dutton Children's Books, a division of

Penguin Putnam, Inc. *The Long Season of Rain* by Helen Kim, © 1996 by Helen Kim. Reprinted by permission of Henry Holt & Co., Inc. *Midnight Encores* by Bruce Brooks, © 1986 by Bruce Brooks. Used by permission of HarperCollins. *My Louisiana Sky* by Kimberly Willis Holt, © 1998 by Kimberly Willis Holt. Reprinted by permission of Henry Holt & Co., Inc. *Notes For Another Life* by Sue Bridgers, © 1981 by Sue Ellen Bridgers. Used by permission of Random House, Inc. *One Bird* by Kyoko Mori, © 1995 by Kyoko Mori. Reprinted by permission of Henry Holt & Co., Inc. *Only My Mouth Is Smiling* by Jocelyn Riley, © 1982 by Jocelyn Riley. Used by permission of William Morrow, division of Lothrop, Lee & Shepard Books. *Over the Water* by Maude Casey, © 1994 by Maude Casey. Reprinted by permission of Henry Holt & Co., Inc. *Pick-Up Sticks* by Sarah Ellis. Copyright © 1992 by Sarah Ellis. Reprinted with the permission of Margaret K. McElderry Books, an imprint of Simon & Schuster Children's Publishing Division. *The Pig-Out Blues* by Jan Greenberg. Copyright © 1982 by Jan Greenberg. Reprinted by permission of Farrar, Straus & Giroux, Inc. Excerpts from *The Rain Catchers* by Jean Thesman. Copyright © 1991 by Jean Thesman. Reprinted by permission of Houghton Mifflin Company. All rights reserved. *The Revolution of Mary Leary* by Susan Shreve, © 1982 by Susan Shreve. Used by permission of Random House, Inc. *Shabanu* by Suzanne Fisher Staples, © 1990 by Suzanne Staples. Reprinted by permission of Random House, Inc. *A Share of Freedom* by June Rae Wood, © 1994 by June Rae Wood. Reprinted by permission of The Putnam & Grosset Group. *Shizuko's Daughter* by Kyoko Mori, © 1993 by Kyoko Mori. Reprinted by permission of Henry Holt and Company, Inc. *The Silver Kiss* by Annette Klause. Copyright © 1990 by Annette Klause. Used by permission of Delacorte Press, a division of Random House, Inc. *Someone's Mother is Missing* by Harry Mazer. Copyright © 1990 by Harry Mazer. Used by permission of Dell Publishing, a division of Random House, Inc. *Star Baby* by Joan Lowery Nixon, © 1989 by Joan Lowery Nixon. Used by permission of Bantam, a division of Bantam, Doubleday, Dell Publishing Group, Inc. *The Star Fisher* by Laurence Yep, © 1991 by Laurence Yep. Used by permission of William Morrow, division of Lothrop, Lee & Shepard Books. *A Star for the Latecomer* by Bonnie and Paul Zindel, © 1980 by Bonnie and Paul Zindel. Used by permission of Harper Collins. *Sweet Whispers, Brother Rush* by Virginia Hamilton, © 1982 by Virginia Hamilton. Reprinted by permission of The Putnam & Grosset Group. *Thief of Hearts* by Laurence Yep, © 1995 by Laurence Yep. Used by permission of HarperCollins. *Thunderwith* by Libby Hathorn, © 1979 by Libby Hathorn. Published by William Heinemann Australia. Reprinted by permission of Hathorn Enterprises. *The Tower Room* by Adele Geras. Copyright © 1990 by Adele Geras, reprinted by permission of Harcourt Brace & Company. *Truly Grim Tales* by Patricia Galloway, © 1995 by Priscilla Galloway. Used by permission of Dell, a division of Bantam, Doubleday, Dell Publishing Group, Inc. *Walk Two Moons* by Sharon Creech, © 1994 by Sharon Creech. Used by permission of HarperCollins. *The Wrong Way Home* by Liza Fosburgh. Copyright © 1990 by Liza Fosburgh. Used by permission of Bantam Books, a division of Random House, Inc. *Zel* by Donna Jo Napoli. Copyright © 1996 by Donna Jo Napoli. Used by permission of Dutton Children's Books, a division of Penguin Books USA Inc.

Introduction

The Daughter–Mother Relationship in Adolescence: A Significant Relationship

We will mark this place as a crossroads in women's development: a meeting between girl and woman, an intersection between psychological health and cultural regeneration, a watershed in women's psychology which affects both women and men.

—Brown and Gilligan

The different experiences of being a daughter and the mother of a daughter have been so much a part of my personal and family life that I did not question or think about the significance of the relationships with my mother or daughter. They just were there—part of my everyday living. The seeds for this book were sown while I was teaching a course on young adult literature. There were comments from members of the class that some of the stories that they were reading about teen daughters and their mothers did not accord with the relationships they enjoyed or had experienced with their own mothers during adolescence. Their personal responses were congruent to comments made in articles about how the daughter–mother relationship *as* a relationship seemed to be absent or not fully developed as a topic in young adult novels.

The serious treatment of this relationship, Lou Stanek wrote in 1975, was one of the "literary gaps" in literature. She hoped that this would change in the literature that was emerging for adolescents—particularly through the agency of women writers who had daughters (236). Yet in the 1990s, it was still noted that there was a lack of young adult novels that dealt meaningfully with the relationships between daughters and mothers and that a mother's physical and emotional absence was a frequent element of story.[1]

1

An obvious question, of course, is why a relationship that is so significant in girls' and women's lives has been perceived as a gap—an absence—in contemporary young adult literature. The most frequent explanation is that there is less emphasis on telling stories about relationships between young people and parents in young adult novels because of the literary convention of absenting parents. Stories portray teen protagonists who prove that they can be independent and responsible; they are thus represented as good role models for a youthful audience. This convention of story is congruent with an understanding of adolescence as a time when young people are engaged in conflict with their parents as they seek to become more independent—a perception of adolescence that has been generally reproduced in contemporary novels depicting American youth.[2] The lack of emphasis that has been placed on the importance of the daughter–mother relationship would thus seem symptomatic of a more general cultural valuing of independence that has been perceived as a breaking away of dependency on parents—the story of adolescence that has been dominant in male coming-of-age stories.[3]

One year after Stanek had written about the absence of mother–daughter literary models in women's literature, Adrienne Rich's ground-breaking work, *Of Woman Born: Motherhood as Experience and Institution,* was published in which Rich made her oft-quoted statement that the "cathexis between mother and daughter—essential, distorted, misused—is the great unwritten story." In writing to understand her own relationship with her mother, Rich explored not only her own feelings but also how the mother–daughter relationship has been socially constructed under patriarchy. She wrote that the relationship that she perceived as so important to her emotional life had been "minimized and trivialized" in discourses of art, sociology, and psychology. The relationship between a mother and her daughter is no longer an unwritten story. Since Rich's work, feminists have been giving voice to the significance of the mother–daughter relationship. The diverse experiences of this relationship have been documented in feminist studies in many disciplines as well as in biographies, letters, essays, poetry, fiction, film, and television sitcoms.

It has taken a while for feminists to catch up with their daughters. If anything, the relationship between teen girls and their mothers has been perceived as even more conflict-ridden and *non*significant than the relationships between adult mothers and daughters that has been the focus of attention in feminist studies. During the last decade, however, the story of the relationship between teen girls and their mothers has been addressed and re-visioned in the context of feminist studies on female adolescence.

Terri Apter's study of mothers and teen daughters in *Altered Loves: Mothers and Daughters During Adolescence* and studies by Carol Gilligan and others under the auspices of the Harvard Project on Women's Psychology and Girls' Development have been central to the formation of a new social construction of female adolescence. Mary Pipher's *Reviving Ophelia: Saving the Lives of Adolescent Girls* and Peggy Orenstein's research in *SchoolGirls: Young Women, Self Esteem, and the Confidence Gap* have also drawn attention to girls' coming-of-age in American society particularly addressing issues such as loss of esteem and the way girls are placed at risk in a society that has been labeled sexist and violent.[4]

In this new discourse on female adolescent development, girls are said to be at a "watershed in female development" and in "danger of drowning or disappearing" (Gilligan Preface 10).[5] At a time when issues of independence and individuation are said to be foremost, Gilligan and her colleagues have particularly centered on the way girls lose voice as they disconnect themselves from relationships. Girls are said to disassociate from what they really feel and know as they come up against "a wall of shoulds in which approval is associated with their silence, love with selflessness, relationship with lack of conflict" (Brown and Gilligan 97). In a male-centered culture, girls are said to feel pressured to take themselves out of relationship with girls and women (Brown and Gilligan 216). The relationships between teenage girls and their mothers are thus situated at the crux of that crossroads that girls are said to reach during adolescence.

BACKGROUND TO THE STUDY OF THE DAUGHTER–MOTHER RELATIONSHIP

The relationship between an adolescent daughter and her mother has been perceived as fraught with difficulties since Sigmund Freud's pronouncements on the necessity of girls loosening their attachment to their mothers and on the inevitable accompanying anger and hostility as girls do so (Femininity 121). A daughter's continued attachment to her mother was described in terms of regression; it was a bond to be severed.[6] Freudian adolescent psychology perpetuated this description and explanation of daughter–mother relationships together with the gender bias deeply entrenched in Freudian psychoanalytical narratives. In *Mother Daughter Revolution: From Betrayal to Power*, Elizabeth Debold, Marie Wilson, and Idelisse Malave refer to the myths of female development that tell us that adolescence is a time when daughters struggle to become separate from their mothers, a time when daughters do not listen to their mothers or like them, and a time when girls may be hating their mothers or otherwise they may have "serious problems" (29).

In re-visioning the relationship between teenage girls and their mothers, feminists have primarily drawn from feminist theories of difference which argue that explanations of human development have emphasized and valued male rather than female patterns of development. Jean Baker Miller's *Toward a New Psychology of Women* drew attention to the way women have made connections and relationships central to their lives and to the way these qualities have been devalued in a culture that has placed value on independence and autonomy. In her seminal work, *In a Different Voice: Psychological Theory and Women's Development*, Gilligan argues that girls' development is viewed as "problematic because of the continuity of relationships in their lives" (39). Young people's perceived failure to adhere to a model of development that is premised on separation and individuation is thus viewed as regressive.[7]

In *The Reproduction of Mothering: Psychoanalysis and the Sociology of Gender*, Nancy Chodorow, writing from the theoretical stance of the Object Relations school of psychoanalysis, argues that girls both personally identify with and have a "real relationship" with their mothers from whom they learn their model of femininity—unlike boys who must disidentify with their mothers in order to identify with cultural prescriptions of what it is to be masculine (175–76).[8] Feminists assign value to the attachment and continuity of connections that so often have been de-emphasized in explanations of the relationship between adolescent girls and their mothers. Emphasized in feminist accounts are patterns of development in which young people grow up in relationships with others. In her model of development, for example, Gilligan explains that a concept of development based on interdependence, rather than on a view of development based on independence linked with detachment and separation, is a means of empowering "both the self and the other, not one at the other's expense" (Remapping 14).

In new discourses on female adolescence, the move is being made from discussing the psychological dynamics of the relationship to showing how this relationship is constructed through gender, class, and race in different socioeconomic contexts. The relationship between teenage daughters and their mothers stands at a site of contradiction as girls and mothers both contend with the intertwined issues of power and gender. Mothers are expected to empower their daughters and to resist sexist practices on their behalf when they perhaps have never had that authority or have lost voice to speak for themselves. Daughters expect their mothers to mother and protect them in a culture where mothers have not always had the social and economic means to do so. Following feminist pathways, the personal becomes political as mothers are being called upon to empower their daughters to resist sexist practices and cultural scripts that speak of domination and separation. In *Mother Daughter Revolution*:

> Of all the crossroads in the life of a woman, becoming a mother is one of the most powerful and the most political. Raising a daughter in a society that has been largely constructed by white men and is still, for the most part, run by them and by their desires is a political act. (Debold, Wilson, and Malave 6)

There is an unmasking, in this text, of how adolescent daughters and their mothers have been subordinated through the organization of gender relations in a patriarchal culture. One can make connections between the metaphors of revolution used by Debold and her colleagues and the rhetoric of French feminist Luce Irigaray. Irigaray speaks of the "mother/daughter, daughter/mother relationship" in Western culture as a "highly explosive nucleus. Thinking it, and changing it, is equivalent to shaking the foundations of the patriarchal order" (*Irigaray Reader* 50).

What is certainly revolutionary is that theories of female adolescence are being re-visioned through listening to the voices of girls and young women as they talk about their own experiences of adolescence and their relationships.[9] Authority is thus being granted to the voice of young females to construct their own ways of understanding what it is like to grow up female rather than being subjected to the normalizing discourses of traditional adolescent development.[10] In *Altered Loves*, Apter reports that after listening to the voices of adolescent daughters and their mothers talking about their experiences of the relationship, she came to the conclusion that "a model of adolescent development involving separation and conflict was either inadequate or inappropriate" (14). In studies by Gilligan and others, the voices of daughters from other cultures and from different socioeconomic contexts are gradually infiltrating what was a dominant white Western construction of female adolescence.[11]

For professionals working with young people and literature, the advent of mother–daughter book clubs, in which mothers and girls join together to discuss and share books, acknowledges the attention paid to the relationship between mothers and daughters in feminist writings. The concept of girls and their mothers joining voices in circles of mutual support and enjoyment is an example of the emphasis now being placed on the connections maintained between girls and their mothers. There has also been a noticeable increase in novels for young adults that represent the relationship between an adolescent daughter and her mother from a feminist perspective

Interdisciplinary studies addressing the mother–daughter relationship cross the fields of psychoanalysis, sociology, cultural, and literary studies. The relationship between mothers and daughters has taken a central place in both black and white feminist studies. There have been a number of critical literary studies of the mother–daughter relationship. In *The Mother/ Daughter Plot*, Marianne Hirsch uses insights from feminist psychoanalytical theories to analyze narrative plots of the mother–daughter relationship in nineteenth- and twentieth-century women's writing.[12] *Double-Stitch: Black Women Write About Mothers and Daughters*, edited by Patricia Bell-Scott et al., is an anthology of short stories, poems, and critical essays on the African American mother–daughter relationship—one of several works that provides critical approaches for looking at the black mother–daughter relationship.[13] In *Lives Together/Worlds Apart: Mothers and Daughters in Popular Culture*, Suzanne Danuta Walters looks at how the relationship is re-represented in popular culture, including film and television, from the 1930s and 1990s. There has been an increased interest in looking at how relationships between younger daughters and their mothers are represented in children's and young adult literature.[14]

In this study, I examine how relationships between adolescent girls and their mothers are represented in one hundred young adult novels plus short stories selected from the category of books marketed by publishers for an audience of young adult readers and published between the years 1965-1998.

THE DAUGHTER–MOTHER RELATIONSHIP AND YOUNG ADULT NOVELS

The central characters in young adult novels are teenage daughters and sons working through different kinds of conflicts and relationships in their lives including their relationships with parents. Since the emphasis in the young adult novels in this study is on daughters, I use the term daughter–mother relationship to reflect this bias. I have chosen to identify the young adult novel as a specific generic form in that it is most often written (although this is not always the case) for young people and marketed specifically for teenage readers. Using Anne Cranny-Francis's definition of the term genre to "identify texts that exhibit a special format or formula or set of conventions" (16), the young adult novel can be defined as a generic form that encodes an ideological discourse about adolescence through a number of narrative conventions. Their texts socially construct for a teenage audience the "reality" of what it is like to be an adolescent in a variety of different contexts. The *raison d'être* for adolescent literature is to tell stories "about making the passage from childhood to adulthood" (Donelson and Nilsen 28). Questions of independence, identity formation, and relationships with parents and peers have been identified as central to stories in discussions and evaluations of young adult literature.

In young adult novels, stories tell what it is like to grow up as a female and as a daughter in different sociohistorical and cultural contexts. In the female coming-of-age stories chosen for this study, daughters prove that they are independent and responsible for self. If a daughter is shown to be placed in a marginal position because of gender and socioeconomic circumstances, she is "liberated" in the sense that she gains an inner strength to survive although, she may not, like Shabanu in the desert culture of Cholistan, escape the circumstances in which she is placed (Staples *Shabanu*). Likewise, it cannot be assumed that the presence of daughters and mothers in a text is a liberating text for girls and their mothers. As Kay Vandergrift points out, the presence of girl protagonists in a text— "no matter how feisty or independent"—is not enough to make a text a feminist text (Journey 21).[15] The relationships between girls and their mothers are, in selected novels, produced through a gender-biased discourse. Freudianism continues to inform family romances in contemporary fiction for young people.

Cultural Narratives of the Daughter–Mother Relationship

The recent increase in multicultural materials for children and young adults emphasizes the imperatives of respecting cultural diversity and of being aware of the issues in writing about, discussing, and defining those who are outside the dominant culture.[16] Some of the more plural and feminist representations of the daughter–mother relationship are found in African American novels such Virginia Hamilton's *Sweet Whispers, Brother Rush*, Angela Johnson's *Toning the Sweep*, and Jacqueline Woodson's *The Dear One* and *I Hadn't Meant to Tell You This*. Black feminist critics have written about the inadequacy of employing white, Western theoretical approaches to analyze the black mother–daughter relationship.[17] I have, therefore, addressed African American daughter–mother narratives in a separate chapter. I have also devoted a separate chapter to discussing daughter–mother narratives in novels set in other cultures including Maude Casey's *Over the Water*, Helen Kim's *The Long Season of Rain* and Kyoko Mori's *Shizuko's Daughter* and *One Bird*.

Stories "structure the meanings by which a culture lives" (Cohan and Shires 1). The stories in young adult novels cannot be considered separately from stories in other popular cultural forms and from the attitudes and cultural beliefs that are encoded in them. Young adult novels may be marketed to a potential audience of adolescent readers, reviewed and written about in academic and professional literature as a separate phenomenon, and shelved in special sections of the bookstore and the local library, but they are only one of a plethora of media available for young people. Although I have separated young adult novels out as a medium in which to look at the relationship between teenage girls and their mothers, this is an artificial division. The daughter–mother narrative in young adult novels forms part of a larger discourse on mother–daughter relationships and on mothering. Found in stories about teenage girls and their mothers are descriptions and explanations of the relationship that are also present in fairy tales, adult fiction, and feminist writings—cultural narratives about daughters and mothers.

In Rose Glickman's *Daughters of Feminists,* there is a wonderful anecdote about the author's adolescent daughter dismissing her mother's lectures about feminism: "Lighten up, Mama, lighten up" (xii). As Glickman points out, however, feminist mothers have made enormous gains for their daughters. The daughter–mother narrative in young adult novels, by virtue of its focus on daughters and mothers, raises a range of issues that are highly significant to the lives of young women. These include debates about the responsibilities of mothering, the difficult choices to be made in wanting to both raise a family and have a professional career, abortion versus the right to life, and surrogate motherhood. These are all issues crucially relevant to adolescent daughters who will be making choices and decisions within a climate of moral, political, and societal pressures. Through the voices of daughters and mothers, topics are raised that are pertinent to adolescent daughters relating to sexuality, gender, and body image. From a feminist perspective, the representation of the daughter–mother relationship itself is often problematic in young adult novels. However, issues addressed by feminists and the Women's Movement are frequently used as consciousness raisers in female coming-of-age stories.

A Narrative Analysis of Daughter–Mother Stories in Young Adult Novels

Composing story involves raising questions about what is "felt to be narratable by both literary and social conventions"—about what kinds of stories can be told and how they are to be resolved (DuPlessis 3). In regard to this study, this means looking at what kind of stories can be told about teen girls and their mothers given how this relationship is socially constructed in different racial, ethnic, and socioeconomic contexts. I look at these stories as narrative. Steven Cohan and Linda Shires define narrative as recounting a story. A narrative analysis involves looking at the ways in which stories are mediated by the telling of story (1–2). I examine how the relationships between teenage daughters and mothers are mediated through narrative strategies and conventions used in telling stories in young adult novels paying particular attention to questions of agency and dialogue. In *Lives Together/Worlds Apart*, Walters writes that:

> The themes we take to represent psychological truths about the [mother daughter] relationship need to be seriously and rigorously questioned: they need to be deconstructed to uncover and reveal the ideological agendas inscribed within many common understandings of this relationship (11).

Using this approach, I look at the discourses and cultural scripts that provide us with common-sense ways of talking and thinking about the relationship and unpack some of the language, concepts, and the ideologies embedded within them that are often used in presenting this relationship in fictional texts. I look at how this relationship has been represented in relation to traditional Freudian theories of adolescent development and in relation to feminist theories of the daughter–mother relationship. These include feminist revisions of female adolescence and revisions of the relationship between adolescent daughters and their mothers by Apter, Gilligan, and the Harvard Project on Women's Psychology and Girls' Development, along with the work of feminist theorists from the Object Relations school of psychology and from the French feminist school. I have drawn upon traditional and feminist theories of adolescent development; psychoanalytic and sociological feminist theories of the mother–daughter relationship; writings on mothers and motherhood; and critical literary studies of the daughter–mother relationship in adult and young adult literature.

I chose to examine a fairly large number of novels because it soon became apparent that the daughter–mother narrative in young adult novels is produced through a number of different and conflicting discourses. Young adult texts are complex and multidimensional; there is more than one side of story to be told. Since young adult fiction is replete with teenage daughters whose mothers flit in and out of their lives, I had to develop some overall criteria for the choice of novels. I first delimited my choice of novels by focusing on those novels that featured a female protagonist of twelve to eighteen years of age. After reading widely, it was soon apparent that although a teenage girl and her mother might be present as characters in story, this did not mean that their relationship was treated meaningfully.

The first task was to determine what makes a daughter–mother relationship a significant element of story in a particular novel. The criterion that I finally chose was basic and broad in scope but did work in identifying those texts in which the relationship was treated at some level of depth. The important factor was that the daughter–mother relationship is treated with some degree of self-reflexivity in the sense that a teenage daughter questions what her relationship to her mother means or has meant to her. In novels in which the daughter–mother relationship is treated with significance there is often a generational story of mothers and daughters, in which a teenage daughter's mother, as adult daughter, thinks back to her own relationship as a teenager with her mother. The relationship is significant in a story about a mother's death or absence if this event in story is more than a plot device. Emphasis is placed, for example, on what a mother's loss means to her daughter in Zibby Oneal's *A Formal Feeling*.

Because young adult novels are composed of a number of different discourses and incorporate different themes, in placing emphasis on daughter–mother relationships in texts, I de-emphasize, or sometimes disregard, other elements of story. In reading these novels, young people may well focus on other aspects of these stories; certainly they will construct their own meanings from these texts. In writing about these novels, I chose examples that would best illustrate a particular narrative strategy or a point that I wanted to make.

SUMMARY OF CHAPTERS

In chapter one, it is shown how the voices and relationships of teenage daughters and their mothers are mediated through narrative conventions used in telling story. Chapter two focuses on the fairy tale daughter–mother narrative in re-tellings of Snow White and Rapunzel for young adults. Chapter three demonstrates how a cultural script of adolescent psychology informs stories about daughters and mothers. Chapter four discusses how Freudian romances of family relationships also continue to inform daughter–mother stories. Chapter five examines the ways in which conflict has been made an integral element of fictional accounts of the relationship. Chapter six emphasizes how daughters' expressions of love and need for their mothers are mediated in story. Chapter seven discusses the discourses of mothering through which daughter–mother narratives are produced. The focus in chapter eight is on grandmother–daughter–mother narratives and popular discourses of the mother–daughter relationship. Chapter nine discusses stories of daughters and mothers set in other cultures and cross-cultural contexts. Chapter ten focuses on the African American daughter–mother narrative with a discussion of Nancy Farmer's novel, *A Girl Named Disaster*, which is set in Africa. Chapter eleven addresses feminist narrative strategies of telling story and how they are being used in telling stories about adolescent daughters and their mothers. Some of the implications of this study for those who work with young people and their literature together with suggestions for book discussions are also discussed.

Chapter one addresses a central paradox of the daughter–mother narrative in young adult novels. While it is a literature in which we celebrate the strong voices of daughter protagonists, the conventions of telling story in young adult novels often work toward granting a daughter agency to tell her side of story while suppressing the voice of her mother.

NOTES

1. See Nadeau; Nilsen and Donelson 116.
2. See DeMarr and Bakerman.
3. See Stanek 232; Vandergrift "Journey" 25.
4. See, for example, The American Association of University Women; Bank and Hall; Orenstein; Sadker and Sadker.
5. For criticism of the AAUW Report and research on female adolescents, see Sommers 137-56.
6. See, for example, Deutsch *Selected* 113; Blos *On Adolescence* 66 and "Modifications."
7. For discussion and criticism of Gilligan's work and her reply, see Kerber et al.
8. Chodorow's account of female development and the mother–daughter relationship has been read variously as a positive affirmation of connections and continuity between mothers and daughters or more negatively by those, such as Jane Flax, who see this very continuity as a disadvantage to daughters seeking to establish autonomy. See, for example, Flax "Mother-Daughter Relationships" 20-40.

9. See, for example, S. Rich; Brown and Gilligan.

10. For an extended discussion on the relation between women and girls and voice, power, and authority, see Goldberger et al., eds.

11. See, for example, Taylor, Gilligan, and Sullivan; Ward.

12. See, for example, Davidson and Broner, eds.; Natov.

13. See Collins *Black Feminist Thought: Knowledge, Consciousness, and the Politics of Empowerment* and "The Meaning of Motherhood in Black Culture and Black Mother–Daughter Relationships"; Joseph, "Black Mothers and Daughters: Their Roles and Function in American Society."

14. See, for example, Agee; Erol; Gerlach; Kertzer "Reclaiming"; Nadeau.

15. Vandergrift's "Model of Female Voices in Youth Literature" sets out themes and criteria that are useful in identifying feminist literature for youth, see Vandergrift "Journey" 19; see also Trites.

16. See, for example, Vandergrift "A Feminist Perspective" 354-77.

17. See, for example, Collins *Black*; Joseph *Black Mothers and Daughters: Traditional and New Perspectives* 97.

One

Listening to the Voices of Daughters and Mothers

You probably think I spend a lot of time talking and thinking about my mother
and you're right.

— Pascal

Listening to the voices of daughters and mothers has been a primary activity in feminist research studies that address the development of female adolescents.[1] In talking about their relationships with their mothers, teenage daughters have acknowledged the centrality of this relationship in their lives.[2] Listening to the voices of teenage daughters and their mothers in young adult texts also involves bringing a conscious attention to how interpersonal relationships between daughters and mothers are mediated in story.

Feminists have drawn attention to the potential of children's literature to provide literary experiences for young people in which young protagonists have agency (that is, they are represented as having the potential to take action or exert power) compared to the relative powerlessness of children in their day-to-day lives in contemporary society.[3] The question of voice—an important aspect of feminist studies—is especially crucial in discussing female adolescence. The loss of voice that girls experience as they come of age in a sexist culture has been well documented.[4] Female adolescence is said to be a time of "relational crisis" when girls, afraid to voice their own thoughts and feelings, lose both voice and relationships (Brown and Gilligan 2–3).

It is important then to consider in daughter–mother narratives who is narrating a particular story in a particular time and place and from whose perspective that story is told. This includes noting the racial, social, and cultural contexts in which voices speak. It is also important to note whose voices are absented, whose voices are privileged and have agency, and to see how power relationships between mothers and daughters are negotiated through dialogue. In this chapter, I critique traditional narrative theories for their usefulness in looking at voice and subjectivity in daughter–mother narratives and suggest an alternative model of analysis using terms and concepts extrapolated from poststructuralist narrative theories. The emphasis is on how voice and relationships in daughter–mother narratives are mediated by the narrative strategies of telling story.

TRADITIONAL NARRATIVE THEORIES: CRITICISM AND LIMITATIONS

The questions of who is narrating and speaking, and from what perspective, have usually been confined in analyses of young adult novels to those theoretical models of narrative theories that employ the terms "first-person point of view" or "third-person point of view." These terms are often further defined through determining whether there is an omniscient narrator—one who sees all—or a limited omniscient narrator, defined as a narrator whose perspective is limited to the perspective of one or more characters. Traditional narrative strategies are, however, limited in their usefulness on several accounts. Writers have employed a number of different strategies in telling story that allow events to be seen from more than one subject position in the text. Indeed, one of the trends in literature for youth is an increase in texts that provide multiple viewpoints for a reader by setting up more than one narrating agency in a text. I have identified five main strategies used in mediating story in daughter–mother narratives:

- a first-person character-bound narration of a daughter protagonist.
- texts narrated by an anonymous narrator—traditionally characterized as a third-person narration.
- a split-narrative pattern in which an anonymous narrator shares the telling of story with a daughter who is a first-person character-bound narrator.
- a plural narrative in which different chapters are narrated by an anonymous narrator from the differing viewpoints of more than one character in the text.
- a plural narrative in which story is told by more than one first-person character-bound narrator.

The characterization of narrative strategies of telling story as either first-person or third-person narratives is inadequate for these more complex narrative structures. The employment of traditional narrative analyses tend to mask the way in which dynamics of the daughter–mother relationship are mediated by narrative strategies of telling story. For example:

1) the term "third person narration," as Cohan and Shires point out, is a contradiction in terms since it obscures the narrating agent of story since in grammatical terms a "third person cannot narrate" (92). In this type of narration it is neither the author nor the characters who are the agents responsible for the narration within story. Narration is, rather, as Mieke Bal points out, provided by a "linguistic subject which expresses itself in the language"—not by a person (*Narratology* 119). This function is frequently referred to as an anonymous narrator or as a narrative voice in the text rather than a "third-person." Using only the latter does not enable one to distinguish clearly enough between who is responsible for the point of view being presented in the text. When one picks apart this difference, it is often easier to detect the bias of a narrator's voice in a text that may be over and above bias that is associated with a particular character's viewpoint. One needs, in effect, a narrative method of analysis that allows one to see the position of the narrating agent in relation to the characters in a text in order to determine how the daughter–mother relationship is being presented and how values are being assigned to the different viewpoints of characters.[5]

2) in using the third-person narration we are also encouraged to assume that the "third person"—when functioning as an omniscient narrator—undertakes a unifying function in the text. We need, rather, to be able to articulate how viewpoints—often conflicting—are constantly rearranged between a narrating agent and characters in the text.

3) problems with the limitations of traditional theories of narrative analysis are compounded by the fact that many of the narrative practices that have been employed in telling story in young adult texts *are* formulaic. A reader is often encouraged, especially in a first-person narrative, to identify with one subject position in the text, namely, (in regard to the daughter–mother narrative) a daughter. A reader can thus be potentially aligned with a daughter's particular ideological stance in the text including attitudes toward mothers and practices of mothering.

Unpacking how ideologies and power relationships are constructed through strategies of telling story is important in determining how daughter–mother relationships are represented in texts. The method of analysis outlined below clarifies how the relationships between teenage girls and their mothers are enunciated through the signifying practices in the text. One can discern, for example, when a daughter's or a mother's voice is decentered in a text; and when a mother's subjectivity is not constructed solely through her daughter's narration but is also constituted through other voices from alternative positions in the text.

FOCALIZATION

Narrative theorists Bal, Cohan, Shires, and Seymour Chatman agree that a narrative analysis using the terms first-person and third-person viewpoint obscures the vital difference between a narrator who is telling story and a character who is "seeing" from a position within story—the difference between "who speaks" and "who sees" (Chatman 145). As Cohan and Shires point out: the "narrating agent of a text and its 'point of view' are not the same. Agency raises the question of who supplies the narration, while point of view raises the question of whose vision determines what is being narrated" (94).

These theorists differ, however, in their choice of terms and in the complexity of analyses that they use. I have chosen, therefore, only those terms and levels of analysis (from the work of theorists quoted above) that I perceive as being most useful for the purposes of this study. Bal in *Narratology* and Cohan and Shires use the term "focalization" to refer to the spatial relationship between the agency of narration and the perspective from which story is told. Cohan and Shires define focalization as "a triadic relation formed by the *narrating agent* (who narrates), the *focalizer* (who sees), and the *focalized* (what is being seen and, thus narrated—[which is] in the case of mental life: emotion, cognition, or perception)." Using focalization as a method of analyzing narrative structure allows one to show whether there is similarity and proximity or dissonance and distance constructed between narrating agent, the focalizer, and what is focalized (95).

In applying this analysis to the daughter–mother narrative, the first-person character-bound narration of a teenage daughter taking up the speaking position of "I" is dominant if she maintains this subject position throughout the text. It is her language, attitudes, and viewpoint that are prevalent. Because the reader has access to what the daughter thinks, knows and sees, but only has access to the mother's thoughts and feelings through the daughter's focalization and quoted or paraphrased dialogue, the reader, in principle, will tend to identify with the daughter. In this instance, a mother's subjectivity and the representation of the daughter–mother relationship are primarily mediated through the biased focalization of the daughter.

The focalization within story can also shift from one character to another, so that the reader, positioned differently, can perceive how different characters "view the same facts" (Bal 104–5). A reader may, in the course of a daughter–mother narrative, also be positioned by a narrator to identify with a mother who focalizes her daughter and the daughter–mother relationship from a different position in the text. It is also important to note that secondary focalizations by other characters can produce other perspectives, particularly through directly quoted dialogue. Vandergrift points out, "a great deal of dialogue from a particular character may reveal point of view in addition to or in contrast to that of the narrator" (*Child* 112). A daughter's or a mother's subjectivity is, thus, constructed discursively across a number of different positions in the text. The daughter–mother relationship also may be focalized from a plurality of positions in the text.

Depending on the distance between narrator and characters, on the shift of focalization both from narrator to character, and from characters themselves within story, there is, as Cohan and Shires point out, a "textual movement" in which "narration cannot be centered in a fixed and single point of view or personified by a narrator whose viewpoint is totally responsible for what is said, seen, and shown" (103). The "textual movement" that results from these shifts of perspective and differing positions has the potential to decenter or reinforce the focalization of an adolescent daughter at different points in the text. This point becomes particularly important when determining how much legitimization may be given to the voice and behavior of a mother in the text despite, perhaps, a daughter's criticism.

NARRATION AND AGENCY

The narrator as "narrating subject" is the "agency responsible for the telling of an enunciation"—an anonymous narrator, for example, or a first-person narrator. This narrating subject has a different function than the author of the text, of course, and should also be distinguished from characters who do not have agency. Characters (unless taking up a subject position "I" as narrator) are subjects of narration in that they are signified by the narrating subject (Cohan and Shires 108). In other words, a character is bespoken by the narrator responsible for the narration. These distinctions can be useful in reference to a split narrative in which, for example, a teenage daughter's mother is the *narrated subject* of an anonymous narrator in selected chapters of the text while her daughter takes up first-person narration in the other chapters. In some chapters, therefore, the daughter–mother relationship is focalized by the mother (as main focalizer), although she is not a speaking subject.

This distinction does make a difference. In a review of Hila Colman's *Claudia, Where Are You?* a reviewer, using the accepted practice of first and third narrator distinctions, states: "In alternate chapters, they speak, Claudia in first person, her mother in third" (Sutherland 84). While the split narrative of the text divides the voices of daughter and mother into alternate chapters, Claudia's voice, as strong-daughter protagonist, is dominant as she narrates her own side of story. Her mother's side of the story, narrated anonymously, is thereby given less weight in the text. The mother does not speak in the sense that she is a narrating agent in these alternate chapters, because she does not, as does Claudia, take up an "I" position and narrate her own story. Thus her voice is not accorded as much weight as her daughter's, and her voice and representation as a mother are subject to the bias of the narrator.

The strategy of using an anonymous narrator raises the question of mediation and distancing in the text that depends on the extent to which the narrator's presence is visible or effaced. As Chatman points out, an anonymous narrator very often incorporates in the telling of story attitudes and a set of beliefs toward what is being narrated. Chatman prefers the term "slant" (139–46). A narrator's slant can be revealed through commentary, judgements, and attitudes on and towards the mother, daughter, and the relationship. A narrator does not stand outside a "locus of ideology" (143).

HARMONICS OF RELATIONSHIP

In addition to determining who is speaking in the text and from which place, whose voice is absent, and from which perspective the daughter–mother relationship is focalized or slanted, this study is concerned with the harmonics of their relationship.[6] This involves noting the absences and silences between daughters and mothers and noting the way in which their relationships are constructed through dialogue. It also involves examining the values and assumptions encoded into story through the voice of a narrator and how these affect the harmonics of relationship between a girl and her mother.

The compositional element *tone* has been used to describe how attitudes toward characters and relationship and toward ideas and opinions are produced in the text. As Vandergrift writes: "Literary tone corresponds to tone of voice in spoken language" (*Child* 123). Tone does not usually seem to be considered as part of the theoretical structure in theories of narratology. For example, tone is not mentioned as a separate element by Bal nor by Cohan and Shires. Chatman, however, in using and discussing a narrator's attitudes as slant is, arguably, talking about tone.

Susan Lanser points out that there is need for a "poetics" that goes beyond the usual "formal classifications" particularly in distinguishing between voices in the text. She argues that a theory that would "define and describe *tone* in narrative" would be useful (617). Pointing out that feminist criticism and the "formal poetics" of narratology have usually been regarded as incompatible, Lanser argues that a revised narratology "should be of particular interest to feminist critics because fiction is the dominant genre in the study of women and literature" (614). Lanser's suggestion of an extension of poetics in order to distinguish between different voices in a text through employing the concept of tone may be usefully applied in listening to the harmonics of relationship between mother and daughter.[7]

The following examples are used to demonstrate how narrative strategies mediate relationships between daughters and mothers. In the first example I use excerpts from Marilyn Sachs's novel, *Just Like a Friend,* to demonstrate how narrative strategies are used to mediate a daughter's changing relationship with her mother from a relationship in which their voices are in harmony to a relationship in which their voices are no longer in affinity. At the beginning of the novel, teenage daughter Patti describes the friendly communication between her mother, Vi, and herself: "Vi grabbed me and danced me around the room. Both of us were laughing and talking and acting crazy" (58). A relationship characterized by openness between daughter and mother: "'Sit down! Sit down!' Vi says to her daughter. 'Tell me everything, from the beginning. Don't leave anything out'"— changes to a more closed relationship in which the daughter's voice criticizes her mother (58).

> We went to the Courtyard for dinner, and Vi kept trying to get me to tell her about Dan. I didn't want to tell her about Dan or about anything else. I didn't want to be with her. I looked at her pretty, silly face, and I felt suddenly that I didn't like her. It was scary (109).

Patti and her mother are shown to move from a relationship of harmony to one characterized by disharmony and distance through Patti's judgmental commentary. Patti's mother becomes the disparaged object of discussion (25). The relationship is changed to one of disjunction as Patti no longer communicates her thoughts and feelings to her mother. When one character does not have the "insight into feelings and thoughts" of another character and thus cannot respond to "or oppose them," an "inequality" is reproduced between the characters. "Unspoken words—thoughts, internal monologues—no matter how extensive, are not perceptible to other characters" (Bal 110). The relation between what is said to the mother and what is *not* said to the mother but is directed towards the reader becomes important in determining the attitude towards the mother and, thus, in determining the tone of the relationship.

The following passages from Colman's *Claudia, Where Are You* are used to demonstrate how some of the narrative strategies discussed above work together to construct a relationship of total disharmony between an adolescent daughter and her mother. Colman's narrative is characterized by the use of a split narrative that contributes to the disassociation of a daughter's and mother's voice, and by the effective use of monologue and dialogue so as to privilege a daughter's voice and negate that of a mother. The opacity between daughter and mother is structured in an exchange over college. From the position of first-person character-bound narration, Claudia reports her mother's side of the conversation:

'And where will you be? If you think we're going to send you off to Europe, you're very much mistaken. Your father and I think you should work this summer and earn some money toward your college education. That is, if you get into any college next fall,' she added haughtily.

I smiled. The whole argument was so ridiculous. We were two people discussing trivia when one of us was going to throttle the other. And damn it, I wasn't going to be done in. I wasn't a sweet piece of sweet butter that she was going to pat into one of her fancy molds and serve up with a gleam in her eye for her friends to admire.

'If you want me to go to college, you'd better let me do my homework,' I said calmly. What else could she do, but walk out of the room? (17–18)

In this passage, the daughter shows her attitude towards her mother through the use of the negative tagged word "haughtily" (her interpretation), her choice of language—"throttle"—and by her negative summing up of her mother's motives and behavior. Distance is created between daughter and mother through the use of interior monologue. Claudia's mother may see her daughter's smile but the rest of Claudia's words are unspoken, and her mother is unable to respond to what is *not* said to her.

She only hears Claudia's apparent "smiled" agreement and Claudia's evaluation of how she, herself, speaks is a positive one—"calmly."

The conversational style in which Claudia addresses the reader also constructs a reading position from which to approach the text: "I'm only a kid and 'disturbed' as they say. You know, one of the statistics in the *New York Times* about teenagers who freak out" (1). The tone of her different voice, in conversation with her mother, is thus set up to place more distance between daughter and mother than the voice used to address a potential reader. Readers are potentially invited to identify and sympathize with the dominance of Claudia's voice and her bias against her mother through the extensive use of interior monologue. It is a powerful example of how a daughter's voice is used to distance and disparage a mother as she negates her mother's actions and feelings through her interpretations.

Although her mother is granted a measure of focalization in the text through which both her love for her daughter and the misunderstanding of her daughter are expressed, her story is narrated through the judgmental comments of an anonymous narrator whose slant reinforces Claudia's critical and sarcastic comments against her mother. The narrator's comment that: "Although the realized relationship with her daughter had been far from close for some time, the fact that Claudia was home permitted Mrs. Nichols to indulge in some wishful, gay dreams" conveys how out of touch Claudia's mother is with her daughter (29). Through her narrated monologue, Mrs. Nichols is revealed to be an invasive and vicarious mother as her thoughts revolve around how she may actively plan and be included in Claudia's life. The novel is a powerful exemplar of how narrative and discursive strategies are used to structure alienation between a daughter and her mother. Claudia refers to herself as a "stranger in her own home" (21). Her mother is described as crying out in "frustration and anger" as she feels as though she has "a stranger in the house, which was not what she had dreamed of when her baby daughter had been born" (65). Phrases such as the "veiled blank eyes" used by Claudia more than once to describe the way she looks at her mother and Claudia's comment that her mother never knew about the really important things about her emphasize the utter lack of mutual recognition and understanding that is constructed between an adolescent daughter and her mother. Her mother, narrates Claudia, "never knew where the inside me, my thoughts, the important Claudia, not just my body, ever was" (21). Passages of dialogue between Claudia and her mother are restricted to the first and last chapters. Many of the strategies used here— the personal address to a reader, a narrator's slant, and the use of monologue to privilege a daughter's voice—are frequently used to construct the

harmonics of relationship between daughters and mothers in young adult
novels.

In other texts, disjunction is lessened between the voices of daughters
and mothers through a narrative structuring of voice that evokes, along with
a daughter's criticism of her mother, a tone of sympathy. A passage from
Joan Lowery Nixon's *Overnight Sensation* illustrates this alternative narrative model:

> 'They're not your friends!' Cassie hesitated when she saw the hurt in Abby's
> eyes. 'Mom, sure, a few of them—like Paul—are your friends, but most of
> them aren't. They're only here because you're a star! . . . If you weren't the
> famous Abby Grant, they wouldn't care anything about you!'
> As Abby gasped and stepped back, Cassie stammered. 'Oh Mom. I'm sorry.
> I—I didn't mean it.' She knew, with a sick feeling in her stomach, that she
> had gone too far (15–16).

The overt criticism, the sympathetic slant of the narrator's comments on
Cassie's mother's hurt feelings, and Cassie's apology evoke a sympathetic
tone towards Cassie's mother producing a very different harmony of relationship than that mediated between Claudia and her mother in Colman's
Claudia, Where Are You?

Revisiting a Relationship

In Nancy Honeycutt's *Ask Me Something Easy*, Addie, who is nearly
seventeen years old, tells her sister, Dinah, that she will have to go back
"nearly ten years. To when you were ten and I was seven years" to understand what had happened to them (1). This going back to the past involves
Addie re-experiencing her painful relationship with her mother. As in other
first-person narratives, Addie is both the autobiographical narrator of story
and is also a character in story. With the difference in timeframe, Addie's
"going on seventeen" voice is split from the voice of seven-year-old Addie
at the beginning of her reminiscences—although these voices appear unified through the "I" position in the text.[8]

Depending on the kind of relationship that is described between an adolescent daughter and her mother, one can read and interpret a daughter's
narrative as the reconnection of her voice with that of her mother's or conversely as a daughter's way of working through their relationship so as to
finalize it. In some texts, for example, a daughter, at closure, is celebrating her independence from her mother; in other novels, a daughter's inter-
rogation of her mother's past and their relationship is shown to be a source

of strength for a teenage girl. At closure of *Ask Me Something Easy*, Addie narrates that her relationship with her mother continues to be an uneasy one since she is "still a disappointment" to her mother and finds herself "backing away when she's friendly" (150). Addie's relationship can, therefore, be read as unresolved. Emphasis is placed on the differences and conflicts between mother and daughter rather than on reconciliation. There are three narrative strategies that particularly affect the representation of the daughter–mother relationship: addressing the reader; mother as *narrated* subject in the text; and mother as *narrating* subject in which a mother takes up a first-person narrative in a text.

Addressing the Reader

"You probably think I spend a lot of time talking and thinking about my mother and you're right" (Pascal 20). A pervasive textual strategy used in young adult texts is the use of the personal address to a potential reader. The conversational tone is used to entice the reader into the text and to identify with the subjectivity of a teenage daughter through her first-person character-bound narration. The style of address to a reader can be colloquial, thereby reinforcing the identification. This practice implies that there is a common experience of adolescence that both reader and the "I" in the text can share. This works toward constructing a "societal ideology" and particular ways of seeing and understanding the world (Stephens 57). In regard to the daughter–mother narrative, this practice can work to invite a reader to identify with a daughter's views about her mother (mothers, in general), and what a mother should be for her daughter. In selected texts, this means identifying with a daughter who criticizes or negates her mother. This kind of textual address is, therefore, ideologically powerful.

Talking about Mother: Mother as Narrated Subject

In Colby Rodowsky's *Hannah in Between,* a mother says to her daughter, Hannah: "I guess you had a fine time talking about me, didn'y? Is that what you and your father do, when I'm not here, or even when I am? Talk about me like that. Talk, talk, talk" (90). This, in fact, is exactly what teenage daughters do in daughter–mother stories in young adult novels. They talk and talk and talk *about* their mothers. While a mother's voice may be heard through reported speech or through her narrated voice, the mother is not a narrating agent in that she does not take up a subject position (an "I" position) in the majority of the young adult novels in this study. Adapting Molly Hite's point that in telling story, the "coherence of one line of narration rests on the suppression of any number of 'other sides'" (4), a mother's story is often the "alternative version" that is either not told, or is often told only in segments with many gaps and frequently through the voices of others, especially by a daughter. The daughter's voice as narrating subject is often dominant in these young adult novels since it is her story, and not her mother's, that is the main focus of story. This is one of the most prevalent conventions used in the genre of young adult literature—as it is in children's literature. Adrienne Kertzer has pointed out how this practice colludes with an "avoidance of maternal voices" in Western culture (160). The absenting and controlling of the maternal voice that Kertzer found in picture books for children is found in the texts of many of these young adult novels.

The formulaic conventions of telling daughter–mother stories in selected young adult texts bear analogy to cultural and Freudian psychoanalytic narratives in that they exclude the voice and subjectivity of the mother. As Hirsch points out, in psychoanalytic narratives:

> *the child* is the subject of both study and discourse. While psychoanalytic feminisms have added the female child to the male, they have not succeeded in inscribing the perspectives of adult women. The adult woman who is a mother, in particular, continues to exist only in relation to her child, never as a subject in her own right. And in her maternal function, she remains an object, always distanced, always idealized or denigrated, always mystified, always represented through the small child's point of view (167).

Jessica Benjamin writes that this "distorted view of the mother" is "deeply embedded in this culture as a whole" (23–24).

One of the most powerful examples of a text in which a mother is represented as object is in Jocelyn Riley's novel, *Only My Mouth Is Smiling*. Through the first-person narration of thirteen-year-old Merle, a harrowing story is told about a mother, who is represented as "crazy" by her daughter and her own mother, as she goes back and forth from home to mental hospital. Merle's mother is constructed as an object of pity, and sometimes, ridiculed by Merle and her younger siblings. She is frequently observed and discussed behind her back by her children. Her daughter Merle comments:

> Sometimes, I get the creeps when I think of the way Mother's always telling us that 'they' are talking about her behind her back and we're always saying that's not true. When we do talk about her behind her back, we always pretend that we aren't. As though we have something to hide (142).

Merle's mother is discussed by those in authority—"they"—whom she states have "taken my job, my land, and now they're after my children"

(209). Subjected to the voices, language, and power of others, she is represented as "paranoid" as she refers to the "evil forces" surrounding her. Her delusions, however, are not groundless. The physical removal of the mother from her daughter and other children—silenced, tied, and powerless in a straitjacket—is perhaps a nadir of the representation of the silenced, negated, and powerless mother in the texts of these novels. There are other mothers who are represented as literally absent and without voice. Dialogue between an adolescent daughter and her absent mother in selected novels can be described, in the words used in one novel, as a "one-way connection" (Deaver 12). This one-sided communication from a daughter to a mother is frequently produced through the narrative form of letters or in the form of diary entries addressed to an absent mother. One effect of this narrative strategy is to place value on the psychological dimension of a daughter's inner fantasy of connections and relationship to her mother while emphasizing the actual empty spaces and separation between them through the elimination of a mother's voice.[9] Another effect is, of course, to tell all story from a daughter's side. There are, however, novels in which different narrative practices of telling story do give legitimacy and space to a mother's voice—a voice that is not absented, suppressed, or objectified to the same extent in fictional texts as in traditional psychoanalytic narratives.

Placing Value on a Mother's Voice

Jean Davies Okimoto's novel, *Molly by Any Other Name*, is a good example of how the employment of an effaced narrator with a sympathetic slant toward a teenage daughter's mother can be used to place value on a mother's character and voice. Okimoto's story about Molly and Karen is one of several stories about an adopted daughter's search for her birth mother. Okimoto reinforces the value and presence of Molly's birth mother through using a split narrative in which the five consecutive chapters focalized by Karen are entitled "Part Two: Karen." The close relation between the anonymous narrator of story, the focalizer (Karen) and focalized (Karen's thoughts) creates a sympathetic representation of a mother who loved her daughter but was unable to keep her. "I love you, that's why I can't keep you, and I'm not a bad person, and I wasn't a tramp she wanted to tell her daughter" (194). At the closure of the novel, the voices of Molly, Karen, and Molly's adoptive mother are heard together in "Part Three: Children of a Common Mother." Okimoto thus places value on maternal voices in her text as well as on the voice of a daughter.

In her novel, *Shizuko's Daughter*, Mori employs an anonymous narrator and a plural narrative. While Yuki, her daughter protagonist, and the members of Yuki's family are all narrated subjects, every important member of her family has a chapter or part of a chapter in which he or she is the main focalizer of events. Even though Yuki's mother, Shizuko, commits suicide at the beginning of the novel, her quoted monologue, with which the book begins, as she dreams about herself and Yuki immediately foregrounds both her importance to story and the strong emotional relationship between mother and daughter.

Mother as Narrating Subject

In five young adult novels and in one short story selected for the study, a teenage daughter's mother is granted agency to narrate her own story in a selected chapter or chapters. In these particular chapters, she is the narrating subject of the text—the teller of her own story. The use of the "I" position encourages a reader to identify with the subjectivity of a mother rather than a daughter. This narrative strategy has the potential to be a disruptive and contradictory site in a fictional genre marketed to teenage readers.[10]

Each of the following texts has a distinctive narrative structure so that the agency given a mother to narrate her own story is used to a very different effect in each novel. Alice Childress's *Rainbow Jordan*, one of three African American novels in which a mother narrates some of her own story, is an interesting example of how allowing a mother to tell her own story does not necessarily grant a mother agency. Her first-person narrative reveals her entrapment and actual lack of agency in a relationship with a man who abuses her and upon whom she is dependent.

Johnson's African American novel, *Toning the Sweep,* is the only grandmother mother–daughter narrative in the study in which both a mother and grandmother are given agency to speak in separate chapters. Emily, for example, introduces her grandmother's voice in a chapter in which "Ola remembers":

> The moment my granddaughter was born, I must have been planting the rosebush that I would name for her. My mama used to name her rosebushes after new babies. My daughter called me half an hour after the baby was born and said that they had named her Emily, and did I think the name was okay (88).

Johnson thus liberates how a mother and grandmother experience the daughter–mother relationship from the domination of a granddaughter's voice. The above passage illustrates well how Johnson builds harmonies of relationship and continuities between daughters and mothers through the first-person narration of a grandmother. It is important, however, to note that these chapters form a small segment of the total novel. There is still a clear hierarchical structure of voices in the text dominated by the strong voice of a teenage daughter.

In Woodson's novel, *I Hadn't Meant to Tell You This,* Marie's mother's free-verse poems, written in first-person narrative on postcards that arrive from all over the world, are inserted directly into her daughter's first-person narrative. Marie, longing for more personal communication from her mother, narrates that she cannot read her mother's poems for "real messages between the lines, at least nothing that [she] could decipher" (100). The poems have the effect of presencing Marie's mother in a way that disrupts her daughter's narrative and the effect of freeing a mother's subjectivity from the domination of her daughter's voice. Marie's mother also controls the communication between herself and her daughter since the postcards are sent with no return address. Woodson's daughter–mother narrative is representative of those in which a daughter fantasizes having conversations with a mother who is absent. The longing for a mother's love is a controlling fantasy in stories about teenage girls and their mothers.

Donna Jo Napoli's *Zel*—a retelling of the Rapunzel story—contains one of the most powerful mother's voices to be heard in any novel in this study. The text is an example of a split-narrative strategy in which an anonymous narrator shares the telling of story from the focalization of Zel and the prince with the first-person narration of Zel's sorceress mother. Through the narrative strategy of granting "Mother" agency to tell her own side of story in comparison to the more distanced anonymous narration of Zel's story, Napoli sets up story so that there can be a close identification with Zel's mother. By placing weight and value on a mother's voice and side of story, Napoli is able to redress the unequal balance in the power relationship between a teen daughter and her mother that results from narrative strategies conventionally employed in young adult texts. Feminist retellings of fairy tale frequently employ this narrative strategy of telling story from the subject position of a mother. In "A Bed of Peas," for example, Priscilla Galloway tells the tale of Rapunzel entirely from the side of her birth mother whose voice is silenced in traditional versions of the tale.

In her novel, *Julie's Daughter,* Rodowsky also uses a split plural-narrative in order to place weight on mothers' voices. Her daughter–mother narrative is composed of alternating the first-person narration of an adolescent daughter, Slug, with the first-person narrative of Julie, her mother, who had abandoned her as a small baby, and with the first-person narrative of an elderly woman artist who had left her small daughter in order to pursue her art. Through the strategy of granting agency to the unmediated voices of two mothers who are able to voice their own experiences and stories, Rodowsky reinforces the authority of mothers' voices despite Slug's anger and criticism of her mother's behavior

A Feminist Daughter–Mother Discourse

There is a discernable paradox in feminist theorizing of voice in children's literature—a paradox that runs through the analysis of daughter–mother narratives in this study. While we may applaud the strong voices and agency of teenage girls who are presented as role models for teen readers, their voices have frequently been produced through a Freudian gender-biased discourse that blames and negates mothers. In listening to the voices of daughters and mothers in texts, it has, therefore, been important to consider to what extent a daughter-centered narrative colludes with the child-centered narratives of psychoanalysis and to what extent a daughter's voice is decentered in order that a mother's voice be heard and legitimized.

Hirsch has defined a feminist daughter–mother discourse as a plural discourse in which mothers speak as well as daughters (196). "Rather," she writes, "than daughters having to 'speak for' mothers, mothers would be able to speak for themselves, perhaps with 'two voices'. Only thus can mothers and daughters speak to one another. Only thus could the plots of mothers and daughters become speakable" (197). Throughout this study, feminist revisions of female adolescence have particularly focused on reclaiming the voices of adolescent girls *in relationship* with the voices of mothers and other women. Emphasis is being placed in new narratives about female adolescence on the need for girls to come of age through models of development based on interdependence. In the five young adult novels and short story described above, there is certainly a move away from narrative structures that have made daughters' voices dominant in texts at the expense of erasing the voices and subjectivities of mothers. There is evidence in recent young adult novels of more plural-narrative structures in which a daughter's voice is decentered so as to allow space for a mother to tell her own side of story. There is also a move in more feminist daughter–mother narratives toward granting a mother multiple identities rather than a subjectivity that is dominated by her daughter's view of her as *only* a mother.

Listening to the voices of teenage daughters and mothers through examining the strategies used to tell story is only one approach that can be employed to examine the daughter–mother narrative in young adult texts. Chapter two discusses the daughter–mother narrative in fairy tale—in particular, the tales of Rapunzel and Snow White—two of Grimm's folktales that have been adapted and retold in novels marketed for young adults.

NOTES

1. See, for example, Brown and Gilligan; Taylor, Gilligan, and Sullivan; Gilligan et al., eds.

2. See, for example, Apter; S. Rich 259.

3. See Trites 29.

4. See, for example, Brown and Gilligan; Debold, Wilson, and Malave.

5. For a visual depiction of the distance between the narrating agent and characters, see Bal 102-3.

6. I have borrowed this term from a description of the methodology used in listening to girls' voices. See Brown and Gilligan 18–41.

7. The example Lanser uses is one in which she makes the distinction between the different voices of one woman writing a letter written for two readers. See Lanser 616–19.

8. Cohan and Shires make the distinctions in a character-bound first-person narration between the "narrating subject of the text, its teller, and the character who narrates [who] also functions as a subject of narration because he or she is an actor in the story." See Cohan and Shires 109.

9. Letters, however, are a narrative form that has sometimes been used for intimate dialogues between mothers and daughters. See Payne.

10. The concept of the "reading position" in the text is useful here. It is the "position assumed by a reader from which the text seems to be coherent and intelligible. . . ." See Cranny-Francis 25.

Two

The Daughter–Mother Narrative in Fairy Tale and Young Adult Novels

Whatever's the point of a stepmother . . . if she isn't wicked?
—Geras *The Tower Room*

In the version of Snow White most often retold, Snow White's birth mother dies in childbirth, and Snow White is brought up and betrayed by a wicked stepmother.[1] In the Brothers Grimm's versions of the Rapunzel tale, Rapunzel's mother, bound by the bargain her husband makes when he is caught stealing the plant that she craves, hands over her daughter to a woman identified as a sorceress. The daughter–mother narratives in these tales are shaped through conventional narrative forms. These include, for example, the story elements in which a daughter's maternal mother is absented from the plot; the substitution of a stepmother or witch/mother; and the eventual separation of a daughter from this negatively portrayed figure.

Grimm's folk tales have been read and interpreted from various theoretical approaches. Psychological and sociological reasons have been used to explain the absenting of a daughter's birth mother and the substitution of another mother in traditional tales. Bruno Bettelheim, whose Freudian psychoanalytic approach to fairy tales has been one of the best-known interpretations of fairy tale narrative, has explained that the stepmother plot that splits the mother into "a good (usually dead) mother and an evil stepmother serves the child well." This fantasy device enables the "image of the good mother" to be preserved while allowing the child to feel anger when experiencing mother as a bad mother (66–70). Bettelheim's explanations have been criticized on the grounds that they offer universal and timeless

31

psychological explanations that do not acknowledge the reality of how mothers were situated in specific historical contexts. Shari Thurer writes, for example, of the social and economic circumstances in which a stepmother "may well have been wicked in early modern Europe," because it was also a time of high death rates when mothers were often replaced by stepmothers whose own children became rivals for a father's status and wealth (151–52).

Feminist criticism of fairy tales has centered on exposing the gender ideology that is perpetuated through these traditional tales. Daughters may be the heroine protagonists but their fates are determined, in several tales, by their being found and wakened by the kiss of a prince on whom their happiness and future security depends. Jack Zipes points out that the Brothers Grimm, while editing the tales they collected, reinforced the construction of gender and the reinforcement of sex roles according to the "patriarchal code" of their time (xxviii). Since their tales were to conform to certain codes of moral and social values, the Grimms were also concerned with preserving the figure of the good, ideal mother as "symbol of the eternal feminine, the motherland, and the family itself as the highest social desideratum" (Warner 212). They, therefore, replaced villainous birth mothers in earlier editions of the tales with a stepmother or witch/mother figure. The birth mother of Snow White, for example, was the original villainess of the tale in the 1810 and 1812 editions of Grimms' text but her "murderous jealousy" was transposed onto that of the stepmother figure in their 1819 edition (Warner 211).[2] The realization by the Grimm Brothers that their tales were to reach the ears of children also influenced their editing of the tales. Wicked stepmothers were easier to accept than evil mothers (Tatar 37).[3] Disneyesque representations of the evil stepmother have certainly continued to generate powerful images of maternal malevolence. These representations have also provided us with particular descriptions and explanations of how daughters, who are in the process of becoming sexually mature young women, relate to their mother(s).

Kertzer has pointed out that revisions of fairy tales that "reinstate" the traditional role of mothers or continue to absent and silence the voice of mothers only reaffirm the status assigned to them in traditional tales. In some tales, the role assigned to mothers is that of dutifully inculcating their daughters into patriarchy (20). Another consequence of absenting the birth mother has been the marginalization of the emotional attachment and *relationships* between daughters and their mothers. This is seen, for example, in tales that are congruent with oedipal patterns of family and social relationships in which daughters align themselves with fathers and other men rather than their mothers. The relationships between wicked stepmothers and their daughters in selected tales have been described as poisonous—literally so in Grimm's tale of Snow White.

This chapter discusses the daughter–mother narrative in Grimm's tales of Rapunzel and Snow White (although there are references to earlier Neapolitan, French, and German editions of the Rapunzel tale) and the ways in which the Rapunzel tale has been intertexualized into selected young adult texts. The focus is on Napoli's retelling of Rapunzel in *Zel;* Galloway's retellings of the Rapunzel and Snow White tales in her *Truly Grim Tales;* and on Adele Geras's adaptation of Rapunzel and Snow White in her trilogy, *The Tower Room, Watching the Roses,* and *Pictures of the Night.* This chapter summarizes how a particular daughter–mother narrative in fairy tale remains a popular way of imagining and describing relationships between daughters and mothers. I begin by discussing the Brothers Grimm's 1857 edition of Rapunzel in *Kinder-und-Hausmarchen* (Children's and Household Tales) translated by Zipes.

THE DAUGHTER–MOTHER NARRATIVE
IN BROTHERS GRIMM'S *RAPUNZEL*

Rapunzel, Rapunzel, lass mir dein Haar herunter.
—Jacob Ludwig Karl Grimm

The story of Rapunzel was included in the first volume of Grimm's *Kinder-und-Hausmarchen* issued in 1812 and has remained one of the tales that is consistently reproduced and retold in picture book versions and in fairy tale collections for children. It is also one of the tales in which a daughter–mother narrative forms a major portion of the text. The daughter–mother narrative in the Rapunzel tale is shaped by two major elements of story that are retained in retellings of the tale: the transference of a daughter's care to a mother other than her birth mother, and the triangular relationship between a mother, daughter, and a daughter's lover.

Grimm's 1857 version begins with the story of a woman who, after long wanting a child, craves the "rapunzel lettuce" that she sees growing in the walled garden next door that belongs to a powerful "sorceress." Her craving for the lettuce is such that she tells her husband that she will die without it.[4] On his second visit to the garden to steal more rapunzel for his wife, he comes face-to-face with the sorceress who demands her price for letting him have as much as his wife cares to eat—she will have the child who is to be born. The text gives no hint of a mother's protest or signs of refusing her husband's bargain after wishing so long for a child. Absent from the text are signs of maternal love, remorse, or grief when the sorceress appears and takes the child away. The loss of the daughter is described without emotion. A mother, bound by her husband's promise, is represented as merely exchanging her daughter, whom the sorceress names Rapunzel, for the rapunzel she had craved.

In accordance with other daughter–mother narratives in selected folk tales, the care of a daughter is transferred to a substitute mother—in this case an unknown "sorceress" rather than the usual stepmother figure. This sorceress figure in Grimm's text is certainly not representative of the figure of the stereotypical wicked stepmother that has been so criticized in fairy tale. She identifies herself with a caring mother as she assures Rapunzel's father that he need not "fear about the child's well-being, for" she will "take care of it like a mother." She, moreover, in opposition to Rapunzel's seemingly uncaring birth mother, "must have the child" (47). Rapunzel, indeed, later refers to the woman who has taken care of her as "Mother Gothel." [5] It is at this point in Grimm's tale that the sorceress figure is identified *as* "Mother" by Rapunzel.

Rapunzel's childhood with the woman she knows as mother is passed over in Grimm's story. All that is told is that she grew "to be the most beautiful child under the sun" and that, aged twelve years old, she was taken by the sorceress to a tower in the forest and locked away. There were no doors only a window high up in the tower. The fact that the sorceress/mother had visited her daughter every day is revealed through Rapunzel's dialogue with the prince. Also revealed through their conversation is the implication that Mother Gothel had shown at least some love for her daughter, since when the prince asks if she will have him for her husband she decides that he would love her "better than old Mother Gothel" (48). There are only a few other hints given in Grimm's text about Rapunzel's time in the tower and her relationship with her sorceress mother. Rapunzel obeys her mother's daily commands to "let down" her hair that is described as "long and radiant, as fine as spun gold" so that her mother may visit her (48).

Rapunzel's voice is described as "sweet" as she sings to pass her lonely days away. She is said to be "afraid" of the prince who climbs up Rapunzel's hair—for she had never met a man before. It is with the advent of the prince that Rapunzel is first shown to be deceitful as she meets, willingly, with him every "evening" when she knows her mother will not be there. Rapunzel is not a passive maiden in Grimm's text. Although, in alignment with the social and cultural mores of patriarchal courtship, she must wait for the arrival of the prince to rescue her from the tower, there is the suggestion in the text that Rapunzel is an active, intelligent girl as she suggests that she undertake the task of weaving a ladder from the skeins of silk that the prince must bring her so that she can elope with the young man who is now named as her "husband."

Rapunzel's illicit love affair and loss of innocence is revealed in Grimm's 1857 edition only through her lack of discretion as she comments on the contrast between feeling the weight of her mother and the weight of the prince as she pulls each one up to the tower by means of her hair. Zipes explains that in the first Grimm edition of the tale (published in 1812), Rapunzel had asked the "fairy" why her clothes had "become too tight" and no longer fit her (xxvi–xxvii).[6] The original text certainly makes more visible Rapunzel's loss of virginity and pregnancy that is masked in the text of the 1857 edition. One can also speculate that the introduction of the term "husband" that does not appear in the 1812 edition may have been introduced by Grimm Brothers in the 1857 edition in order to give the private troth of Rapunzel and the prince a public legitimacy.

The entry of the prince, whose access to Rapunzel is achieved through the means of observing her witch mother, is a significant marker in that it is shown to change the relationship between Rapunzel and her mother. Indeed, the most dramatic scenes described in Grimm's story are that in which a sorceress mother expresses her rage on discovering her daughter's secret love affair. The fact that Rapunzel was, indeed, no longer a virgin and was expecting a child explains the intensity and passion conveyed through the text in the scene where she calls Rapunzel a "godless child," accuses her daughter of deceiving her, and cuts off her braids with scissors. The powerful emotions and drama in this passage and the scene in which Rapunzel's sorceress mother lies in wait for the prince contrast, for example, with the passages describing the advent and courtship of the prince. It is at this point that sorceress/mother is described as becoming a witch —"a cruel sorceress"—to her daughter as she thwarts the rescue or elopement of her daughter by the prince.

Rapunzel is taken to a "desolate land" where she lives in "great misery and grief" and gives birth to twins—a boy and a girl. A grief-stricken prince is met in the tower by the "vicious" looks of an angry mother and told that he will never see Rapunzel again. The "beautiful bird," she tells him, "is no longer sitting in the nest," and she will not be "singing anymore." She continues with: "The cat has got her, and it will scratch out your eyes" (49). Stylistically at odds with the rest of the text, this is perhaps an example of the "rustic, natural tone" characteristic of the original telling of the stories that were retained by the Brothers Grimm in their revisions of the tales (Zipes xxv). A sorceress mother's prediction of the blinding of the prince comes to pass as the prince jumps from the tower in fear and his eyes are "pierced" by the thorns into which he falls. After Rapunzel and the prince have spent a number of years in "misery" and "wretchedness," the prince finds Rapunzel and their children and his blind eyes are healed by Rapunzel's tears. At the closure of story, the family is making their way to the prince's father's kingdom.

Left behind in narrative are the figures of the birth mother and sorceress mother for Rapunzel is now recognized as a legitimate birth mother and wife. In accordance with other fairy tale narratives, Rapunzel, originally the daughter of peasants, gains access to a higher social rank through marriage. The Grimm version, in effect, can be read as a series of substitutions or exchanges: Rapunzel for rapunzel, a mother for a 'mother', and a lover for a mother that keeps the narrative moving forwards. The final substitution reproduces the expected destination of a young woman in a patriarchal society—the love of a mother exchanged for that of a prince with the value at closure placed on the legitimization of marriage and family.

THE RETELLING OF A TALE

The tales collected by the Brothers Grimm were successively edited by them for the edification and suitability of a child audience and for those who wished the tales to be censored for children (Zipes xxv). Changes were made to the tales in terms of style and theme, and "erotic and sexual elements that might be offensive to middle-class morality" were eliminated (Zipes xxviii). As Marie Tatar points out, it is clear that the Grimm Brothers eradicated from their versions the open acknowledgement that Rapunzel become pregnant in the tower made in earlier versions of the Rapunzel tale (45).[7] The process of editing, reinterpreting, and retelling of the tale of Rapunzel continues, of course, today—particularly in picture-book versions for young children. Glossed over is the full significance of a tale that can be read as a story about female sexual desire and maturation. Rapunzel's pregnancy is particularly masked in texts and visual representations in media marketed for children.[8]

The Brothers Grimm, however, also omitted from their versions details present in earlier editions of the tale that give a very different spin on the representation of "Mother Gothel" as witch/mother. Stripped from Grimm's version are descriptions of the "fée's" care of Rapunzel that are present in earlier French and German versions of the tale. In Mlle. De La Force's story "Persinette," for example, which is frequently referred to as an early Rapunzel tale, the fée who takes the small Persinette from her mother in exchange for the herb parsley ("persil") brings up the young girl with all the care imaginable (Lüthi 97).[9] Rapunzel is ensconced in a silver tower and provided with jewels, fashionable clothes, and delicacies for her meals.[10] In an early German version of the tale by Friedrich Schulz, which is very similar to the story of "Persinette," the fairy places Rapunzel in the silver tower to protect her because she knows that an unlucky star shone at her birth (Lüthi 101). Rapunzel's pregnancy, in this version, is her "fate" that, despite a sorceress mother's caution, could not be avoided (102).

In "Persinette," the fée's mother's heart softens and she takes pity on the reunited family of Rapunzel, the prince, and their children who are near death. She takes them in a shining wagon of gold and precious stones to the prince's father and his kingdom (Lüthi 99). The story, thus, closes with acceptance, love, and forgiveness of a mother for her daughter and her family. As in the version by Schulz, after a mother metes out punishment to young lovers, she is restored to the position of a loving, caring mother (and mother-in-law). She becomes the guardian and protector of a moral and social order. It is only at this juncture that the conventional happy romance ending is sanctioned. Grimm's version omits this return of the fairy/godmother plotted in these earlier versions. Grimm's tale presents a more distanced and alienated representation of the sorceress/mother. In *The Hard Facts of the Grimm Tales*, Tatar argues that Wilhelm Grimm intensified "maternal malice" and that the plot of Rapunzel is an example of a tale based on the violation of an "interdiction" whereby the "command not to stray is symbolized by imprisonment in the tower" (166).[11] What is clear is that the role of this sorceress/mother figure has been, and continues to be, open to different interpretations including mother as protector, or mother as her daughter's jailer and obstacle to her daughter's development.[12]

Napoli and Geras have written female coming-of-age stories in *Zel* and *The Tower Room*, respectively using the tale of Rapunzel as pretext. Keeping to the broad outlines of the original tale, Napoli and Geras imagine the daughter–mother narrative very differently though both their stories are filled (as are the traditional tales) with passion, love, jealousy, and anger—as daughters grow into beautiful young women who desire, and are desired by, young men. In the retellings of the Rapunzel tale by Napoli and Galloway, a daughter's tale also becomes a mother's tale.

MOTHER IS GOOD, MOTHER IS A WITCH:
THE DAUGHTER–MOTHER NARRATIVE IN *ZEL*

In her young adult novel, *Zel*, Napoli has chosen to retell the tale of Rapunzel in its entirety. In accord with the traditional tale, Zel, like Rapunzel, is brought up by a witch/mother who has exchanged the rapunzel growing in her garden for a daughter whom she locks up in a tower just days before her thirteenth birthday. In contrast to the seemingly timeless and universal setting of Grimm's narrative, Napoli grounds her story within a particular historical, social, and cultural context by situating it in Switzerland in the mid-1500s. By so doing, Napoli is able to draw attention to ideologies of class and gender and belief systems that would seem appropriate and relevant to her setting.

What makes Napoli's retelling of Rapunzel so different from the Brothers Grimm's tale (and various translations and picture-book interpretations based on their tale) is that Napoli writes a female coming-of-age story from a feminist perspective in which emphasis is placed on Zel's growth through puberty into a sexually mature young woman and in which the vital emotional *relationship* between Zel and the woman she knows as "Mother" is made central to story. Napoli fractures the more unified anonymous narrative of folk tale through the strategy of using a plural narrative in which story is narrated from the different positions of three main characters who form a triangular relationship in the text: Zel, Mother, and the prince, Konrad. Napoli, thereby, also breaks with a daughter–mother narrative found in traditional tales and with a conventional daughter–mother narrative found in the majority of young adult novels by making the story of Zel, despite the title, far more than just a daughter's side of story. A mother is given agency to tell her own story. A reader is, thus, invited to directly identify with the vision of Mother.

The relationship between Zel and Mother is constructed from the sides of both mother and daughter through the unmediated first-person narration of Mother and the narrated thoughts and feelings of Zel in separate chapters entitled "Mother" and "Zel," respectively. While Napoli describes a loving relationship between Zel and her mother, a split narrative also serves to highlight the differences between them and constructs from each one's side of story how they understand their relationship. The language Mother uses to tell about her feelings for Zel, for example, encodes a consciousness of daughter–mother bonding that resonates with feminist discourses on mother–daughter relationships: "I have been enjoying the unity of

Mother and Daughter, weaving through the crowds like a single strand of yarn. As I leave Zel with the smith, I feel a sharp loss. I am sacrificing our wholeness, though the sacrifice is all for her sake. The only consolation is that the separation is temporary." She is sure that her Zel will not stray. Zel "is as bereft without me as I am without her" (13). She and Zel "will be together. Mother and Zel. Forever" (19). Zel, however, experiences their relationship differently as narrated in the chapters entitled "Zel."

Described as a bright, creative, and dancingly alive girl at the opening of Napoli's text, Zel is represented as becoming increasingly independent in her thoughts and actions after her encounter with the sixteen-year-old prince, Konrad, at the smithy. From Zel's side of story, it is told how Zel, for example, procures without her mother's knowledge rapunzel seeds so that she may grow the lettuce she loves in her own garden, hiding them in her bed; these are seeds that Zel knows her mother refuses to grow. Napoli transforms the Rapunzel tale into a female coming-of-age story for young adults that describes a girl's increasing awareness of sex and sexual desire from the perspective of a young woman. After meeting Konrad, for example, Zel brings to mind the memory of the youth: "Her skin comes alive as she thinks of him" (47). As in other feminist revisions of the tale, Napoli fractures the association of the long golden tresses with beauty and sexuality.[13] Zel attracts Konrad for her deftness with his horse rather than her beauty (96). Neither are Zel's tresses represented as naturally long, since it is the magical powers of a sorceress/mother that makes Zel's golden braids grow at an unusually fast rate (113).

Grimm's dulcet Rapunzel is reimagined by Napoli as an angry and frustrated young woman who is locked away from the world at the age of fifteen when she would normally be expected to be married "with child, baking bread, and weaving cloth." (158). With the art supplies Mother brings to the tower, Zel draws, for example, a picture of "their billy goat mounting a nanny" in "rapid messy strokes" as she feels "her blood heat." Her "fury fills the page. She stands and runs her hands down her body. She digs her fingers in, leaves the whitest of marks on each thigh." Her mother, she knows, "will not like this picture" (159). The description of Zel inflicting pain on herself and her desire to cut "trenches" down her arms and fill the tower "room with blood" corresponds to contemporary stories of teenage girls experiencing the literal pain of growing up (149). Since Napoli's retelling of Rapunzel resonates with contemporary discourses on the difficulties and pain of growing up female, it is a version to which young adults may relate or identify with more readily than earlier versions of the tale.

As in Grimm's version of the tale, a daughter's sexuality and fascina-tion with a youth are shown to disrupt and change, forever, a daughter's relationship with her mother. Questioning Zel about her meeting with the youth Konrad at the smithy, for example, Mother narrates how Zel's meet-ing with him is causing Zel to be "furtive" with her (59). As explained in chapter two, Napoli constructs a triangular relationship that is central to story both in form and context through telling story from the three subject positions of Zel, Mother, and Konrad. This has the effect of heightening the opposition set up between a daughter's passionate love for her lover and the emotional bond between mother and daughter. While Zel, after a night of love with Konrad, who has found her after two years of searching, talks of the "passion" of lovers, her mother talks of the "bond of passion no one and nothing can break. You have chosen me" (200).

Napoli reproduces all the rage and passion of the sorceress mother in Grimm's tale, who is told of a daughter's tryst with a young man and whose eyes discern her daughter's pregnancy. Mother's cry: "*Oh, God, what sav-age trick you played, to pick for barrenness a woman who couldn't bear to exist without a child*" reproduces the jealousy of a barren mother whose daughter did not have to pay what she herself had paid (205). In keeping with Grimm's text, Mother is, indeed, described as a *witch* mother at this point in story as she tears off Zel's braids with her iron teeth and causes her daughter to be swept away by the branches of the forest (201–2).

One of the strongest components of Napoli's text is the way a reader is positioned to identify with the subjectivity of a woman who grows fully into her double role as caring, possessive mother and witch.[14] Unlike ear-lier tales, Napoli develops the witch side of Zel's mother by giving her the characteristics that are attributed to witches in fanciful tales—iron teeth, the water that runs through her veins, and magical powers. However, the sorceress of earlier tales is demystified and given a personal history as the story is told about a good, barren woman who had to be a mother "with every drop of blood, every bit of flesh, every hair, every breadth of her body" (127). Through her first-person narrative, Mother voices the despera-tion of a woman whose longing for a child and passionate love for a daugh-ter rents apart her very soul; this longing led her to bargain with deviltry and her agreement to persuade Zel, while still a virgin, to likewise become a witch (127–30). Napoli develops one side of Zel's witch mother more in keeping with the caring "fée" in Mlle. De La Force's "Persinette" as she, too, brings her daughter delicacies to eat in the tower.

Through constructing story from the position of the prince, Napoli shows how patriarchy works by showing how princes as well as princesses are constrained by social and cultural laws that have constructed gender-appropriate behavior in a patriarchal society. Unlike the anonymous princes of fairy tale, Konrad's story is fleshed out so that he, too, is a fully realized character. He rebels against arranged marriages and the life of a young noble in order that he may search for the girl, Zel, whom he meets by chance one day at the local smithy. The worst day of his life is when his father announces that he must marry a girl that has been chosen for him, and whom he does not know (41).

Through her representation of a prince who voluntarily resists the expectations of his class and position, who shows concern for the princesses he rejects because of his obsession for Zel, and who would set out, ill and blind, to ceaselessly search for Zel, Napoli transforms the rather unfortunate lackluster prince of Grimm's tale into a prince hero. He displays the necessary characteristics of "compassion" and "humility" that make princes into worthy heroes (Tatar 93). Markedly omitted from Napoli's version is the traditional ending of fairy tale present in Grimm's version and earlier versions of the tale in which Rapunzel and the prince return to his kingdom with their family. Napoli ends her tale as Zel kisses Konrad as her tears fall on his face. In the last sentence of the text, the "we" signifies Mother's sharing the happiness between her daughter and her husband: "And they can see each other and yes, oh yes, we are happy" (227).

In Napoli's story of Rapunzel, the witch mother usually destroyed in fairy tale (Tatar 147–8) is alive in spirit. In *Zel*, she becomes the all-seeing anonymous narrator of the final chapter whose "spirit" interrupts the narrative three times to say that she watches, listens, and touches "the world" but no longer has any power. At closure, a mother forgives a daughter and a daughter her mother. Although she cannot tell her mother directly, Zel admits that Mother had been a "good mother" to her until she was thirteen years of age. She can acknowledge that her mother was a witch and understands what led her to sell her soul (219). Mothers are absolved from blame by a daughter in Napoli's tale as Zel opens her heart also to the unknown mother who had "traded away" her child (220).

One can raise a number of issues in questioning how much Napoli reworks fairy tale. Arguably, she does not fracture fairy tale by merely reversing gender roles—a practice, which does not necessarily result in a feminist text particularly when this reversal is achieved at a surface level. Napoli works within the boundaries of the main plot narrative of the pretext of the Rapunzel tale and within the gender ideologies and belief system of a particular social and historical context. Within these constraints, Napoli reworks the genre of fairy tale by disrupting the conventional anony-

mous (patriarchal) voice of the storyteller and by giving new meaning to
the anonymous "wicked" witch/mother figure of fairy tale.

Fully reclaimed through Napoli's retelling is the passion and sensuous-
ness of young lovers masked in Grimm's tale and the representation of a
young woman who is shown to be a vital and desirous protagonist versus
being represented solely as an object of desire. However, by also extend-
ing the meaning of desire and passion beyond their usual sexual connota-
tions to connote the power of love that a woman can experience for her
daughter, Napoli centralizes and brings new meaning to the daughter–
mother relationship in fairy tale. The passion of a mother's love for her
daughter is written from the side of a mother. Napoli so writes story that a
mother's jealous rage and possessiveness invite sympathy and understanding for a mother as well as for a daughter. Certainly, Napoli's text encodes
a consciousness of the importance of this relationship that is in accord with
a contemporary discourse on daughter–mother relationships.

A MOTHER'S NARRATIVE IN GALLOWAY'S
"A BED OF PEAS"

In transposing her version of Rapunzel to an alternative setting—that of the
desert—Galloway uses a narrative practice frequently used in fracturing folk
and fairy tales. In her short story, "A Bed of Peas," Galloway, like Napoli,
also employs the narrative strategy of fracturing tale by telling story from
another perspective. The tale is told from the side of "Letitia's" birth
mother—a princess who elopes from her father with the slave, Hassan (37).
By reinstating the voice of the mother absented in the tale of Rapunzel and
constructing through her first-person narrative what might, arguably, be
termed a maternal text, Galloway reweaves the Rapunzel tale around a
mother's story. Heard through the voice of a mother whose baby daughter
is taken from her before she has even "kissed the tiny hands and feet" is
her craving for the Lady Grendel's lettuce; the experience of pregnancy and
a difficult birth; the realization after a month spent in delirium that her child
had gone; and her retreat into "madness" as she "wrapped a brick in the
silk shawl" she "had so lovingly embroidered" (44–45).

There is no vindication in this version of the tale for the witch figure,
Lady Grendel. "I have long since been sure that she planned the whole
abominable scheme," narrates the mother of Letitia. "Her enchantments
created that craving. There is no wickedness so great that that lady would
not contemplate it" (44). Galloway does not present the witch mother in

her retelling as a guardian or protective mother figure. Letitia, married and expecting her own baby at the closure of the tale, comments: "I called a woman Mother, but she was not my mother, surely. No mother could have shut her child away as she did me" (59). Galloway twists tale so that Letitia's mother and husband arrange for the death of the mother usurper who had taken their child.

Galloway uses language and imagery that are resonant with a discourse of daughter–mother identity and the continuity of connections between mothers and daughters. A mother tells how she searched for her daughter (with her husband) for seventeen long years. Although on finding her, she waits to make herself known to Letitia, she notes that her daughter's eyes are "twins" to hers thus bringing a different connotation to the "twins" that Rapunzel bears in the original tale (59). She wishes to be a grandmother to her daughter's baby—whom she fantasizes as a "new little princess" who will not be hindered by the "soft body" that had often hampered her own life. Her granddaughter, she narrates, "can learn to sleep on a bed of peas" (59). The narrative practice of intertextualizing elements of the Rapunzel tale with another tale, Grimm's *The Pea Test* (also known as *The Princess and the Pea*) in order to produce variants of story is characteristic of many fractured fairy tale tellings. Geras also uses the narrative practice of intertextualizing various fairy tales in her skillful interweaving of daughter–mother narratives in her trilogy. [15]

GERAS'S DAUGHTER–MOTHER NARRATIVES

Comparing Geras's adaptation of Rapunzel with Galloway's and Napoli's retellings and also with Grimm's text provides an interesting example of how the pretext of Rapunzel and the daughter–mother narrative in Rapunzel can be imagined so differently. In Geras's trilogy, *The Tower Room, Watching the Roses*, and *Pictures of the Night*, Grimm's fairy tale narratives are intertextualized into another genre—the British tradition of the boarding school story. In her contemporary stories about schoolgirls, Geras draws on the tales of *Rapunzel, The Sleeping Beauty, Red-Riding Hood*, and *Snow White* as metanarratives in telling her stories about Megan, Bella, and Alice who share the "Tower Room" at Egerton Hall, England in the 1960s.

What is particularly made visible throughout Geras's trilogy is how powerfully fairy tale is embedded in cultural narratives of white Western culture, for Geras not only adapts and makes use of narrative plot elements of fairy tale but shows throughout her trilogy how fairy tale continues to inform the inner fantasies and imaginations of young women. Geras's young adult texts certainly raise the question of in what ways a reader's recognition of narrative plot elements, quotes and allusions from fairy tale affects a reading of Geras's novels.[16]

Love and Jealousy in *The Tower Room*

> If a young woman is locked away, as you are locked away, at the top of a
> tower for years and years . . . imagine what can happen.
>
> —*The Tower Room*

Geras, as does Napoli, writes in her adaptation of Rapunzel about a young woman's sexual desire and secret, forbidden love within the context of a relationship between a daughter and guardian mother. In Geras's *The Tower Room*, Simon Findlay, the new lab assistant at Egerton Hall, climbs up the scaffolding, that is currently in place, in order to hold trysts with Megan in the "Tower Room." Megan had fallen instantly in love with him when she saw him out of the tower window. The concept of love at first sight is used by both Geras and Napoli—an element of Grimm's story that is incorporated into their respective stories. There is a delicious irony, of course, in using a girl's boarding school as setting for stories about sexual passion and illicit love. The convention of out-of-bounds used in school stories takes on another dimension in Geras's novels. The elderly and perceptive Miss van der Leyden points out that parents pay to remove their daughters from the "real world" to live only among girls. Now, however, a young man has "come from the outside," who promises to be a "cat among the doves" (corrected by Megan to "a cat among the pigeons"). Geras uses, here, a linguistic marker to the verse uttered by Rapunzel's sorceress/mother in Grimm's text (34).

Retained as part of story is the daughter–mother plot of the Rapunzel tale in which a mother transfers a daughter from the care of her birth mother to the care of another woman. However, when recontextualized into a contemporary middle-class setting in England, the nature of the transaction is redefined and so is the nature of the daughter–mother relationship. Megan recounts, for example, how her mother left her at Egerton Hall seven years before so that she could accompany Megan's father to Africa. Both of them, Megan narrates, tried not to cry when it came time to part. Megan had been told since she was a small child that she would, one day, be entrusted to

Dorothy, a former neighbor and now a teacher at Egerton Hall (*The Tower* 3). Dorothy, she goes on to explain, had provided her mother with the asparagus from her garden for which she had had a craving (4). The way in which allusions to the Rapunzel tale (which may, or may not, be recognized by a reader) are intertextualized into Megan's narrative is representative of the kind of narrative strategy Geras adopts in using the pretext of fairy tale in her trilogy as a metanarrative.

Geras plays differently with the double identity of Grimm's sorceress mother than does Napoli. In contrast to Napoli's daughter–mother narrative, Geras places emphasis on the representation of Dorothy as a substitute mother figure by characterizing her as passionless and not all motherly. As Megan narrates:

> It was only during the holidays that Dorothy turned by magic into my adoptive mother. In my heart I regard her only as a guardian and never think of her as a real mother. . . . She did try to be like a mother to me during the holidays, but it was as though she were copying maternal behavior she had seen in other people, and not quite succeeding (74).

The actual relationship between Megan and her guardian "mother" is described as cold, distant, emotionless. Indeed, the guardian mother in Geras's story seems less warm than the figure in Grimm's tale who is made more motherly through the use of the term "Mother Gothel." In contrast to Napoli's reworking of the Rapunzel tale, Geras makes use of the more conventional strategy found in young adult texts of telling story from a daughter's side of story. The distancing of Dorothy is, thus, also achieved through her position of narrated subject in the text: a woman who does not tell her side of story—in contrast to the witch/mother who tells her personal story in Napoli's *Zel*.

Geras retains the second major plot element of the daughter–mother narrative in the Rapunzel tale, namely, a triangular relationship between a "mother," daughter, and a young man. The relationships within this triangle are, however, aligned very differently. The uncovering of illicit love takes on a different dimension in Geras's text as Simon is shown to be the object of the love of both daughter and mother. Geras draws on a popular theme in the discourse on daughter–mother relationships that is reproduced as an archetype in different narratives and contexts from fairy tale to contemporary popular culture: the rage and jealousy of a mother in competition with a daughter for male love and attention.

All the drama of Grimm's and Napoli's tower room scenes is reproduced in Geras's story as Dorothy confronts Simon and Megan. Dorothy is transformed into an angry, shrieking, weeping woman accusing the lovers of "wallowing in" their "own filth"—and Megan of betrayal (144). The description of Dorothy beating against Simon's "chest with her hands fixed into claws" is analogous to Grimm's description of the transmutation of Mother Gothel into a witch figure. The blinding of the prince scene takes another form as Dorothy asks Simon if he had cared for her at all and smashes his glasses that fly to the floor by stamping on them. "She stamped and stamped until the lenses were ground to dust on the Tower Room floor" (145). Following Grimm's story line, Simon and Megan are banished by a guardian mother in disgrace. However, in Geras's story, the young lovers leave Egerton Hall together.

Included as part of Geras's story is the period of time spent in a symbolic wasteland that is a central element of the Rapunzel tale.[17] Recontextualized in Geras's retelling, this interim is used to show how romantic love can also imprison a young woman as Megan describes herself sitting alone in Simon's attic room in London feeling as though she were in a "desert" and missing Dorothy (39). In Geras's female coming-of-age story, romance is also disrupted and delayed—but this time through a young woman's own decision—as Megan decides to return to Egerton School to continue her schooling. Geras places a different emphasis on the symbol of the "tower" in a young woman's life: Megan writes that she sometimes feels as though she has spent "years and years in one room at the top of a winding flight of stairs, looking out of the window of life, instead of taking part in it like everybody else" (149). The daughter–mother relationship between Megan and the teacher who stands in place of her mother is described as remaining "chilly" despite a daughter's wish for reconciliation. Megan explains in a letter to Simon that although she cannot love Dorothy as a mother should be loved, she does feel "sorrow" for Dorothy because she understands how much she must have wanted Simon (149).

Through interweaving the stories of Megan, Bella, and Alice, Geras presents three very different daughter–mother narratives. In *Watching the Roses*, Geras draws on the Sleeping Beauty and the Red Riding Tale to tell the story of Alice who was raped by the wolflike Angus. Alice's mother is shown to be caring and loving toward her daughter telling her that "Nothing was [her] fault" (13). In *Pictures of the Night*, Geras deals more fully with the third in a trio of mothers—the wicked stepmother figure.

A Wicked Stepmother

"Once upon a time," Bella tells her friend, Greg, "I had a mother, but I killed her." Her mother had died when she was born, she explains (Geras *Pictures* 3). The pretext of Snow White and her wicked stepmother is tightly interwoven into Bella's relationship with her stepmother, Marjorie, forming the central narrative in *Pictures of the Night*. Although Snow White is not referred to by name, those familiar with Grimm's version of the tale would certainly make associations between Grimm's tale and Geras's novel through linguistic markers. Belle, for example, who is said to have lived happily with her father until Marjorie came along, is said by her father to have: "Skin like untrodden snow" (100).

Episodes from Grimm's narrative plot are tightly integrated into *Pictures of the Night* and adapted to a contemporary setting. There is, for example, the episode in which a woman, named Em, beguiles her way into the house where Bella is staying with seven members of a band and ties a belt so tightly around Bella that Bella cannot undo it and collapses after she has left (19–20). There are the incidents when Bella nearly chokes on one of Marjorie's apples (108); and when a woman who does Bella's hair pushes a decorated comb so tightly into her head that Bella is sick and dizzy. Could the comb have been poisoned, a doctor asks her (103–4). In the final scenes of *Pictures of the Night*, Bella sings with the band at "The Glass Menagerie" for a party at which her father and her stepmother are present. Marjorie's identification with Snow White's stepmother is reinforced through her comment while dancing that: "Every step" she took was "absolute hell" and that her shoes felt as if they had "been soldered to" her "feet with red-hot irons. . . ." (176).[18] As Bella sings, suspended within a cage of glass, she faints and receives the "kiss of life" from Mark, the young man with whom she has fallen with love (180).

Geras retains the theme of jealousy and envy of a stepmother for her beautiful stepdaughter in the story of Bella and Marjorie. In one confrontational scene, for example, Bella openly accuses Marjorie of her envy after Marjorie has told Bella that a dress she plans to wear looks "cheap and tawdry." Marjorie is mistaken, Bella tells her. She, Bella, looks "terrific" in the dress because it flatters her figure and her "white skin with not one wrinkle in it." She looks: "Vibrant, alive, sexy, dangerous, sparkling, beautiful, and above all *young*." Bella goes on to say that Marjorie cannot "bear it" now that she is no longer young and so beautiful and accuses Marjorie of trying to "hurt" her. Marjorie has "*not* been a mother" to her, she proclaims when Marjorie protests at her outburst (*Pictures* 170–71).

The well-known mirror scene in Grimm's tale is reproduced in an episode in which Megan watches as Bella and Marjorie compare their reflections in a mirror at the hairdressers. Megan narrates and focalizes daughter and stepmother as Marjorie pats her own hair and asks: "But honestly,
Armand, tell us what you think. Which do *you* think looks prettier?" As
Megan looks at the faces of Marjorie and Bella "nearly touching in the
mirror" she notices the differences between Bella's "almost incandescent"
skin and that of Marjorie's that has begun to coarsen and wrinkle. She observes the "gray streaks" in Marjorie's hair compared to the "blue sheen"
in Bella's. It "must have struck" Marjorie "like a warning," Megan comments (*The Tower* 93).

Megan narrates: "Marjorie wasn't exactly wicked. Not really. Even Bella
admitted this. But she was small-minded, critical, and jealous of the relationship between Bella and her father . . . and especially of the relationship that had once existed between Bella's father and mother" (*The Tower*
92). Bella is shown to be subject to her own doubts and fantasies about what
she imagines and what is true. Is Marjorie at the "bottom" of those episodes with the belt, the poisonous comb, and the apple Bella wonders in a
letter addressed to Megan (*Pictures* 108). She knows, however, that Megan
will tell her that she has an "overactive imagination" (109).

Bella is certainly not the sweet, passive, virginal Snow White figure of
the Grimm tale. She has an affair with Greg before she is swept off her feet
by Mark. Her time spent as a singer with Greg and Pete's seven-man band
and other scenes in Geras's adaptation may remind readers of Fiona
French's picture-book version of Snow White.[19] The substitution of young
men for dwarfs, of course, is perfectly apt for the novel's contemporary
setting and audience.[20] Through Bella's first-person narrative, Geras shows
that illusion and reality are not always easy to tell apart. It is this slippage
that works toward subverting the story of the wicked stepmother. Geras's
text, unlike that of Grimm's, is open to a reader's active speculation and
interpretation. Is Marjorie *really* a wicked stepmother?

In Galloway's retelling of Snow White, "A Taste for Beauty," Snow
White's stepmother takes up the subject position in the text to narrate events
from her side of story. She tells about her cruel home where her father beats
her mother and her attempt to run away. She tells about her job in an abat-
toir where she soon graduates to the top of the line where she slaughters
the animals. After the foreman suggests that she try out for a beauty contest that pays a large reward for the winner, she works at deportment, dancing, dieting, and working-out at the gym until she meets Esmeralda and

seals with her the bargain that will make her queen. Esmeralda—a descendant of a line of Romany queens—will train her in the arts of spells and potions while Snow White's future stepmother's part of their pact is to murder the king's young daughter, Snow White. By so doing she will play a part in avenging the death of Romany queens at the hands of ancestors of the king. No female of the king's line is allowed to survive beyond ten years, Esmeralda tells Snow's stepmother. "Few brides of the king" survive a "second decade of marriage" (104).

As in Napoli's *Zel*, Galloway's retelling of a fairy tale is not used to absolve the actions of a stepmother (a mother) but rather to explain them. "A Taste of Beauty" shows how context, personal life history, and what is presented as fate, shape and mold a mind that becomes capable of murdering a child. Indeed, Galloway, in giving Snow White's stepmother agency, makes the horror of a murderous act, distanced in the Grimm version through intermediaries (the hunter and the anonymous narrator), more terrifying. She will not ask the huntsman to do the task for her. "I have sharpened my long steel knife and my little pointy one. I think all the time about Snow White lying dead. I can take care of her myself. It won't be difficult at all" (106).

Galloway thus subverts those versions of Snow White, noted by Tatar, that have depicted the father of Snow White in the place of the hunter in the tale or those interpretations of the tale that have associated the hunter with the king (154). Galloway absents the figure of the king from the immediate scene by placing Snow White's murder in the context of a matrilinear tale of revenge rather than a tale in which a stepmother's jealousy and envy for her husband's attention are shown to be the only motive. Galloway's version of the Snow White tale offers no seduction into a tale of romance. Snow White is no romantic heroine. The very cruelty of the tale would seem to lie in the way a young daughter is made victim to the assertion of power and revenge by women whose line has been dominated and marginalized by patriarchy—represented by the king's lineage. Through her representation of the wicked stepmother, Galloway's text opens up for discussion the question of just how much women in this story are represented as colluding in the separation of mothers and daughters in the name of revenging the sins of patriarchy. Galloway's text provides a different way of looking at the poisonous relationship between the stepmother and Snow White. Galloway brings right to the forefront issues about gender and power—a power that is stitched seamlessly into the traditional tale so that it is well masked.

FRACTURING TRADITIONAL DAUGHTER–MOTHER
NARRATIVES OF FAIRY TALE

Napoli, Galloway, and Geras all fracture, in different ways, the convention of fairy tale in which an anonymous narrator tells the whole tale—a narrative practice—which has had the effect, as Cranny-Francis points out, of making the discourses and power relations constructed within fairy tale to seem neutral and value free (89). They have, for example, centralized those voices that have been marginalized in story by giving voice to women so that story is told from the side of mothers. Galloway and Napoli demystify and give voice and agency to the wicked stepmother and sorceress/mother of fairy tale in that they are able to express their feelings and explain their actions. This provides alternative perspectives from which to think about the figures of a sorceress/mother.

Daughters, of course, also get to tell their stories. While Galloway has focused exclusively on giving mothers' sides of story, Napoli and Geras have written female coming-of-age stories for a contemporary young adult audience in which young women are subjects of their own desire and sexuality. Geras has written fairy-tale romances for young adults that retain much of the traditional framework of fairy tale while making visible, for example, the ways in which beauty and sexuality can work for and against intelligent and passionate young women who are, as Bella describes herself: "Vibrant, alive, sexy." [21] While traditional fairy tale has minimized or absented the relationship between daughters and mothers or has represented them as one dimensional, Napoli, Galloway, and Geras have, in their various stories, made the daughter–mother relationship a central part of their stories. Napoli and Geras bring the daughter–mother relationship alive in their narratives as they write about the emotional and relational dynamics between young women and mothers.

THE DAUGHTER–MOTHER NARRATIVE OF FAIRY TALE
AND A CONTEMPORARY DAUGHTER–MOTHER
DISCOURSE

The daughter–mother narrative in traditional fairy tale is intertextualized into popular cultural discourses that continue to inform contemporary representations of adolescent daughters and mothers in young adult novels. As a conventional narrative form it has been incorporated into young adult novels as pretext and metanarrative. In some instances, there may be only an allusion to a familiar daughter–mother fairy tale narrative such as in Sheila Klass's young adult novel, *To See My Mother Dance*. In this novel, Klass describes the feelings and attitude of thirteen-year-old Jessica toward her new stepmother, Martha. In one scene, Jessica, enticed down to the kitchen by "a delicious baking smell," narrates how she resists the temptation to push the newly instated Martha into the oven (42). A reader may gain a richer appreciation of how Klass emphasizes, with humor, the difference between the traditional wicked/crone stepmother and Jessica's new stepmother by knowing the Hansel and Gretel story. The mother/stepmother opposition is one that many young readers might well be familiar with from the discourse on daughters and mothers in traditional tales.

As in the tales of Rapunzel and Snow White, stories told in young adult texts about daughters and mothers have something to say about a young woman's relationship with her mother as she grows toward sexual maturity, about the role of mothers, and about the position of the daughter–mother relationship in familial relationships set in various historical and cultural contexts. Several aspects of the relationship in fairy tale narrative are congruent with contemporary discourses on the daughter–mother relationship found in young adult texts, although these aspects are, of course, contextualized with concerns and issues reproduced in a contemporary discourse on adolescence.

In young adult novels, the daughter–mother narrative continues to be composed of themes such as the splitting of mothers into good and bad representations of motherhood. There are jealous mothers, mothers who wish to protect daughters from the dangers of the "outside" or (using the vocabulary of current daughter–mother discourse) refuse to "let go" of their daughters. Mothers continue to be viewed as impediments to their daughter's development. In young adult texts, daughters also gaze into mirrors in order to check out their reflections against those of their mothers. Nixon's novel, *Star Baby*, for example, contains a classic Snow White type mirror scene reproducing the stereotype of the jealous and competitive mother who dreads her daughter's coming-of-age.[22] As Abby stands by her mother in front of a mirror, she challenges her mother: "Who would guess that behind that little Cookie Baynes costume lurks the real Abby Baynes who—in less than four years, ladies and gentlemen—will legally be an adult." Abby sees the "flash of terror in her mother's eyes" as her mother preens "at her own reflection" in the mirror. "You're still a child," she replies to her daughter. "Look at me. My goodness, I'm much too young to have a grown-up daughter" (71–72).

These types of representation and themes fit well into texts in which stories are told about daughters who are represented as growing towards independence and maturity during the stage of development known as adolescence. Traditional adolescent psychology is another cultural narrative that has influenced the kind of stories that are imagined and told about adolescent daughters and their mothers. Chapter three addresses the ways in which language and imagery of the psychodynamic narrative of adolescence are used in the telling of daughter–mother stories in selected young adult novels.

NOTES

1. This is the version, for example, in the 1857 version of Grimm's tales. See Grimm, Jacob and Wilhelm, *The Complete Fairy Tales of the Brothers Grimm.* For resources on variant editions, criticism, and scholarship on Snow White, see Vandergrift *Snow White.*

2. For Grimm's 1812 version of "Little Snow-White" see Ashliman.

3. For a discussion of maternal evil in the guise of stepmothers, witches, and mothers-in-law in Grimm's tales, see Tatar 137–55.

4. The identification of the "craving of the pregnant woman" as a folklore motif is made by N. M. Penzer in reference to Giambattista Basile's tale, "Petrosinella." Pre-dating Grimm's Rapunzel tale, this Neapolitan version was published in the collection of tales, *Lo Counto de li Cunti,* or *Pentamerone* (1634). See Basile 140.

5. In other translations of Grimm's text, the word "Godmother" is used—a nomenclature that carries an even more positive description of the witch figure in Grimm's *Rapunzel.* See Grimm, *Tales for Young and Old,* trans. by Ralph Manheim; *The Juniper Tree and Other Tales from Grimm,* trans. by Lore Segal and Randall Jarrett.

6. This version of story is, in fact, close to an earlier German version of the Rapunzel tale by Friedrich Schulz in which it is noted that Rapunzel's dresses did not fit anymore. See Lüthi 102.

7. For Mlle. De La Force's French version "Persinette" and an early German version by Friedrich Schulz, see Lüthi. See also Basile.

8. For example, the version retold for younger children in *Favorite Fairy Tales Told in Germany,* see Haviland 21–31.

9. I have translated from the French version of "Persinette" given in Max Lüthi's "Die Herkunft des Grimmschen Rapunzelmarchen." See Lüthi 96–100.

10. In Mlle De La Force's tale, the "fée" receives the infant Persinette in a swaddling cloth of gold and transforms her into the most beautiful creature in the world by sprinkling water on her face from a crystal vase. When Persinette reaches her twelfth year, the fairy/mother, aware of Persinette's fate, determines to steal her

away from her destiny. Rapunzel is placed in a tower of gold with jewels, fashionable clothes, and delicacies for her meals. See Lüthi 97.

11. For other examples, see Tatar 36–37 and 137–55. In Giambattista Basile's Neapolitan version of the tale "Petrosinella," the witch/mother figure, represented as an ogress, is destroyed by the magic acorns that Petrosinella and the prince throw into her path as they flee the tower. This collection was certainly known to the Brothers Grimm, since Jacob Grimm wrote the preface to the German edition of Basile's tales by Felix Liebrecht in 1846. See Basile lxix–lxx, 135–39.

12. For an interpretation of "Rapunzel" using a psychoanalytic approach, see Bettelheim.

13. The visual image of Rapunzel with her long golden tresses, for example, is a familiar icon in popular culture. Other feminist retellings of the tale also fracture the association with Rapunzel's tresses and codes of sexuality and beauty. See Claffey 36–41; Velde 71.

14. For another example of a young adult novel in which the witch figure has been revisioned, see Napoli *The Magic Circle*.

15. Intertextuality is specifically defined here as "the production of meaning" from the interrelationship between a specific text and an earlier pretext signified by a quotation or an allusion from a pretext. For a fuller definition and explanations, see Stephens 84–119.

16. Kay Vandergrift's model of "contextual void" explores meaning making in reference to how readers experience literary texts. Response to a text may depend on a reader's "literary knowledge and literary allusions." See Vandergrift "Exploring" 356.

17. An exception is the version "Petrosinella." See Basile 138.

18. In Grimm's 1857 version, the queen is forced to put on "red-hot slippers and dance until she fell down dead." See Grimm *The Complete* 204.

19. Elements of story that Geras seems to have also recontextualized in her novel are the seven-man band with whom Belle sings, the party where she is given a cocktail by her stepmother, and the young man with whom she falls instantly in love. See French.

20. For the various ways the dwarfs have been depicted in the Snow White tale, see Vandergrift, *Snow White*.

21. Geras intertextualizes the tale of Red Riding Hood in her retelling of the tale of Sleeping Beauty in which Beauty is raped. See Geras *Pictures*.

22. For an example of how this aspect of the daughter–mother relationship has been popularized, see Friday 160–201.

Three

Flight, Boundaries, and Mirrors: The Imagery and Language of Adolescent Psychology

It's time now for you to step out and live a little. You'll be fifteen soon—it's such a wonderful age.

—Thesman *The Rain Catchers*

The stories of daughters and their relationships with mothers in young adult texts can be read as stories within a story—the story of a daughter's progress through adolescence toward maturity. Represented in these novels are strong daughter protagonists who are described as growing toward independence in which they demonstrate a readiness to take on responsibility for self. The daughter–mother narrative in young adult texts is constructed through and conjoined with cultural discourses about adolescence. It is a narrative that encodes a common-sense understanding of and beliefs about what it is like to be an adolescent, and in particular, what it is like to grow up as an adolescent girl. This chapter is confined to a discussion of Freudian theories about adolescent development and the relation of these to the daughter–mother narrative in young adult novels. Therefore, the discussion is confined to those daughter–mother stories that are set in white, familial settings in North America.

TRADITIONAL THEORIES OF ADOLESCENT DEVELOPMENT

Traditional Freudian theories of adolescent psychology are composed of a number of discourses encoding prescriptive views about how young people should develop into mature, responsible adults. While it is generally recognized that adolescence as a stage of development is a social and cultural construct, the tenets of traditional psychology that have been formulated through the writings of theorists such as Anna Freud, Peter Blos, and Erik Erikson have been used as a hegemonic blueprint for adolescent development.[1] This blueprint has, moreover, been used as an overlay for understanding adolescence in other cultures.[2]

One of the models of traditional Freudian development that has been particularly influential is Blos's model of separation–individuation in which individuation is defined as taking increased responsibility for self.[3] Blos's thesis that adolescents have to relinquish their emotional bonds to parents in order to achieve independence is an understanding of adolescence that has been reiterated in popular psychology texts about teen and parent relationships.[4] A typical statement found in one such text is: "One of the central tasks of adolescence is to extricate oneself from family ties, both psychologically and physically" (Kolodny et al. 313).[5] As Emily Hancock has pointed out in *The Girl Within*, growing-up in contemporary American culture has meant "banishing one's parents" (183). Described in Blos's model and similar models of adolescent development is a view of development that associates attachment with dependency and inequality versus separation with independence and the attainment of equality.[6] An adolescent's need to become independent is constructed in traditional psychology, for example, through a moral discourse prescribing the bounds of healthy and unhealthy relationships between young people and their parents.

This emphasis on independence corresponds to a long-standing North American commitment to individualism. The belief that a young person needs to develop a distinct and separate self is also embedded in discourses about adolescence. Adolescence is characterized as a stage when identity issues are intensified. Finding and establishing one's personal identity has been identified by some psychologists as "*the* developmental task of adolescence" (Donelson and Nilsen 34).[7] Erikson, perhaps the most quoted authority on identity formation in adolescence, describes this process as a "crisis"—a "turning point" in development (96).[8] A belief in the concept of the individual as a separate and autonomous self is central to these discourses.

Independence from parents is said to be achieved through varying degrees of conflict as young people turn, instead, toward forming stronger relationships with peers and move toward establishing sexual relationships.[9] Adolescence has been understood as a period of "storm and stress" and as a time of emotional instability in which the relationships between teenagers and their parents are marked by conflict.[10] This view has been disseminated in self-help texts addressed to teens and their parents that are characterized by a rhetoric of "emotional struggle," "inner unrest," and "turbulent behavior." Adolescence, the titles of some of these texts suggest, is a stage of development to be survived.[11]

The relationship between an adolescent daughter and her mother is especially theorized in Freudian versions of development as one marked by conflict and changes as a daughter is expected to loosen her dependency on her mother and to place distance between them. The daughter–mother narrative in psychodynamic texts is characterized by warnings about adolescent daughters being overly attached and dependent on mothers.[12] Emphasis is placed on a girl's difficulty in separating from her mother and the consequences should she fail to do so.[13]

A Cultural Script

The assumptions and tenets of traditional Freudian adolescent psychology are embedded in a conventional *cultural script* that has popularized a way of understanding issues of identity, independence, and relationships with parents during the teenage years. This includes the relationship between teenage girls and their mothers.[14] This script has been widely disseminated in psychology texts, scholarly and popular articles about adolescence, and is reproduced in articles and discussions about young adult literature. It has been used, for example, to explain the portrayal of parents in young adult novels.[15] It has also been suggested that the writing of fiction for adolescents is influenced by an author's common-sense knowledge and beliefs about adolescent development.[16] Perhaps, most of all, this script has contributed to a way of thinking and talking about teens and parents in certain circumscribed ways using a ready vocabulary of terms and definitions that encode assumptions and values that have not always been closely examined.

This script encoding the tenets of traditional adolescent psychology is used in a number of ways in young adult texts. It is used, in selected texts, as an underlying script for describing, explaining, and plotting the entire story of a relationship between a teenage girl and her mother. Stitched seamlessly into story, the script has the effect of naturalizing the kind of relationship that is imagined between them. In other texts, a portion of this script is used to highlight a particular aspect of the relationship between a teenage daughter and her mother—inviting a reader to recognize "yes—this is just how it is." In selected stories, a cultural script of traditional adolescent psychology is used as a conflicting viewpoint against which other sides of a girl's relationship with her mother are told.

This chapter demonstrates in what ways the script and imagery of traditional adolescent psychology are used to construct and explain the relationships between adolescent girls and their mothers in young adult novels. The
stories of daughters and mothers discussed in this chapter are set in white,
middle-class America from the 1960s to the 1990s. Initial discussion begins with Lynn Hall's *Letting Go* because the text is so centered on the
daughter–mother relationship that it almost functions as a treatise on the
subject. The timeframe of the novel takes place over one weekend during
which sixteen-year-old Casey and her mother engage in a debate about the
status of their relationship as they travel to and take part in a dog show.
Representative of other novels included in this book, Hall's novel encodes
the assumption that a girl's relationship with her mother is marked by
changes and tension as she grows into womanhood.

The minimal narrative plot is constructed around Casey's decision
whether she wishes to, or should, continue to spend her time in an interest
that she shares with her mother. The relationship is represented as a double–
bind for Casey who enjoys the world of dog showing but also feels anger
towards her mother for the disadvantages that she experiences through having the same interests as her mother—namely, estrangement from her peers
(35–36). Casey explains her understanding of how relationships between
adolescents and their parents should be as she and her mother discuss their
relationship. "Kids my age," she informs her mother, "aren't supposed to
get along with their parents. We're supposed to be cutting loose and learning to be independent and all that stuff. We're just going through a stage"
(93). The assumptions that adolescents are in conflict with their parents and
that adolescents must separate from their parents in order to become independent as part of a stage theory of adolescent development is reiterated
by Casey's mother:

> I know we have something special, and I know we have to go through this
> separating craziness for a few years. She has to be independent, and I have
> to loosen up on the leash, and if we don't cut each other up too badly in the
> process, maybe we can be friends ten or fifteen years from now (53).

Clearly reproduced in this cultural script are a set of mandated practices
for how young people and their parents are "supposed," as Casey puts it,
to structure their relationship during adolescence. In Hall's daughter–mother
narrative, the script of "separation–craziness" is questioned as an adequate
model on which to base the way a teenage daughter and her mother relate
to each other. In its place is an explanation of the relationship as a bond-

ing between a daughter and mother. *"No matter what we say to each other,* Casey narrates, *"the need is there on both sides, more strongly on mine than on hers. It's part of the love, and the love is embedded in both of us"* (101). The italics in the text show the emphasis placed in Hall's text on this social construction of the daughter–mother relationship that is further discussed in chapter six.

The dynamics of relationships between white, North American daughters and mothers in selected texts are frequently mediated by recurring patterns of language, metaphors, and visual imagery that are found in the narratives of adolescent psychology.[17] In the following sections, examples illustrate how issues of separation, differentiation, and identity are mediated by recurring patterns of metaphors and imagery grouped (for purposes of discussion) into three main categories: flight, boundaries, and mirrors.

Flight

The relationship between the adolescent and his or her parents is discursively formulated in the classical psychodynamic narratives through a figurative language of freedom in which the young person is freed—"loosened"—from an emotional bondage and dependency on his or her parents. The theoretical writings of Blos, Helene Deutsch, and A. Freud are replete with such terms as "detachment," "emancipation," "liberation," and "flight"—terms that are used to describe the process in which an adolescent separates from his or her parents. Separation from parents, for example, is mediated by language and concepts from biology in a text directly addressed to adolescents in the following passage:

> Even young birds, as they prepare to leave the security of their nest, are cautious and show concern about being able to fly on their own. You too may be concerned about being able to leave the safety of your nest, and yet a part of you is wanting to be on your own (Elchoness 22).

Blossom Turk, in *Living With Teens and Enjoying Them Too*, also makes the analogy between a baby chick stretching its wings and adolescence. "How many of you," she addresses parents, "love your children enough to let them try their wings? There is something frightening about letting them go" (48–49).

Phrases such as "letting go," "cutting loose," and "loosen up on the leash" are examples of a conventional language used in young adult novels to describe the process in which a daughter is expected to separate from her mother in order to be independent; in which a mother is expected to "let go" of her daughter. The wishes of daughters to lead their own lives and be responsible for self reverberate through many texts. Phrases such as a "life of my own," "I can't live my life according to your plans," and "I can't do it your way," and a daughter's wish to "try her wings" are all found in the texts of young adult novels.

In a number of novels, younger teenage daughters express their need to take care of themselves now that they have reached this new "stage" in their lives. They chafe about restrictions on their freedom and about being treated like babies. Fourteen-year-old Cassandra in Colman's *Rich and Famous Like My Mom* states that she is "sick and tired of being kept on a leash" by Agnes, who looks after her in her rock star mother's absence (21). She has "reached a new stage" in her life, she narrates, and "wasn't going to be treated like a baby anymore" (22). "But thirteen, well, you're a teenager and finally you're going to be treated with respect," narrates hopeful thirteen-year-old Cornelia Griswold in Julie First's *Look Who's Beautiful!* (8). These particular novels are representative of others in which the script of adolescent psychology is naturalized into the daughter–mother narrative, and in which stories are plotted around events in which younger teenage girls prove to their mothers that they are capable of being independent and responsible for self. Metaphors of flight encoding assumptions of independence and separation are frequently interrelated with imagery and metaphors that construct a daughter's fear that she will be unable to differentiate herself from her mother.

Boundaries

"I want to be myself, as I am. To know myself," wishes the adolescent daughter of Beya Rete in Stephanie Smith's fantasy novel, *Snow-Eyes* (159). Her statement neatly sums up a key element found in narrative texts on adolescence—a young person's search for identity. The relational problems that a girl is supposed to experience in her relationship with her mother are set out by Chodorow. A daughter:

> identifies with and is expected to identify with her mother in order to attain her adult feminine identification and learn her adult gender role. At the same time she must be sufficiently differentiated to grow up and experience herself as a separate individual—must overcome primary identification while maintaining and building a secondary identification (*The Reproduction of Mothering* 177).

Explanations of how girls identify with their mother are characterized by a figural language of boundaries. In relation to their mothers, for example, girls are said to "experience themselves as overly attached, unindividuated, and without boundaries" (Chodorow *The Reproduction* 137). Apter writes that the "main impediment to the daughter's development, either sexual, intellectual or professional, has been seen to be permeability—the blurring of boundaries between mother and daughter" (97). Evidence of the popularity of this view of daughter–mother relationships can be found in fears of the invasive mother and in warnings about the overidentification of teenage girls and their mothers that are frequently encoded in the daughter–mother narrative in young adult novels.

The apprehension that a daughter will not be able to distinguish herself from her mother is a recurring motif in Nixon's generational stories of daughters and mothers. Teenage daughter Cassie in *Overnight Sensation* tells her friend that she wants her "own identity. It's as simple as that" (58). She "wanted to scream at all of them" that she was not the "shadow" of her mother. "I'm me," she proclaims (98). In *Encore*, sixteen-year-old Erin confronts her mother, Cassie, with her fear that her mother does not want her to be her own person: "What you want is for me to live the kind of life you lived, to be a carbon copy of you! . . . You want me to be your kind of success, but I want my own kind of life!" (105). A daughter's need to draw boundaries between herself and her mother is, not surprisingly, a central theme of the daughter–mother narrative in adolescence. It is treated with a dash of humor in Tanith Lee's fantasy novel, *Black Unicorn*, in which a sorceress mother's magic leaks over and spoils her daughter's breakfast and turns her fountain water into "berry wine" (7). Nevertheless, Tanaquil's anger at her mother is real enough to want her to leave her mother and the fortress where she feels imprisoned.

One of the more serious treatments of the theme of mothers encroaching upon their daughters' lives is found in Deborah Hautzig's novel, *Second Star to the Right,* which is one of two novels in this book that directly associates a teenage daughter's eating problems with a mother's behavior.[18] Hautzig's novel is an intense fictional account of fourteen-year-old Leslie's downward spiral into anorexia nervosa. Through her first-person narrative, Leslie recounts her emotions and her attitude toward her mother and their relationship. The conversational style in which Leslie shares her secrets with an implied audience potentially invites a reader to identify with the position of an adolescent daughter against her mother. Leslie's mother is described by her daughter as pretending to be "so selfless yet manages to suck me dry till I don't even feel a person. Till I can't tell us apart" (120). Leslie's subjectivity is shown to be under threat of erasure by an overbearing mother. As indicated in her narrative, she is, at times, unable to experience herself as a distinct person: "Mother, me, we, are, one, none, goodbye Leslie" (98).

She wishes, she narrates, to "fly" to "never-be-Mom-land, always-be-me land" (144). Leslie reveals in first-person narration the difficulties she has in fighting with her mother. She is "old Leslie-keep-the-peace Hiller who always plays the game" (126). She can fight with her mother over the "dumb things all the time, but when it comes down to important stuff, somehow" they "always agreed" (15).

Leslie's battle with anorexia is told in the context of a story told to her by her mother. Leslie is named after Margolee, a cousin of her mother's, who was killed because, narrates Leslie, of her selfless act of following her mother to the gas chamber instead of trying to save her own life. Relating the story to her own situation, Leslie now feels selfish in wanting to establish a sense of self separate from her mother. Leslie's dilemma is displaced, in the text, onto an eating problem. "Suppose someone said, 'If you don't starve, your mother will be killed.' Imagine it. That's not why I do it, of course, but just imagine it. If you eat, she'll die. And if your mother dies, you die. I would. Eating=greedy=selfish, and selfish is dangerous" (120).

The blaming of a mother for finding it difficult to allow her daughter to separate—to let go—is also part of a discourse that constructs female adolescence as a time when a daughter has difficulties in extricating herself from her mother. A psychologist tells Leslie's mother that she is "worried about" her, not her daughter (73). While this is the only novel included in this book that is built directly around this particular association, the discourse that constructs too close an attachment and overidentification with a mother as unhealthy, as discussed later in this chapter, structures other stories about daughter–mother relationships.[19] How much this understanding of the daughter–mother relationship in adolescence is normalized into popular culture is apparent from a review of Hautzig's book that refers to the depiction of the relationship as "psychologically sound."[20] The mother who threatens a daughter's individuality and difference, who is written about in terms of the engulfing and devouring mother, appears in feminist writing as well as in popular literature including the genre of young adult literature. Paulina Palmer refers, for example, to the recurrent imagery of engulfment and mirrors as archetypal because their use is so pervasive in texts and novels (114–15).

Mirrors

In the narratives of psychoanalysis and psychology, a discourse of identity and differentiation is also characterized by a visual imagery of mirrors.[21] Gilligan notes that the concept of identity as constructed through the "recurring image of the mirror" is prevalent in the writings of psychoanalytic literature ("Remapping" 7).[22] The description of the adolescent girl gazing into a mirror is, of course, a prevalent image in fictional accounts of growing up. The reflecting image of the mirror has been shown, for example, to contribute to the encoding of a code of beautification in young adult texts.[23] It is also used to address the question of "who am I" for the teenage girl. One of the clearest examples of how mirror imagery is used to depict a self as "separate and bounded" is found in Madeleine L'Engle's novel *Camilla*.[24] As she stands in front of a mirror, Camilla narrates: "This is me. I am Camilla Dickinson. I'm me, and this is what I look like standing on the floor with my feet just off the edge of the rug, staring into the mirror in my room." She repeats that she is "Camilla Dickinson and no one else and no one else is me" (125).

From Snow White to young adult novels, the mirror has served to reflect and also to divide the images of daughters and mothers.[25] Issues of identity and differentiation between teenage girls and their mothers are particularly mediated in young adult texts by a visual mirroring in which daughters compare themselves to their mothers. Representative is Zöe's comment in *The Silver Kiss* that "she had always been compared to her mother." She has "the same gray eyes, long black hair with a slight curl, and deceptively pale skin that tanned quickly at the slightest encouragement" (Klause 2). Identified below are examples from specific texts illustrating the way in which mirror scenes are used to show how daughters construct their subjectivities in relationship or in separation from their mothers based on a visual mirroring of their similarities or differences, respectively. Girls and mothers are also shown constructing their relationship to each other through gazing at the juxtaposition of their double images reflected back to them by the ubiquitous mirror "on the wall." [26]

Mirror Images

A. E. Cannon's *Amazing Gracie*, Linda Fosburgh's *The Wrong Way Home*, and Sachs's *Just Like a Friend* are exemplars of novels in which the imagery of mirroring is used extensively as part of the daughter–mother narrative. These mirror scenes contribute toward constructing a formulaic patterning of the daughter–mother relationship (found in these and other selected novels) that characterizes a girl's relationship with her mother at the beginning of story as close. In Cannon's *Amazing Gracie*, for example, Gracie's mother is described as exactly the "same size" as Gracie and has "identical taste in clothes." As Gracie comments, they "have the same taste in a lot of things—food, movies, movie stars. We both love the way Mel Gibson looks, for instance" (9). Gazing at their mirrored images, Gracie's mother comments: "We really *do* look alike, don't we?" as she smiles at the mirrored reflection of herself and her daughter (15). "Everybody says we do," she continues. Gracie agrees: "We're both short and small with long permed black hair, dark eyes, and fair skin that always burns in the sun" (15).

In Sachs's *Just Like a Friend*, a daughter is also identified with a mother who is represented as looking and behaving like her teenage daughter. Fourteen-year-old Patti and her mother are described as sharing each other's interests and buying similar clothes. In a scene in which mother and daughter stand together at the mirror, Patti, looking at their reflected images, notes how "alike" they look (5). Patti and Vi hang out together during the summer (7). They buy identical sweaters (3). The behavior and conversation of daughter and mother in the beginning chapter of the novel leads a sailor to ask whether they are sisters (2). It is also made clear in these texts that this is not an appropriate kind of relationship for teenage girls and their mothers, reiterating advice given in self-help texts about the daughter–mother relationship in adolescence. [27]

In each novel, mothers are shown not to be adequate role models for their daughters. In *Amazing Gracie,* Gracie's mother is described as having suffered severe bouts of depression since the death of Gracie's father. During these times, Gracie has had to take care of herself and her mother, a caring that continues after Gracie's mother recent remarriage, when Gracie also finds herself partly responsible for her small stepbrother, Sinjian. As story continues, however, Gracie narrates how she feels anger and hate against a mother who has lied to her about relocating after her marriage, attempts suicide, and is not represented as nurturing or empowering her daughter.

Set in the context of a family situation in which Patti's young-looking mother and her older husband live with Patti's maternal grandmother, Patti's mother in *Just Like a Friend* is accused by her daughter for failing to carry out her duties as a wife in failing to care adequately for her husband when he has a heart attack. Patti tells her grandmother, for example: "She's hopeless. She's like a baby—no—not like a baby, because she's a grown woman. She's nearly thirty-two. It's crazy for a woman her age to act so silly and to think of nobody else but herself" (Sachs 116). The critical voice of the daughter, the tone of disparagement through choice of language—"silly," "a baby," and "crazy," and the representation of the mother as childish are all narrative conventions used in this and other texts to lessen the stature of a mother. She is not going "to be silly and empty headed" like her mother, Patti narrates (142). Although Patti's grandmother defends Patti's mother and herself when Patti blames her for her mother's failings, Patti's narration and focalization of events dominate the text. Patti's development into a mature person depends on her growing beyond her mother whom she criticizes as dressing inappropriately as a "teenage punker" (151). Their mirrored image as teenage look-a-likes is fractured at the closure of the novel as Patti is described as disassociating herself from her mother, because her mother, as a character foil, is associated with dependency and immaturity.

Fracturing Daughter–Mother Images

The novels by Cannon and Sachs are representative of texts that use the convention of visual imagery to show how a daughter moves from an overly close identification with a mother to a splitting of their mirrored image and a splitting of self as a young woman differentiates herself from her mother. In *Just Like a Friend,* Patti narrates how she used to sometimes cry because she was worried that she "might not look exactly like" her mother: "But now here I was, looking at myself in the mirror, at me, with my brown eyes, and my tall, slim figure, and my face that was something like Vi's and yet completely different, and I wasn't upset at all. I liked what I saw in the mirror" (Sachs 43).

In *Amazing Gracie*, Gracie's fear that she is her "mom all over again" is foregrounded as Gracie looks at her mother's photo in a yearbook and narrates that her "insides went dead cold" as she saw her mentally depressed mother as "just a normal regular kid" when she was Gracie's age. "I keep this fear like a hard little seed buried deep inside me. Mostly I ignore it," she narrates. "But it's always there" (Cannon 103). Gracie's stepfather, Pete, tells her: "Well you *look* just like her. But no. You're not like her *at all*," and laughs in response to Gracie's further worry that she will be like her mother when she is "her age" (183). His assurances leave Gracie feeling separate from her mother—"as free as wind" (185).

Mirroring is used extensively in this text to show the need for a daughter to fracture her identity with her mother. After her mother attempts suicide, Gracie is unable to bear her days of sadness and the pictures in her head of her mother lying unconscious on the bed where she had found her (162). She leaves her unhappy stepfather and the equally desperate and angry little boy, Sinjian, to go and live with her friend, Sarah, who lives where she had formerly lived with her mother (165).

Grace, however, is not a mirror image of her mother. In a scene in which Gracie re-enacts her mother's attempted suicide, Gracie almost fails to step off the railroad tracks before an oncoming train. "You could have been killed. Is that what you wanted?" Sarah yells at her. It is not what she wants, replies Gracie (172). Later, she dreams that she had left Sinjian, only a few inches long, in a drawer with just enough food and water to last until she returned home. In her dream, Sinjian had "turned blue because he couldn't breathe" (174). "I don't care," she had flung out at Pete when she left home (165), but after passing the home where she used to live with her mother, Gracie begins to cry—missing her mother—and makes the decision to return home. She does care. Gracie is represented as "amazing" in comparison to her mother. Her stepfather tells her that she is "tough" unlike her mother who cannot fight. She is "so competent" that he been "real scared of her" (183). In Cannon's daughter–mother narrative, it is made clear that a daughter comes of age through surpassing her mother—a conventional motif in daughter–mother stories.

Matrophobia is a term used by A. Rich to explain the "fear" of "becoming one's mother." It is defined as a desperate wish to become free of the mother when boundaries are blurred and a daughter dreads complete identification with her mother. It involves, she writes, a "womanly splitting of the self" (235–36). The splitting of the daughter's sense of identification from negative representations of the maternal body would seem to be a crucial issue in adolescence, particularly since adolescence is constructed as a stage in which issues of body, gender, and identity are central concerns for adolescents.

The most haunting nightmare of a daughter seeing herself as her mother in these novels is found in Fosburgh's *The Wrong Way Home* in which fifteen-year-old Bent's mother suffers from Huntington's chorea, a genetically transmitted disease. The vivid descriptions of Bent's mother's diseased and wasting body and her lack of agency as she is able to utter only "spastic garbled sounds [that] rarely sounded coherent anymore" (9) are used to heighten a daughter's fear that she will inherit her mother's genes: "The disease was there waiting, biding its time before it struck with its insidious and deadly force. . . . So many times she had felt this fear" (16).

In visual imagery that is definitive of matrophobia, Bent is lost in the "hideous maze" of a dream as she runs after the "hunched and stumbling figure of her mother." Swinging her mother's "body around," Bent screams as she comes "face-to-face with her own image, her fifteen-year-old self, stooped and shaking, her hair white and stringy" (17). The fear of being unable to construct a sense of self separate from that of her mother is reproduced through the further incongruity and grotesqueness of juxtaposed images of mother and daughter who are focalized as being "like two peas in a pod, one not yet fully formed, the other shrinking in the mildewed shell" (16). Bent, in one scene, agrees with a friend that she and her mother look "just alike."

> The gray, almost white, hair above the colorless face, sagging cheek muscles, slack mouth, unfocused eyes behind thick glasses. 'Pictures of her at my age show her to be prettier, but we look alike.' She brushed the golden hair back from her forehead and it hung in soft waves from the center part (64).

While the mirror scenes in Fosburgh's novel produce extreme examples of how mirror imagery is used to evoke a daughter's nightmare vision of becoming her mother, this fear is frequently reproduced as an underlying theme in other daughter–mother narratives in young adult texts. Themes of independence, difference, and the process of a daughter's separation from her mother are interrelated in the psychodynamic literature with the concepts of idealization and deidealization.

Idealizing and Deidealizing Mother

The move from idealization to deidealization is a dynamic that is frequently used to describe and explain the changing relationship between a daughter and her mother in which a daughter moves from a state of idealizing her mother to a more critical and distant view in which she sees her mother as "other" to self. Attachment, identification, and idealization are conceptually linked together in the psychodynamic literature. The concept of deidealization is described by Louise Kaplan in terms of a daughter "recognizing that the woman on whom she has modeled her own self is far from a divine creature fashioned in heaven" (181). An older adolescent girl, she explains "reappraise[s] her mother for what she really is and is not" as she becomes more sure of her own independence and self-identity (182). The move from close attachment and idealization of a mother to a more distanced position in which a daughter views her mother more critically is also a strong structuring dynamic in fictional accounts of daughter–mother relationships in selected young adult novels.

The textbook definition of deidealization is reproduced, for example, in L'Engle's novel *Camilla*. As fourteen-year-old Camilla struggles with the knowledge of her mother's extramarital affair with Jacques Nissen, Jacques tells her:

It's a very difficult thing to realize that your parents aren't the completely perfect human beings that parents ought to be, isn't it? . . . And I include your father in that statement as well as your mother. As for me, I'm not your parent, so there wasn't ever any reason for me to be perfect, was there? (276).

Camilla tells her friend that her mother "used to look like a princess in a fairy tale, and now that's gone. I suppose she's still beautiful, but it's different" (64).

The novel *To See My Mother Dance* by Klass is an exemplar of how the language and imagery of child and adolescent psychology (including concepts of regression, idealization, and deidealization) are used in a novel for young people. Klass's family romance is set in the context of a story in which thirteen-year-old Jessica's divorced father wishes to marry again. Jessica, however, is described as unable to relinquish a fantasy of idealized love for her mother, who had abandoned Jessica on her first birthday.

In a series of short vignettes that are framed and break up the linear flow of the narrative plot, Jessica describes Karen, the mother she adores, in her dream fantasies: "She sits very straight in a beautiful blue velvet chair. A tiara of gardenias crowns her honey-brown hair, and she is more lovely in her long ivory satin gown than any queen ever was" (1). Through taking up the speaking position of the absent Karen, Jessica fantasizes a daughter–mother dialogue signifying the love and unity between daughter and mother: "She looks up. Joy lights her face. Jess—how glad I am to see you. I've been thinking of you. This morning I wrote a poem about you. . . . It's called, 'My Daughter, Lovely Child of Me'" (25). The practice of using vignettes in order to divide a daughter's inner fantasies from the surface narrative is also a good example of how Freud's concept of inner and outer consciousness is employed to literally structure the physical layout of a text as well as story.[28]

Her fantasies are fractured when Martha, her stepmother, decides to take her to find her actual mother. She had asked Jessica's father: "You want her to live her whole life this way? You want her to believe in a fantasy mother?" (111). Jessica finally sees her mother (now Sita Kumari) in the gaudy and exotic setting of the house of the Children of the Lotus where she is described as abasing herself in prayer to "Sita Ram" and speaking like a "programmed doll." Jessica comments that the mother she had spent years dreaming about was nothing like the woman she has just met (149). The beautiful young Karen who had been her mother was "unreal, a photograph mother" (141). Jessica is represented as moving from a fantasized attachment to a mother she never really knew to the reality of a relationship with her new stepmother.[29]

Healthy and Unhealthy Relationships

The discourse that constructs teen relationships with parents around the opposition of dependency and independence and attachment and separation has provided a way of talking and thinking about family relationships that has been absorbed into everyday conversation and reading material about adolescence. In *Lives Together/Worlds Apart* Walters notes that the discourse about mothers and daughters in the 1980s was particularly structured through a "psychological litany" of terms such as "independence, autonomy, individuation, separation" (190). In the context of the daughter–mother narrative in adolescence, however, this litany has been doubly used since it is integral both to the traditional narratives of adolescence and to cultural scripts of the daughter–mother relationship. Excerpts from C. S. Adler's novel, *The Shell Lady's Daughter*, Sachs's *Just Like a Friend*, and Sheila Schwartz's *Like Mother, Like Me* illustrate how fictional accounts of the daughter–mother relationship in adolescence are constructed through a discourse that addresses issues of attachment and the dangers of dependency. Emphasis is placed on the need for a daughter to be independent.

A clear example of how a model of development that equates dependence and attachment with a failure to mature is encoded into texts is seen in. Adler's novel, *The Shell Lady's Daughter*. The story tells how the dependency and overattachment of a mother to a daughter can thwart the development of a teenage girl. Fourteen-year-old Kelly Allgood's mother breaks down and attempts suicide as her daughter, described as her mother's "best friend," meets with other friends, including a boyfriend, rather than spending time with her. Kelly explains:

> The truth is, lately it's begun to scare me that I'm my mother's best friend. Not that I don't still love her and think she's the warmest, most wonderful mother in the world, but I don't plan to spend the rest of my life with her. Kids are supposed to go away to college and leave home to get married aren't they? (11).

However, when her mother is ready to come home from hospital, Kelly tells her paternal grandmother that she is not going to boarding school but is planning on staying home to help take care of her mother. She has to give her mother her "love and support." Her grandmother does not agree. Kelly will be "sacrificing" her life for her mother instead of "realizing" her "potential" (134). There are others who voice the opinion that letting her mother become too dependent on Kelly will slow down Kelly's development. Kelly is warned by a Ph.D. psychologist that her plans could have "negative effects":

Well, while I agree that it might benefit your mother to have you home in
this early part of her recovery, I do see some danger to you. That is, if you
allow your mother to become dependent on you and feel responsible for keeping her company, when you should be out socializing with your peers, that
could stunt your emotional and social development (137).

It is made clear in the text that Kelly's plan to stay home is sanctioned on
the contingency that Kelly is strong enough to withstand her mother's dependency on her. Her mother might, warns the psychologist, have a "re-
lapse" (138).

The same concern that a mother be not too dependent on her daughter
is encoded into Schwartz's young adult novel, *Like Mother, Like Me.* Jen
is represented as her mother's helper and supporter as she takes over the
household duties when her mother experiences a breakdown. Jen narrates:
"Part of me watched what was happening to her with loving concern. But
I have to admit that another part of me began to be annoyed and resentful"
(148). Jen eventually tells her mother that she would like to "feel happy
and free, not worried all the time." She feels too "guilty" to go out and enjoy
herself (152). Her mother's response is: "Of course, darling. You go along
and have a good time, and I promise you things will be different when you
return. I promise you. You don't have to worry anymore" (153). Emphasis
and value in the text is placed on the attainment of independence versus
dependence for both a daughter and her mother. Jen narrates at the beginning of the novel: "I want to tell you about the year he was away, and how
my mother turned into a teenager and then grew up" (3).[30]

The novels by Adler and Schwartz are representative of young adult
novels in which the daughter–mother relationship is shown to be one of
contradiction and contention. It is a site where expressions of love and attachment between a daughter and her mother conflict with a cultural discourse that perceives attachment of mothers and daughters as "unhealthy"
in a culture that "values independence and rationality over closeness and
emotionality" (Caplan 114).[31] A concept of self, defined through relationship, is placed into contradiction with a concept of self that is separate and
autonomous.

In a text on female adolescence entitled *All That She Can Be,* for example, we are told that a girl should not be best friends with her mother
since this not a healthy kind of relationship for either a teen daughter or
her mother. A girl who is her mother's "best friend" is characterized as
"passive"—the "good girl" who has difficulty in achieving independence
from her mother. A " 'best-friend mother' " is characterized as a mother who

is using her daughter to obtain the "love and companionship" she is unable to gain from "more equal relationships" because of her insecurity (Eagle and Colman 86).[32] The inappropriateness of a daughter being her mother's best friend is a pervasive script in texts on adolescent psychology. It is precisely this set of risks that are encoded into the texts of novels by Adler and Sachs. While much of this advice may be viewed as common sense, it also forms part of a cultural script in which attachment to a mother is represented as problematic.

Adolescence has been popularly understood as a stage when adolescents turn away from their parents and turn instead to others for friendship and support.[33] This script for this model of development is heard in Adler's text through the voice of a woman doctor who tells Kelly that: "A girl your age is supposed to spend time with her friends. That's part of growing up and becoming independent, which is what you're supposed to do in the normal course of your development into adulthood" (104). At the beginning of Sachs's *Just Like a Friend,* Patti describes her relationship with her mother in terms of friendship: "She's more like a friend than a mother," she tells a peer friend, Emily (22).

Patti spends the summer away from home with Emily and her mother, whom Patti admires. The description of the daughter–mother relationship in Sachs's story bears relation to Deutsch's description of female adolescence in which a daughter makes "energetic attempts to be different from her mother" that includes idealization of another woman (1:7 and 8). Her mother, Patti narrates toward closure of the novel, is "not" her "friend" but her "mother" (132). Similarly, in *The Shell Lady's Daughter,* Kelly is warned that she is her mother's daughter, "not her friend," and that her mother "has to have her own life" (Adler 137). In a society in which "loving one's mother is linked with dependency, passivity, and regression" (Pipher 103), the very term—*relationship*—is a contradiction. In so many young adult novels, the concept of relationship—and what it means in respect to the daughter–mother relationship—is put into question.

Authorizing a Script

In Adler's *The Shell Lady's Daughter*, the privileged first-person narrative of Kelly gives voice to the love and attachment between Kelly and her mother. However, a cultural script prescribing what the appropriate healthy relationship between a daughter and her mother should be during adolescence is strongly presented in the text through the mediation of voices who carry authority. The representation of fictional characters as psychologists or counselors, whose expert advice is sought and given, is a narrative convention used in several texts to authorize the ideological stance taken in a text. Adler uses the script of adolescent psychology verbatim in her novel through the voices of fictional characters who are represented in the texts as medical experts. Their voices are legitimized through the acknowledgement of the expertise of a psychologist on the verso of the title page. In Adler's text, the question could be raised to what extent a daughter's voice is used to soften the experts' opinions. Emily's mother in *Just Like a Friend*, who is a psychologist, is also represented as an authorizing voice as she advises Patti that her family needs professional counselling (142). She tells Patti that she is going to have to be more independent and be ready to solve her own problems (143). Emily, whose mother was not always available to meet her needs, is clearly represented as a role model for Patti. Patti narrates how she is going to manage on her own like Emily (143).

The practice of constructing an alternative daughter–mother relationship, between a best friend and her mother, is frequently used to endorse a particular ideological viewpoint in a text or to demonstrate a different, sometimes preferable kind of daughter–mother relationship. In this way, different positions are created in the text from which to compare and contrast alternative experiences of the daughter–mother relationship. Described in *Just Like a Friend* is the more healthy, and therefore more acceptable relationship between Patti's friend, Emily, and her mother, which is based on the assumption that a certain amount of distance in which they can allow each other to "breathe" is healthy. The emphasis in the text on self-reliance and independence from a mother is reinforced through Emily's mother's refusal to take Patti "under her wing." Patti later asserts her independence and her difference from her mother (147).

At the closure of Sachs's novel, a lacuna exists between Patti and her mother as shared laughter changes to a halting conversation filled with silences and ellipses (153–54). As in all the other novels chosen for this study, adolescence in Sachs's novel is fantasized as a crucial stage during which issues of independence and subjectivity are foregrounded and in which a daughter's relationship with her mother is marked by changes, differences, or conflict as a girl grows into womanhood.

Growing Away from Mother

Daughters are represented as growing up toward maturity in the young adult novels chosen for this study. If narratives are said to be motivated by "desire," this can be said to be at least part of the dynamic that motivates narrative plot. Daughter–mother narratives emphasize the importance of independence and responsibility. Indeed, it can be said that a generic convention of young adult texts is the representation of daughters as strong protagonists who become increasingly self-dependent and learn to take responsibility for themselves—and often for their mothers—and others. This female coming-of-age story can also be told as a teenage girl's growth toward self-understanding and her understanding and acceptance of others.

The narrative script of traditional adolescent psychology, however, has also been influential in disseminating the belief that daughters and sons must separate themselves from their mothers in order to mature. The result has been that little attention has been given to daughter–mother loving connections because of the emphasis on individuation and separation. Sachs's *Just Like a Friend* has been used as an exemplar of how this script, articulated in the text as a means of empowering an adolescent girl, is used as a mandate to describe how the relationship between a teenage daughter and mother *should* be during this stage in a girl's life.

Stephens suggests that "all developmental paths are ideologically constructed"(4). Such ideological positions may be incorporated into literature for young people in such a way that they imply that this is how things are—this is how it is (9). When stitched seamlessly or explicitly into story, without contradiction, the tenets of adolescent psychology contribute towards constructing a certain ideological "truth" about adolescence, the daughter–mother relationship, and the construction of subjectivity during adolescence. The choice of using a formulaic convention, for example, that includes getting "rid" of parents "so that the young person will be free to take credit for his or her own accomplishment" (Donelson and Nilsen 24) encodes a conceptualization of adolescence that places value on independence and responsibility that de-emphasizes growing up through interdependency with others.

Pipher's statements that adolescent girls are "socialized to have a tremendous fear of becoming like their mothers" and to "reject" identification with their mothers give voice to a popular cultural narrative that is also reproduced in daughter–mother stories in selected young adult novels (103). The daughter–mother narrative in young adult texts, of course, is also socially constructed from other narratives. As demonstrated in many of the excerpts from the young adult novels discussed above, a narrative script of adolescent psychology frequently colludes, for example, with a popular cultural discourse about the mother–daughter relationship found in fictional accounts and other texts about the relationship included for adult audiences.

One of the least openly acknowledged premises of traditional adolescent psychology has been its inherent gender bias. According to traditional Freudian theories of adolescent development, a girl must detach herself from the "confining" dependency of her mother and turn to her father (Blos 232–33). These theories, authored by men, tell a side of human development that has, for the most part, been patterned on male experiences and held up as the norm against which female development is judged and compared (Belenky et al. 6–7) [34] Chapter four discusses how Freudian fantasies and family romances continue to inform daughter–mother narratives in selected young adult novels.

NOTES

1. Blos has been referred to as "the most influential writer in the psychodynamic tradition" of adolescent development. See Adelson and Doehrman 110.

2. For the view that "adolescent development is basically uniform in all societies" and in all historical periods, see Kiell 1–20.

3. Blos draws upon Margaret Mahler's concept of separation-individuation. See Blos "The Second" 157; Mahler 307–24.

4. Blos characterizes adolescence into different phases during which adolescents experience a time of "emotional turmoil," a time of "slow severance of the emotional ties" from their families, and a time of "mourning" their loss. See Blos 10, 12, 187.

5. For another example of how Blos's theory is reproduced in a self-help book on adolescent psychology, see Gardner 24.

6. See Gilligan "Remapping" 14.

7. For explanations of stage developmental theories developed by Blos, Erik Erikson, Lawrence Kohlberg, Jane Loevinger, and Robert Kegan that address the formation of identity in adolescence, see Kroger.

8. Identity "crisis" is described as an adolescent's task in forming a new "kind of identification" that involves "subordinating" childhood identifications, and which is achieved (for a male) through an adolescent's assimilation into society and recognition by the "community." See Erikson 155–58. For Erikson's explanation of female identity, see 283.

9. See Coleman.

10. Adolescence was characterized by G. Stanley Hall as "the most critical stage of life" that recapitulates "some ancient period of storm and stress when old moorings were broken and a higher level attained." See Hall I: xiii. He described adolescence as a period when youth "experience hot and perfervid psychic states" and search for "excitement." See Hall II: 74.

11. See, for example, titles by Bruggen and O'Brian, Elchoness, Gardner, and Kolodny et al.

12. For an example of a discourse that brings into contiguity daughter–mother attachment, the problems of idealization, and incestuous relationships, see Kaplan.

13. See, for example, Blos *On Adolescence* 66, 232–33; Blos "Modifications" 16–17; Deutsch 1:244.

14. A script is defined as incorporating "patterns of learned behavior that are culturally and historically specific." See DuPlessis 2.

15. See, for example, Atkinson.

16. For examples of how authors of young adult novels draw upon their knowledge of adolescent psychology, see Atkinson 315; Small 282.

17. It is reported in *Between Voice and Silence* that interviews with adolescent girls show that the themes, language, and visual imagery of adolescent psychology are readily available to young women for constructing and shaping their experiences of their relationships with their mothers. See Taylor, Gilligan, and Sullivan 315–17.

18. See Greenberg *The Pig-Out Blues*.

19. For an analysis of *National Velvet*, in which the daughter–mother relationship is linked with eating problems in adolescence, see Tyler 154–58.

20. See Sutherland (1979-84) 182.

21. Both Lacanian and Object-Relations theorists use the language and visual imagery of mirrors in theories of identity development. See Lacan; Winnicott.

22. Criticism of the image of mirroring as used to understand the conception of self is made by Gilligan as she points out that it is a static, nonrelational way of understanding self and other. See Gilligan "Remapping" 7.

23. For specific examples from texts illustrating how "romance, sexuality, and beautification" form part of a feminine discourse in young adult novels, see Christian-Smith 43–55.

24. See Gilligan "Remapping" 3.

25. For an example of how mirror imagery is used in the daughter–mother narrative, see the essay poem by Irigaray "And."

26. D. W. Winnicott stresses the role of the mother in the construction of self-identity in his concept of "maternal mirroring." According to Winnicott, the mother's face as mirror reflects back to the child what he or she sees. See Winnicott 112.

27. For the view that "Changing fashions and the youth cult of the 1960s was the beginning of this trend," see Hammer 110; for the view that the prenubile, adolescent look "becomes a way of controlling the adult woman's sexuality," see Coward 77.

28. For the argument that Freudian theory with its emphasis on the "inner consciousness" was influential in the development of adolescence, see White 44; Witham 13.

29. For the view that there has to be a "loosening of pre-oedipal fixations" in regard to an adolescent daughter's "liberation" from her mother, see Blos "Modifications" 17.

30. It is interesting to note that Schwartz's novel was released as a television movie under the same title. Walters describes the movie as a "mother's feminist

coming of age" story that "is paralleled with that of her adolescent daughter." It is clear that elements of story have been changed, and that formulaic conventions have shaped the representation of this daughter–mother relationship in a somewhat different form in Schwartz's text. See Walters 132–33.

31. Caplan also refers to the homophobic discourse that warns against too close a relationship between mothers and daughters. See Caplan 117.

32. See also Secunda 312–13.

33. For the view that adolescents set themselves apart from the adult world and form a "subculture" of their own as they turn to friends and peers, see Coleman.

34. For criticism of traditional Freudian psychology, see Adelson and Doehrman; Greenberg, Siegel, and Leitch; Youniss and Smoller.

Four

Daughters, Mothers, and Freudian Romances

If we live in a Freudian culture, it is not because most people have studied Freud, but because institutions of cultural production have so absorbed Freudian thinking that it has become part of the foundation of how we tell a story or perceive a character's motivation.

—Walters

The stories we are told about family relationships engage the imagination and provide us with different ways of knowing how these relationships may be experienced. Freudianism, as Walters points out, has been influential in the way family relationships have been imagined and talked about in our everyday discourse. Freud's use of the Oedipal myth on which to base his theories of human development has resulted in a paradigm for development that valorizes the need for adolescents to separate from parents in order to attain maturity. In developing a theory in which a boy's masculinity depended on his separation from his mother in order to take up male identification through his father, Freud saw a different developmental path for a girl because of her identity and attachment to her mother. Classical accounts of female adolescence ask that a girl reject her mother on the grounds that she does not possess a penis—a marker of power and authority—in order to mature and to take "her place with her father." This was acknowledged by Freud as a difficult task, and probably one never fully completed.[1] Freud's conception of development has been directly transposed into traditional theories of adolescent development.[2]

In *Mother Daughter Revolution*, Debold and others argue that Erikson and other psychologists have built on Freud's theories so that these interpretations of human development are regarded as "objective truth" (68). As Gilligan points out, gender bias is inherent in Freudian versions of female development because the development of girls and women did not fit into accounts based on male experiences. The strength and continuation of women's "pre-Oedipal attachment to their mothers" was seen by Freud as a developmental difference and the cause of a "developmental failure" (*In a Different* 6–7). If, as Chodorow argues in *The Reproduction of Mothering*, the establishment of a boy's masculinity has been seen as depending on his rejection of dependency, attachment to his mother, and his identification with her, one can see how problematic this model of development has been for girls. The work of traditional developmental theorists is filled with dire warnings should a girl fail to liberate herself from her mother and make the "turn" toward the father. In a discourse that describes a mother as an obstacle to her daughter's development attachment to a mother and the figure of the mother becomes associated with regression and dependence. This is characterized by language that devalued the figure and place of the mother.[3]

As discussed in chapter three, a narrative script of adolescent psychology has informed the description of the daughter–mother relationship in selected young adult novels. A relationship has also been drawn between narratives of white Western theories of adolescent development and the narrative plotting of young adult novels. The argument is made that both narratives are formulated through a linear plot of development in which adolescence is theorized and written about as a stage of growth between childhood and adolescence.[4] As Vandergrift has also pointed out, many of the classic coming-of-age stories in American literature follow the paradigm of a male journey (Journey 25). The heroic journey of the hero in the form of the *Bildungsroman*—a hero's separation from family in order to achieve independence and a separate identity—is a basic narrative plot in many young adult novels.[5]

While, of course, fictional accounts about adolescence correspond in only some respects to linear narratives of psychoanalytic development, one can argue that if the narrative plotting of a story about adolescence is congruent in some respects to a Freudian linear narrative of adolescent development and encodes some of the assumptions of that narrative, the gender bias of Freudianism can be stitched discursively into story.[6] In this chapter, I argue that the tenets and gender ideology of Freudianism are encoded into a set of narrative and plotting conventions used in telling stories about daughters and mothers in selected young adult novels. Because Freudian narratives and romances have been used to represent white Western adolescence and familial structures, the novels discussed in this chapter are limited to stories about white North American daughter–mother relationships in various socioeconomic settings.

PARADIGMATIC PLOTS OF THE DAUGHTER–MOTHER NARRATIVE IN ADOLESCENCE

One of the earliest novels included in this study is Colman's *Claudia, Where Are You?* published in 1969. The story of sixteen-year-old Claudia's alienation from her mother, her flight from home, and the culmination of her journey with a romantic involvement with a young man is one of the clearest examples of a Freudian linear-narrative plot. It is analogous to traditional Freudian models of adolescent development as a stage in which independence is equated with emotional separation from the mother. Set in the 1960s, Claudia's rejection of her middle-class parents' "phony values" and her series of adventures towards independence involving drugs and being homeless coheres with the timeframe of the novel's setting. It was a time, as Susan J. Douglas points out, when young, middle-class women were "challenging the status quo" (142). However, the elements of plot such as the emancipation of an adolescent teenager from deidealized parents, conflict and alienation between a teenage daughter and her mother, and the heterosexual romantic plot encode a familiar story of adolescence set within this context.

Claudia's boyfriend states that Claudia has been "pretty damn well protected" for someone who wanted to be "independent" and that she needed to be "*emotionally* independent" from her parents (177). Analogous with Erikson's description of identity formation, Claudia's social identity is constructed in separation from parents. At the closure of the novel, Claudia's statement "My apartment, my job, my boyfriend, my neighborhood. For once I knew where I was" excludes a sense of identity or connection with her mother or childhood (190). She defines self in relationship with the young man, "Papa Steve," who is represented as the new anchoring point in Claudia's life. The turn to "Papa Steve" neatly and obviously doubles the prescribed turn to heterosexuality and the father—a progression that has been viewed as a "natural" journey for a female in a patriarchal society. This description would seem analogous to Erikson's idea that a young woman's identity formation is partly contingent on a future husband (Erikson 283).[7]

In Isabelle Holland's novel, *Of Love and Death and Other Journeys,* published in 1975, fifteen-year-old Meg has lived and traveled all over Europe accompanying her mother in her "vagabond meanderings." Set in Perugia, where Meg, her mother, and her mother's second husband have settled, the story is centered on the death of Meg's mother. Holland shapes the daughter–mother narrative through a linear plot as Meg's father, divorced from her mother, reenters the narrative to take charge of Meg. Her father, Meg narrates, had been "unreal" to her—a "sort of bad joke" between her mother and herself (34). The good name of the father, who is now an Anglican priest, is restored as Meg learns that her mother had been "unfaithful" to him and had left him (63). After Meg has rung the mourning bell for her mother, she leaves the ancient city of Perugia to join her father and his wife, Rachel, in New York—the New World.

Fifteen-year-old Bent in Fosburgh's novel, *The Wrong Way Home*, published in 1990, is taken from the task of caring for her sick mother by her father, who is divorced from her mother. In the context of a story in which a mother is shown to have become dependent on her teenage daughter, phrases such as "She will go soon—to spare you and let you live your new life" (58) and "Was it right to shut a young, healthy person away from the world?" certainly take on significance (145). Bent's father tells his daughter that it is time to "claim" her "home" and "inheritance" with him (179). This is shown through story to be the *right* way home for Bent. A father's conduct and morals are valorized over those of a girl's mother. Bent has idealized her mother who is described by her father (a privileged voice) as "selfish, demanding . . . sometimes tyrannical" (119). She had initiated the divorce, ordering him to leave when she knew the nature of her illness. He is sorry he has to tell Bent this about her mother (175). The linear plot of *The Wrong Way Home* is also constructed through a sequence of plotting in which a mother, who is shown in some way to be a disadvantage to her daughter, is replaced by another mother. Bent's mother is replaced by Bent's father's new wife—a younger and a different mother.

Three different stories about a daughter's growing up—yet told in these stories published nearly twenty years apart and set in the context of the white middle class nuclear family are conventional, generic stories of female adolescence. All the stories, summarized above, could represent family situations centered around events such as divorce, remarriage, and the death of a mother that bear some relation to actual situations that might occur in American family life. However, the narrative and discursive strategies used in telling these particular stories are not "innocent" of Freudian ideology.[8]

As Cranny-Francis points out, it is through the "plotting of narrative, the arrangement of events into a meaningful pattern, that the ideological or political framework of a text becomes apparent" (10). While these daughter–mother stories stand out because they conform so closely to the Freudian linear plot of female adolescence and to Freudian family-romance plots, elements of these daughter–mother plots and similar discursive patterns structure the daughter–mother narrative in novels published from the 1960s through to the 1990s. A staple of the Freudian narrative—the figure of the mother who is an obstacle to her daughter in some way—is a conventional plotting element employed in several young adult novels.

A Mother's Power: Obstacle to a Daughter's Independence

A certain description of mothers and mothering emerges from the traditional psychodynamic literature of child and adolescent development. Mothers have the power to grant or forbid a child's wishes; therefore, mothers are powerful, and mothers are to be feared.[9] In a traditional daughter–mother discourse, this power and fear becomes transposed into narratives of a mother's need to hold on and control a daughter, a mother's refusal to "let go" of her daughter, or a daughter's difficulty in extricating herself from her mother—a story of control and conflict. "How tall" her mother "seemed, how hard," thirteen-year-old Daria comments in *Beyond Another Door* as her mother's "shadow" falls "across the page of her sketch pad" (Levitin 86). Daria's mother, however, like many of the mothers represented in these novels does not possess the markers of social and economic power. She is described as a single parent struggling to bring up an illegitimate daughter in difficult economic circumstances.

Rachel DuPlessis argues that there are no "neutral" conventions in composing story. "Any literary convention—plots, narrative sequences, characters in bit parts—as an instrument that claims to depict experience, also interprets it" (2). A convention of story frequently used in the daughter–mother narrative in young adult novels is that which presents a teenage daughter's perspective of her mother as overbearing and controlling. In a genre in which it is conventional to represent a daughter as a strong and independent protagonist, the controlling mother is, of course, a useful figure around which conflict of story is built in order for a daughter to gain some measure of independence; this story element of a mother's control over her daughter is built into many daughter–mother plots. This convention of story fits well not only with those scripts of adolescent development and cultural expectations that place value on independence and responsibility for self but also with those views of development that construct a mother as an object from whom a daughter must separate in order to attain independence.

The description of the controlling or vicarious mother is found in novels from the 1960s through to the 1990s. Such a mother is to be found in Jean Thesman's *Cattail Moon*. Nearly fifteen, Julia Foster narrates how her mother has hired an "image maker" who is to choose Julia's hair style and clothes—even down to her "pajamas and underwear" (5). Julia's musician friends are unacceptable to her mother as is Julia's wish to pursue a career as a professional musician. She will "spend years studying" her mother tells her, and then, when she fails, she would wish she had listened to and paid attention to her mother "for once" (185).

Representative of other daughter–mother narratives in which mothers are imagined as having no appreciation or time for a daughter's own hopes and dreams, the relationship between an adolescent daughter and her mother is described as one of contention. In a narrative plot in which a daughter moves away from her mother, Julia goes to live with her grandmother and her father, who is divorced from her mother. At the close of the novel, she moves in with a best friend and her family where she can pursue her music. Her mother's decision to move into a condominium too small to accommodate a piano signifies the final break between them. Julia decides that she will find somewhere else to practice (192).

The explanation given for Julia's mother's behavior is one frequently found in the daughter–mother narrative in young adult texts in which daughters are warned about the dangers of mothers trying to reinvent their daughters in their own image. Julia narrates:

> And, I think my mother controls me because of how things were when she was young, when she was a cheerleader and homecoming queen and all those things that don't impress me and never will. I understand what I never understood before. She thinks she can make me happy if she makes me do what she did (177).

The emphasis placed on a daughter's being different from her mother and the avoidance of repeating a mother's life are characteristic of the kind of advice given in general texts about the mother-daughter relationship intended for adult audiences. The representations of Julia's father and her stepfather (who are shown, through Julia's narration, to be sympathetic to her needs and interests) are set against her mother's unreasonableness and lack of appreciation of her daughter's talents. Greg, her stepfather, represented as a kind man, is shown to take her side in her arguments with her mother and to encourage her love of music.

Nixon's *Star Baby*, set in the 1940s, is one of four novels included in this book in which a representation of the stage-type mother, reproduced in fictional and psychological texts, is used to tell a story of a daughter whose independence is thwarted by a vicarious mother—the epitome of an immoral, selfish, domineering mother.[10] Abby's mother manages her daughter's career as the child star Cookie Baynes—even to the point of suggesting that she bind Abby's breasts so that she retains her child-like appearance in order that she can appear in second-rate vaudeville shows (70). "You wouldn't have a career without my sacrifices," she would "snap" at Abby. "You wouldn't be America's favorite little girl if I hadn't given up my own career and dedicated my life to you. How can you be so ungrateful? Why can't you appreciate all I've done for you?" (7).

Published in 1989, Nixon's novel can be likened in some aspects to the "tell-all biographies of evil star mothers written by angry daughters" noted by Walters to be popular in the 1980s except that Abby's narrative voices love for her mother as well as her determination to eventually stand up to her mother (206).[11] Abby's father is described as a good, loving man who, in contrast to his wife, cares about the welfare of his son and daughter and is loved by Abby in return. Just as he is struck by a heart attack, he is literally struck by his wife's arm as he intercepts a blow meant for Abby. Abby's mother had entered the room and seeing Abby with her father had immediately suspected that her daughter was telling her father about her mother's adulterous behavior (167).

A mother is represented as pushing her daughter into stardom through her dancing in Bonnie and Paul Zindel's novel *A Star for the Latecomer*, while in *The Beauty Queen* by Susan Pfeffer and *Representing Super Doll* by Richard Peck, mothers pressure their daughters into the beauty-contest circuit. Described in Peck's novel is the loneliness and desperation of Darlene Hoffmeister whose mother has groomed her for beauty pageants since she was small; Darlene can no longer think for herself. The contexts of the novels may change according to the different social and economic contexts and the time periods in which they are set, but a basic premise encoded in daughter–mother stories is that daughters must be free to make their own lives differently.

In Nixon's *Star Baby*, Abby, with the urging of friends, sheds her identity as Cookie and takes on the name of Abby Grant. She tells her mother in a "cold voice" that they "need some distance between" them (173); as she departs on a tour of naval bases as part of a group of entertainers Abby tells her mother that it is now time for her to be making her "own decisions" (178). The equation of geographic distance with physical distance is a frequent motif in plots of daughter–mother separation—a literal marking of boundaries between daughter and mother. As teenage daughter Kit informs her mother in Pfeffer's *The Beauty Queen*: "I can't live my life according to your plans" (131). The values that are privileged in a generic text are usually visible at closure (DuPlessis 3). In Pfeffer's novel a daughter again distances herself geographically from her mother and her mother's plans for her as she resigns from the state beauty contest and goes to Colorado to take up an acting career (130).

FREUDIANISM AND THE REPRESENTATION OF MOTHERS

Abby's mother in Nixon's *Star Baby* is one of a few mothers who are represented as unmitigatedly bad in the novels chosen for this study. Freudianism, of course, has fostered and disseminated the view that mothers are a disadvantage to their daughters and the belief that women, because they develop along a less clear-cut path than males, develop a lesser sense of justice and are morally inferior to men (Femininity 124–34).[12] Certainly, one can find in young adult texts several examples of mothers who are described as either depressed, suicidal, crazy, or irresponsible as mothers. Examples included in this study are Merle's mentally sick mother in Jocelyn Riley's novels, *Only My Mouth Is Smiling* and *Crazy Quilt*, and the suicidal mothers in Adler's *The Shell Lady's Daughter*, A. E. Cannon's *Amazing Gracie*, and L'Engle's *Camilla*. Henley's mother in Rodowsky's *H. My Name Is Henley* is one of the most unstable mothers described in this book. The little ditty she sings is symbolic of her directionless and irresponsible character: "Round and round and round she goes—where she stops nobody knows" (92). Henley describes her mother's meanness as she teases Booshie, a trusted but mentally disabled woman, and how this makes her feel:

> Flattened back in that corner, I felt a horrid black taste rise up in my throat and I swallowed back against it over and over. I gagged on that taste and on the thoughts that dumped inside me. Thoughts about Patti and the things she did—crazy run around things that kept me chasing after her because I didn't know what else to do. But now there was something else. A meanness that reached out all around me and filled the hall, making me want to fight against it as hard as I could (166–67).

That representations of bad mothers have a history in popular culture is evident through the vitriolic mothers that have been noted in fairy tales, nineteenth-century literature, feminist writing, and popular culture.[13] If, as Cranny-Francis has pointed out, women often have not been given a "real" presence in literature but have been characterized as good or bad depending on how they help or hinder "masculinist practices" so mothers are sometimes represented in young adult texts as good or bad mothers according to how they help or hinder their daughter's progress toward being independent and morally and socially responsible young women.[14]

Replacing Mother: A Freudian Romance

The influence of Freudian stories of development can especially be seen in fictional and psychoanalytic texts that have taken S. Freud's "Family Romances" as a model from which to imagine family relationships. Freud's narrative tells of the child's and adolescent's imaginative "daydreaming" in which he gets free from the parents of whom he now has a low opinion and replaces them with others, who, as a rule, are of a higher social standing (238–39). Freud's "Family Romances" have been incorporated, verbatim, into traditional narratives of adolescent development to explain family relationships.[15] They have been used to explain and interpret fictional plots in literature for children.[16]

Zibby Oneal's *A Formal Feeling,* Klass's *To See My Mother Dance,* and Harry Mazer's *Someone's Mother Is Missing* are representative of a narrative model of plotting predicated on the fantasy of the absence of the maternal mother—a fantasy that has also informed theories of narrative plotting.[17] Set in the context of a middle-class family in a university town, the story is told in Oneal's novel *A Formal Feeling* of sixteen-year-old Anne Cameron, who is described as locked into the controlling patterns set for her by her mother. Extensive use of mirroring is used in the text to emphasize Anne's loss of self-esteem as she defines self as being a less than a perfect replica of her mother:

> 'Anne is her mother's daughter,' people often said, meaning the hair, the height, even the name Anne, which they shared. Eyes, too, and the shape of their noses. And yet it had always seemed to Anne that these features, so similar, were somehow better arranged in her mother's face. Her mother had been beautiful. Anne, looking at herself in the long mirror on the closet door, could by no means call herself that (13).

In another passage as she skates struggling with the figure eight she had always had trouble with:

She could hear her mother's voice saying, 'All right now, get control of your-self and try again.' She could almost see her mother sweeping smoothly through the figure to show her how it ought to be done, in perfect control, calmly. Her mother was able to do it without a ghost of uncertainty.

Then Anne would try—ten, twelve, fifteen times—never getting it smooth enough (91).

Oneal's story shows that a daughter's experience in attempting to con-struct her identity with a mirrored image of a perfect mother is painful and impossible. "Blue. Everything blue," narrates Anne. "Blue and more blue all her life, because, she had been told, it was a color that was pretty with their hair, hers and her mother's." She "hated" that color (139). In terms of narrative sequence, Anne's mother's sudden death is plotted six weeks after Anne arrives at the same boarding school her mother had attended. "I don't want to go there. I don't *want* to go! She remembered saying it more than once. It hadn't mattered. It never had. She had been swept once more on the current of her mother's words until, like a twig, she had come to rest here at this school where she had never wanted to be" (153).[18] In the space of a year Anne's father, a university professor, remarries. His new wife, Dory, is described as "So different. So small. So unlike Anne's mother and Anne herself" (98–99). Value is placed on Dory's difference and re-placement in a positive way throughout the text. She is described as a woman who does not aspire to perfection and who does not find fault so easily. Anne's first unfavorable comparisons of Dory and her mother are partly decentered by Spencer, represented as the older, paternalistic, sen-sible brother.[19]

Characteristic of many other novels, a daughter's strong voice dominates the narrative at closure while a mother's voice is absented. In Rodowsky's *H. My Name Is Henley*, Henley's mother tells Henley that she will be the "storyteller" who will "find the ending" to the story of "Chicken-liken" that she is always chanting to her daughter (103). The daughter, of course, is storyteller in the majority of daughter–mother stories.

A Missing Mother

The absenting of the mother, argues Irigaray, has been encoded into West-ern cultural narratives including that of psychoanalysis (*Irigaray Reader* 39). Despite the differences in form and in sociohistorical contexts, there are interesting questions that can be raised about the similarities between the discursive strategies used in a young adult novel such as Oneal's *A Formal Feeling* and certain Freudian narrative plots identified by Hirsch in nineteenth-century novels.[20] In very different genres written for completely different audiences, it would seem that it is an acceptable social and literary practice to imagine that a mother's voice and subjectivity are erased in order for the daughter to be able to take up her own life.[21] Walters's study of how the mother–daughter relationship has been represented in mass media from the 1930s to the 1990s demonstrates, for example, how Freudianism continues to shape the representation of the daughter–mother relationship in popular cultural forms. When one thinks about how deeply ingrained this story plot is in cultural narratives it is not surprising that fantasies about the absent mother remain strong in contemporary novels for young people.[22] This fantasy, after all, fits well with a popular cultural script of female adolescence that prescribes a daughter say good-bye to an overly close relationship to her mother.

Mazer's *Someone's Mother Is Missing* is one of the most powerful examples of a narrative plot predicated on the absence of the mother. Lisa's mother had stopped functioning when her husband is killed in a plane crash and she is unable to deal with his complicated business and financial deals. She runs away—abandoning Lisa and her younger sister, Robyn. In the following passage, Lisa's hunt for her mother, accompanied by her cousin, Sam, is likened to the child's game of hide-and-seek as they hunt for her mother in her grandmother's apartment:

> *Catch me*, her mother was saying—that's the way it felt to Lisa. Let's play, her mother was saying. Let's play hide-and-seek. Make believe I'm the queen and you're the princess. Make believe I'm the baby and you're the mother. *Come on*, her mother was saying. *Use your imagination. Try to find me!* (88).

"Where are you, Mama? Stop hiding. Come out, come out wherever you are," Lisa calls (88). There is an emphasis on the fantasy of shifting roles and identities between mother and daughter in Mazer's text. Lisa's younger sister, Robyn, surprises Lisa with her understanding about their mother's illness. Robyn sounded "like a little grandmother herself." To Lisa, it seems as if they are all playing a game. "Now Nancy was the mother, now Lisa, now Robyn" (149). After Lisa and Sam have found Nancy in a run-down hotel, Lisa takes her mother to a Quaker home where she must, for now, say good-bye to her (164).

The Fantasy of Role Reversal

Mazer's novel demonstrates powerfully how the narrative convention of a fantasy of role reversal colludes with a narrative plot that fantasizes the absenting of a mother. The fantasy of role reversal is one of the most noticeable narrative conventions used cross-culturally in daughter–mother narratives in the young adult novels included in this book. This fantasy is used to show the growing maturity of a teenage daughter in relation to her mother—a foil against whom a daughter measures herself. There are vignettes in many texts in which daughters are described as seeing their mothers as suddenly vulnerable and defenseless, or in which a mother, for a brief interlude, is seen as child to her daughter. Daughter as her mother's rescuer is a popular motif. The fantasy of role reversal is also used as a narrative plot device in which the power inequalities between daughter and mother are almost, or totally, reversed. In some instances, a daughter is represented as a strong, independent, and responsible protagonist in opposition to a weak and irresponsible, sometimes child-like mother. In L'Engle's novel, for example, Camilla is told by the family doctor after her mother's attempted suicide that her mother is "really still a child" (74). Camilla, however, is "strong" and must be "very strong" for her mother who would need Camilla's "strength" (75). Mazer's *Someone's Mother Is Missing* contains one of the most vivid and complete mirror reversal of mother and child:

> Her mother slept. Her head slid against Lisa's cheek. Lisa's lips brushed across her mother's hair. As her mother breathed she breathed with her, loving the perfect curve of her neck and her cheek and the way her teeth showed through slightly parted lips. Her little mother. She was holding her little mother in her arms. *Her little mother. Her little imperfect mother* (164).

The repetition of "little" reinforces the diminution of Lisa's mother. The role of protector is reversed: "She wasn't the mother. She was the child. Had everyone forgotten that? How had her mother turned into the child and Lisa into the mother?" (148). A strong, independent daughter protagonist is constructed in opposition to the representation of a mother, almost totally diminished in power and stature. Lisa's strength is acknowledged by her mother and by herself. "Why not let her think she was strong? Maybe she was stronger then she knew" (162).

The "game" and exaggerated imagery may emphasize the fantasy of role reversal, the imaginative taking up of other subject positions, and the play of story in Mazer's text, but it is difficult to get beyond the passivity, dependence, and docility of the mother pictured as child in the vignette above. The split narrative in which Lisa's mother is focalized, in alternative chapters, by Lisa's cousin, Sam, serves to double the visual image of Lisa's mother as childlike. She is described by Sam, when found, as looking "like a teenager" who "could have been one of the girls in Sam's class"—another conventional visual image used in texts to diminish the size of the mother (137).

Lisa's mother is compared with Lisa's aunt—an example of how the convention of the split mother is used in the daughter–mother narrative. Lisa's mother was not "strong," not like Aunt Renee. "It was as if," Lisa comments, that Nancy and her sister Renee "had come out of the oven totally different, her aunt rough and ready, and her mother almost carrying a sign. Fragile. Handle, with Care" (164). The fantasy of role reversal, the split representation of the mother into the oppositions of weak/passive/absent and strong/active/presence, and a plot that revolves around the presence and lack of a mother contribute to a text riven by polarities. Mazer's daughter–mother narrative is representative of those that are partly produced through a discourse of mothering in which a maternal mother is associated with lack—in the sense that she signifies the absence of maternal beneficence—and is represented as unable to nurture or empower her daughter.

Lisa might find her mother, but there is no real rescuing of this mother figure in Mazer's story. Lisa's mother not only suffers from depression and low esteem: Lisa finds that her mother had lied to her about her job. She had not been a business partner, as she had led Lisa to believe, but had been fired as a waitress for doing a "lousy" job (77). She tells her daughter that "a dummy" cannot talk and when contradicted by her daughter admits she has to think more positively about herself (140). She has, she tells her, "nothing to give" Lisa and her sister since her husband's business deals were just paper money that had gone when their father had died. "Her face collapsed, her eyes and mouth squeezed shut. The cry, when it came, was buried deep inside her" (142).

Marginalizing a Mother's Voice and a Gender-Biased Discourse

The abjectness of mothers who have "nothing to give" their daughters signifies the loss of mothering for a daughter. Merle's mother is described in *Crazy Quilt* as someone who is "going to lose, lose, lose, just like she always lost, lost, lost" (Riley 46). There are other mothers represented in these texts, who are also represented as literally without voice, and therefore, agency. Gracie's mother in A. E. Cannon's *Amazing Gracie* tells her daughter: "I'm an empty bucket. There's nothing inside of me" (148). In Adler's *The Shell Lady's Daughter*, a mother's story is transposed into the anonymous stories she tells her daughter about the sad shell ladies: ladies who are abandoned by various consorts and which are retold by Kelly. Reproduced in these texts is the silencing of women's voices—a cultural silencing that has been documented in so many contexts in patriarchal cultures. The association of mothers with the terms "crazy," "lunatic," and "crazy-sick" further links the maternal voice with a language of madness. In other texts, the voices of mothers are described as "mean," "selfish," "strident," "angry," and "controlling." Lisa's mother in *Someone's Mother Is Missing* constructs self as "negative," "weak," and "selfish." The voices of mothers are placed in a different relationship to power, culture, and language than those of their daughters in these novels. Daughters speak in these stories on behalf of their mothers. Female adolescence is constructed as site of division between daughters and their mothers as daughters' voices, in selected novels, are estranged from the "crazy" and marginalized voices of their mothers.

Phallocentrism describes the way language constructs the valorization of the masculine over the feminine, the male over the female, the father over the mother through a series of hierarchical oppositions. For example, the association of masculinity with independence and activity and femininity with dependence and passivity in a way that valorizes the first of these oppositions is characteristic of certain narratives in psychodynamic literature.[23] An example of how phallocentricity is stitched seamlessly into a text can be found in Colman's *Sometimes I Don't Love My Mother.* In narrated monologue, teenage-daughter Dallas's mother admits to her difficulties in adjusting to her late husband's demands that she "be social" and "entertain," and that she "share his passion for active sports, none of which she had ever been good at" (44). Her husband had, however, "loved her femininity" (38). He had "liked to see her wear soft, silky robes in the house" and "liked to buy her gifts of jewelry and lacy nightgowns" (38). In Colman's novel these associations are made in a story in which a mother is shown to be dependent on her daughter when her husband dies, and in which a daughter is shown to have had shared a "special relationship" with her father. "No one knew how much that closeness had hurt her as Dallas grew older—the way Hank and Dallas had gone on their special jaunts together, had their secrets, as if she didn't count, wasn't part of the family" (105).

In L'Engle's novel *Camilla,* Camilla's description of her father reproduces the child's perspective of the infallible father figure:

His shoulders are as broad as the shoulders of Atlas on Fifth Avenue near Rockefeller Center, the one who is holding up the world and looks as though he is slipping off his pedestal from the weight of it. But my father's foot would not slip (8).

While these gender oppositions are presented with more than a hint of exaggeration—and may, therefore, be taken with a "pinch of salt"—a phallocentric structuring of the text and narrative plot continues to be reinforced through the continued representation of Camilla's mother as less strong and more fallible than her father. Camilla narrates that it was her father who gave her "a sense of strength and security" and was "the parent who had the power to make things all right" (44). His calm strength and paternal authority are compared to the description of Camilla's mother as a weak, hysterical, and dependent woman requiring "emotional protection." She is presented, moreover, as an immoral woman who has an extramarital affair with Jacques Nissen. Camilla's mother's name, Rose, symbolizes a delicate beauty, and as Jacques comments, "like roses," she can "grow only in cultivated gardens" and "must be shielded from the wind and the cold" (86). More than any other mother in the stories included in this book, she represents the passive, narcissistic woman described by Deutsch in her influential work on women's psychology in the 1940s. Deutsch grounded her analysis of the passive woman and active man in biologism. The nature of men and women was said by Deutsch to be "prescribed organically" (I: 280).[24]

A father and mother are similarly described in Adler's *The Shell Lady's Daughter*. Kelly's father is described as "low keyed, controlled and steady, a sort of foundation person" while her mother is described as "the decorative trim" (14). While the actual charge made by a patriarchal grandmother that Kelly's mother has "bad blood" is contradicted in the text, and it is made clear in the story that Kelly's mother (who has attempted suicide) is valued by her daughter and husband, a father's family name—Allgood— retains symbolic value over a mother's name and working-class background. "You're my granddaughter, Kelly, and an Allgood whether you want to be or not," her father's mother tells her (136). Adler has employed the narrative practice of using Kelly's grandmother to voice a set of stereotypical derogatory remarks against a daughter-in-law in order to have Kelly defend her mother by opposing them. It is questionable, however, if the slurs against a mother are eradicated entirely in this story. Adler's daughter–mother narrative certainly serves as a reminder that the relationships between daughters and mothers are produced through ideologies of class as well as gender.

Inducting a Daughter into Femininity

In the psychodynamic narrative, detachment from a mother, independence, and heterosexuality are linked together in a prescriptive developmental path. In a scene analogous to a daughter's going out on her first date, Camilla's mother assists her daughter's constructed path into femininity as she helps her to "primp," so that she may accompany her father to dinner. She helps Camilla with her makeup, her dress, jewelry, and perfume. Camilla, in effect, takes her mother's place as she wears her mother's "silver shoes" and "pearls" (L'Engle 12–13). It is a clear example of how the role of a mother is understood to be one of assisting her daughter into femininity—a role absorbed naturally into the text. In terms of temporal plotting, it is soon after this incident that Camilla begins dating Frank Rowan.

The most powerful description of a daughter's induction into femininity is produced in Mazer's novel. Although her father is dead, Lisa continues to fantasize and listen to a voice that eclipses the voice of her mother through its immediacy. When Lisa casts interesting looks in the direction of her sister's tennis instructor, she hears her father's voice "so close" and "so reassuring" telling her that she has *"a beautiful smile"* (10). When the instructor does not look at her, Lisa hears her father say: *Be patient, darling. Give it time.* It calms Lisa to hear her father's voice:

> *What are you going to say to him when he comes out?*
> *I'm just going to look at him and smile, Daddy.*
> *That's the spirit. Let things unfold in a natural way* (11).

It is right at this site where girls are socialized into femininity that female adolescence is constructed as a "crossroads." This is where Mazer's text (and others) reproduces in story the division between a daughter's alignment with her mother and her seduction into femininity. It is at this juncture that one can question the practice frequently used in daughter–mother stories in which a daughter is made to look strong and independent by placing her in opposition to a weak, dependent mother as a literary *convention.*

Freudianism continues to inform family romances—imagined and written in a popular cultural form for young people. The dominance of heterosexuality as a naturalized and legitimate narrative in teenage romantic novels is demonstrated in Christian-Smith's study of the teenage romance novel over a period of forty years (20). The daughter–mother narratives in many of the young adult texts included in this book are also stories about love and romance. In Colman's *Sometimes I Don't Love My Mother,* a teenage daughter seeks to free herself from her mother's dependency on her and plans to move away and marry her boyfriend, Victor, who tells her that she has to "break away from her mother" (135). Colman's linear narrative plot is representative of those daughter–mother stories that are congruent to a Freudian narrative plot of female adolescence that tells how a daughter separates from her mother and moves away to the world of her boyfriend/ father—a cultural narrative that has absented and diminished the mother. Perhaps one of the saddest testaments to the narrative of separation to which daughters and mothers are subjected is in the last paragraph of Colman's novel:

> But there was a sad, lonely look on her mother's face that Dallas knew would be a long time in fading. Yet Dallas was certain that she could not be the one to erase it. She could only hope that eventually the pain would diminish and that her mother would find her own way (184).

But at this juncture, too, the contradiction is raised in the text between cultural expectations that adolescent daughters should be independent, that mothers should not be dependent and cling to their daughters, and the need for mothers and daughters to also acknowledge the reality of their relationship. Dallas tells her mother that they will "always be mother and daughter." Again, the term—daughter–mother *relationship*—is put into question in a text that encodes the very tenets of Freudianism.

Setting as Metaphor

Setting is used as metaphor in selected novels to devalue the place of the mother. The entrapment of daughters who wish to escape the restrictions and limitations of their mothers, for example, is symbolized by the association of the maternal home with confining walls and spaces—"a prison," "a fortress," or "a cave." Unable to relate to the values of her parents, particularly to those of her mother, home for Claudia is associated with "deathville" (Colman *Claudia* 120). "No matter what theory you read," Benjamin writes, "the father is always the way into the world" (103). The daughter is theorized as turning to the father because he is the symbol of freedom and independence as the "representative of the outside world—

who is the different 'other' to the mother and, thus, represents autonomy and individuation" (108–9).

Does the fact that a daughter moves from Perugia where her mother dies to New York (the "New World") where her father and his second wife live have symbolic meaning? (Holland *Of Love*). What does it signify that on the jacket of the hardcover of this novel about the death of a beloved mother, only a father is depicted as he journeys to meet his daughter whom he has not seen since his wife left him? In Libby Hathorn's *Thunderwith*, Lara's mother also had run away from her husband taking her small daughter with her. How significant is it that the reader is told that "the Man" (Lara's father) arrives to take Lara to his new farm and stepmother after her mother dies. Lara had "liked" her father immediately: "She knew at once that she wanted to go home with him, wherever home might be" (14). What significance does the title *The Wrong Way Home* carry in a story in which a teenage girl is removed from her mother's apartment to her father's home when she had imagined staying in her mother's apartment after her mother's death (Fosburgh 11).

These linear narrative plots certainly make sense and accord with familial situations in contemporary contexts. However, one can also ask to what extent do the discourses through which these novels are produced and their narrative plots also encode oedipal patterns of family relationships in which daughters are said to turn away from their mothers to their fathers? To what extent do mothers' voices and lives fade away from the central place that they have held in daughters' lives? I suggest that there is, at least, a familiar patterning that can be discerned in selected novels that is congruent to Freudian narratives of female development. Encoded within these patterns is a cultural discourse identified by Pipher, in which mothers are "seen as having great power to do harm with their mistakes," while fathers are viewed as "having great power to do good with their attention" (117).

Freudianism, Literary Conventions, and Stories of Daughters and Mothers

Feminist criticism has particularly drawn attention to the way generic conventions encode gender ideologies that devalue women.[25] Peter Rabinowitz defines formulaic elements of text as those textual elements that recur regularly "without significant variation in comparable texts" (72). As Rabinowitz points out, it is often these formulaic elements of text so taken for granted that reveal implicit cultural values when unmasked and their ideologies exposed (70). In discussing how ideologies are encoded into stories about adolescent daughters and their mothers, attention is drawn in this chapter to a number of literary conventions that are frequently used to tell story. These elements of story when used as a formulaic *convention* of telling story encode a cultural discourse about mothers and mothering that is grounded in a gender-biased discourse of Freudianism. In selected young adult texts, there are divisions, rather than connections, produced between strong, independent, active, adolescent daughter protagonists and weak, dependent, passive, maternal mothers. Feminist gains, as Walters points out, are not achieved through the way some feminists have identified with the "daughter" in overturning the "oppressive mother" (233). This is the kind of story produced in novels in which daughters advance at the expense of mothers, who are represented as weak and dependent or as obstacles to be overcome and left.

Cranny-Francis argues that conventions are "social constructs." They encode that which is socially acceptable (17). One has only to read reviews of books of daughter–mother stories in young adult novels to see that many of the above conventions are accepted as a normal narrative practice. They do, after all, encode views of mothering and of the daughter–mother relationship that are deeply ingrained in American culture. What is at issue is not the representation of mothers who are bad, weak, sick, and mentally ill *per se*. Of course, such representations have a place in literature for young people. These do not necessarily negate mothers or women. It is when it is a *conventional* literary practice to diminish mothers in order to present shining and independent daughters that these kind of conventions can be troublesome.

Daughter–mother narratives in young adult novels are formed from and contribute to a wider cultural discourse on mothers and daughters. The representations of mothers in the novels discussed in this chapter are akin to descriptions of mothers in novels and poetry, written exclusively by women, in *Mother Puzzles: Daughters and Mothers in Contemporary American Literature*.[26] Mickey Perlman comments that mothers are characterized as "missing" in the sense that they are emotionally absent; they also are represented as infantalized, dependent, or depressed. These mothers, Perlman notes, are represented as "disabling" rather than as "enabling" (6).

Fictional texts are multidimensional and the daughter–mother narrative in young adult texts are composed of a number of intersecting discourses. In order to give coherence to one side of the daughter–mother narrative, the way in which stories encode a daughter's love and need for her mother is postponed to a subsequent chapter. An aspect of the daughter–mother relationship in adolescence that is always part of story is the tension, changes, and differences between teenage girls and their mothers. Chapter five discusses the different issues around which conflict is built and the discursive and narrative structures used in the articulation of conflict between the voices of daughters and mothers.

NOTES

1. For Freud's account, see "Femininity" 121–35; for fuller descriptions and explanations of Freudian accounts of the "feminine oedipus complex," see Chodorow *The Reproduction* 111–29.

2. See Blos *On Adolescence* 66 and 232.

3. A mother is said to find it difficult to let go of her daughter and retains "powerful sway" over her. See Blos "The Second," *On Adolescence* 66–67; Deutsch I: 244.

4. See Ross; Small.

5. For feminist approaches to the critical analysis of the male hero journey and *Bildungsroman,* see Abel, Hirsch, and Langland, eds. 10–11; Polster.

6. For the argument that the Freudian linear narrative plot is "sometimes read as the psychoanalytic narrative of 'human' growth and development" that "encodes a male gender bias and linear causal fallacy," see Cranny-Francis 16.

7. Erikson's account of female identity differs from his account of male identity. See Erikson 283.

8. For a review of *Claudia, Where Are You?* in which the story is said to "ring true," see Sutherland 84.

9. For an analysis of how the "fantasy" of the powerful mother has been produced from "a culturally child-centered myth of maternal omnipotence" that also pervades feminist writings about mothers and motherhood, see Chodorow and Contratto 96; Apter 136.

10. For an example of the "stage mother" labeled as a type in a psychological text about the daughter–mother relationship in adolescence, see Eagle and Colman 88.

11. For analysis of film featuring the bad Hollywood mother such as *Mommie Dearest,* see Walters 205–18.

12. See also Gilligan *In a Different Voice* 7.

13. For commentary and references to the representation of the "bad mother," mothers "faulted by daughters," and matricide in women's fiction and feminist writing, see Baym 165; Debold, Wilson, and Malave 27; Hirsch *Mother* 46–50; Thurer 206–07.

14. See Cranny-Francis 24.

15. For an example of how the "family-romance" plot is used to explain the construct of idealization and deidealization, see Kaplan 128–30.

16. In his study of American childhood classics Jerry Griswold identifies elements of a "basic plot" that include separation from parents and "adoption into a second or surrogate family" who are of a "different social rank from the child"—elements of story that he argues are analogous to Freud's "Family Romances," see Griswold 10–11.

17. Peter Brooks, for example, uses Freud's *fort-da* game that enables a child to gain "active" mastery over the "disappearance and return" of his mother in conjunction with Lacan's concept of "desire" to formulate his seminal theory of plotting, see Brooks 9–10; 54–55. See Freud *Beyond* 8–10. For criticism of the gender ideology embedded in Brook's theory, see Hirsch *Mother* 53.

18. For examples of twentieth-century novels in which "killing the mother is the author's 'radical surgery' that severs the mother from her daughter's life," see Gardiner.

19. The brother figure in Oneal's novel resonates with "the-man-who-would understand" fraternal figure in nineteenth-century novels; see Hirsch 57–58.

20. For interpretations of nineteenth-century fictional plots using Freud's "Family Romances," see Hirsch *Mother* 56–57.

21. Hirsch, for example, notes in reference to a paradigmatic Freudian narrative plot that she identifies in women's nineteenth-century fictional texts that: "It is the mother's absence that creates the space in which the heroine's plot and her activity of plotting can evolve." See *Mother* 57 and 170.

22. For the argument that Freudian theory has influenced the way family relationships are portrayed in the novel of adolescence, see White 11.

23. See, for example, Freud "Femininity" 129 and 124; for Deutsch's explanation of nature of woman as passive, masochistic, and narcissistic that is grounded in anatomy and biologism, see Deutsch 1:140, 1:280.

24. See Deutsch 1:280; Freud "Femininity" 128 and 132.

25. See, for example, Cranny-Francis; DuPlessis.

26. See Perlman, ed.

Five

It's Normal to Fight: The Voices of Daughters and Mothers in Conflict

> Because of mixed messages within the culture, conflict between mothers and daughters is inevitable.
>
> —Pipher

In Jan Greenberg's *Exercises of the Heart*, fifteen-year-old Roxie's aunt tells her that "It's normal to fight" with her mother (131). The understanding of the relationship between adolescent daughters and mothers as one of conflict is, perhaps, one of the most ubiquitous adages about the dynamics of this personal relationship. Whatever a teenage girl's personal experiences of her relationship might be, adolescence is socially constructed as a time when a daughter has problems and experiences difficulties with her mother whether this view is produced in psychology texts or in magazines addressed to teens. As fifteen-year-old Jodie notes in *The Pig-Out Blues*, also by Greenberg, *Seventeen*, the popular magazine for teenage girls, "has . . . a story on this dilemma in every issue" (7). Adolescence, writes Pipher, is "scripted in a way that builds conflict between teenagers and their parents" (65).

The view that the relationship between teenage girls and mothers is inevitably one of conflict has, of course, been deeply embedded in the traditional narratives of adolescent development and in general texts about the mother–daughter relationship. The explanation for the anger and rebellion that daughters feel against their mothers is often grounded in a discourse characterized by advice that a daughter needs to disengage from her mother. Conflict, thus, has been viewed as a way of fostering a girl's separation from her mother and a means through which a girl lays claim to her indepen-

99

dence.[1] It has also been understood as part of a normal and expected phase
of development in which adolescents turn from the guidance of parents
toward peer influence. As one text puts it, a young person becomes a "rebel"
who joins up with the "Rebel Army" (Klein and Klein 85).

In recent accounts of female adolescence, criticism, arguments, and fights
are still said to be very much part of the relationship between teenage girls
and their mothers. However, rather than constructing conflict as a necessary corollary to a daughter's efforts to separate herself from her mother,
arguments and fights are being thought about as a way in which daughters
and mothers work toward staying in relationship. From her interviews with
adolescent girls and their mothers, Apter reached this conclusion in her
study of adolescent daughters and their mothers. A daughter, she writes:

> engages in vigorous arguments to correct and redress and defend her mother's
> image of her. She fights not so much for freedom as for her mother's belief
> in her judgement and trust in her independence (75).

A mother, writes Apter, tends to be the parent most often involved in
conflict with an adolescent daughter. She is more involved with exercising
authority over day-to-day matters, and consequently, receives more criticism and more questioning of authority than a daughter's father (111).[2]
Fighting with one's mother, thus, continues to be understood as a healthy
and normal part of a girl's development. Apter's argument that adolescents
"transform" their relationships with their parents rather than abandon them
fits in with other research that affirms young people's connections with their
parents and the attachments that are maintained between parents and teens.[3]
Only when an adolescent fails to receive any validation of self or cannot
work within a relationship that is characterized as confining and inflexible
does separation from parents come to be seen as a necessary part of development (Apter 60).

Feminist accounts of female adolescent development expose the gender
bias embedded in Freudianism and draw attention to the sexism that divides
daughters and mothers. Pipher argues that relationships between adolescent
daughters and their mothers are more conflict ridden than ever in a 1990s
climate in which girls are subjected to sexual harassment and are sexually
active at an earlier age than their mothers. Conflict occurs as mothers, fearful for their daughters, try to protect them from a world in which they are
at risk from date rape, AIDS, and teenage pregnancy—a world that is so
different from the one they knew as teenage girls (104). As Debold, Wilson, and Malave write in *Mother Daughter Revolution*: "Women's relative

lack of power in society creates a bitter complication in mother daughter relationships" (33).

STORIES OF DAUGHTER–MOTHER CONFLICT IN YOUNG ADULT NOVELS

It is, perhaps, not surprising that the fights and arguments that a teenage daughter engages in with her mother are one of the most prevalent aspects of the daughter–mother relationship in young adult novels. Indeed, conflict is considered to be such a healthy and typical aspect of daughter–mother relationships that a narrative practice frequently employed in stories is to draw attention to its absence. This is typically achieved through describing an alternative, and more appropriate, relationship between a teenage girl and her mother in which there is a healthy amount of conflict between them. Conflict with a mother, then, can be regarded as a formulaic convention of story in a genre whose potential readers might be assumed to see this conflict as a normal and inherent part of growing-up. Annette Klause's *Blood and Chocolate* may feature a powerful werewolf teenage daughter protagonist and Lee's *Black Unicorn* a powerful sorceress and her daughter, but the daughter–mother repartee in both fantasy novels is composed of familiar patterns of conflict and repartee that are found throughout the daughter–mother narrative in young adult novels. Conflict is also shown to be an ongoing aspect of the daughter–mother relationship in stories about grandmothers, mothers, and adolescent daughters. In Carol Snyder's *Leave Me Alone, Ma!* fourteen-year-old Jaimie hears her grandmother nagging her mother and listens to her mother answering in the "same fresh voice" that Jaimie uses with her own mother. "Ma, leave me alone, already" is a phrase used by Jaimie and by her mother. "Was nagging hereditary?" Jaimie wonders (63).

The novels chosen for discussion are ones in which conflict is described as a significant aspect of the daughter–mother relationship and that are set primarily in the context of white Western families. In listening to the voices of daughters and mothers in texts, I have identified various scripts and dialogic patterns through which conflict is expressed and also the different issues over which daughters and mothers argue and fight. Examples from selected novels are used to demonstrate how the conflict between daughter and mother in adolescence is produced through divisions of class, race, and sexism. Other examples illustrate how conflict between daughters and mothers is used as a means of valorizing particular values in a text.

Maternal anger in which daughters are physically and emotionally abused by their mothers (as opposed to temporary arguments and fights) is another side to the conflict between daughter and mothers reproduced in some texts. While it is difficult to separate out—like strands in a web—the different ways and issues in which conflict is produced in story, conflict between a daughter and her mother is invariably built around the expectations that daughters and mothers have of each other, including the kind of mothering a daughter expects from her mother. A mother's mothering, or failure to mother, is often a central issue and one of the main loci around which conflict (and story) is centered. However, discussion of selected novels in which issues about mothering and maternal are significant elements of the daughter–mother narrative has been deferred to chapter seven.

Scripts of Storm and Stress

In *The Revolution of Mary Leary*, Susan Shreve uses the hyperbole so often heard in describing conflict between teenagers and parents to delicious effect in her title and chapter headings: "The Declaration of Independence" and "Revenge, Et Cetera." The construction of hostility and conflict between adolescents and parents has traditionally been mediated by metaphors of war and combat in the psychodynamic literature on adolescent development. Deutsch, for example, uses warlike metaphors in referring to adolescence "as a battlefield of various forces" (33). The metaphors and similes of "combat" have been employed to describe the conflict between mothers and daughters. Walters, for example, refers to the description of the mother–daughter relationship in popular culture during the 1980s as one in which "the mother and her daughter are depicted as eternal combatants in a bloody and unavoidable battle" (190).

Terms such as "a wave of hostility," "locked in combat," "two battling women," and "bullets" and "missiles" hurled between mother and daughter are used sparingly to describe conflict between teenage daughters and their mothers in selected young adult novels published since the 1960s and into the 1970s and 1980s. "It's not easy standing between two battling women," a male onlooker observes as he watches a daughter and mother fight (Elfman *House for Jonnie O* 156). These metaphors of war are illustrative of the discourse through which female adolescence has been constructed in Freudian accounts of development. As if reading straight from a Freudian text, a mother asks her daughter: "Why are you so hostile to me? Okay, that's a dumb question. I suppose all daughters sometimes feel that way about their mothers. I just wish you weren't going through that phase now" (Colman *Sometimes* 156–57).

Much of the articulation of conflict between daughter and mother in these young adult texts is constructed through a script of nagging, criticism, blaming, and argument as daughters and mothers blame and reproach each other for their failings. There are scenes, however, in which physical as well as verbal confrontations take place in which mothers are depicted as slapping and pushing their daughters in anger and exasperation. The "proverbial" or "notorious" mother-slap is delivered to daughters in selected African American novels. Daughters are frequently represented as getting mad at their mothers; there are scenes in which they scream and yell that they "hate" their mothers. The term "letting go" generally used in reference to a mother's reluctance to let her daughter individuate can also be thought of in terms of "abandonment" and "child abuse." [4] Some of the most abusive language and violent scenes involving daughter–mother conflict are in a small number of novels represented in this book in which mothers systematically engage in the physical abuse of their daughters.

When dialogue and relationship break down, silences and ellipses in dialogue are used to show misunderstanding and disjunction between mother and daughter. Terms of alienation and estrangement are used by mothers and daughters to describe their feelings of being separate from one another. The words "alien" and "changeling" are used by Jonnie in Blossom Elfman's *A House for Jonnie O*, for example, to describe how she feels in relation to her mother. She and her mother:

> spoke different languages. Different words with different meanings. And then they were both hurt when neither of them understood. If her mother tried soft words, they made her feel worse. And the hard words—she simply threw up a wall against them (92).

Brown and Gilligan found that a figural language of barriers and walls was used by adolescent girls to describe their experiences of shutting down their real feelings, including anger, for the sake of staying in relationship with their mothers (97). Phrases such as "to break through the wall" and a "stone wall of silence" are found in texts to describe the impasse or temporary breakdowns of relationship between teenage daughters and their mothers. The harmonics of relationship between daughters and mothers are described in terms of repressed anger, disjunction—even alienation in those novels in which mothers are represented as controlling or domineering.

Voices of Domination, Submission, and Resistance

Older teenage daughters are frequently described as fighting for space in which to develop their differences and independence from their mothers. "You're ruining my whole life" is a stock daughter–mother phrase used in texts when a mother is seen to rule against a daughter's wishes. One can listen in selected texts to the voices of mothers, instructive and controlling, and to the voices of their daughters who openly comply but who are also heard voicing their resistance. This dialogic pattern, for example, structures the dynamics of relationship between Brooke Hillary's relationship with her mother in Bonnie and Paul Zindel's *A Star for the Latecomer*.

Brooke tells the story of her intense, painful, and emotional relationship with her now-dead mother and her mother's ambitions for her to be a dancing star. When her mother was diagnosed with bone cancer and given a short time to live, the pressure for her to succeed for her mother's sake was intensified. The voice of her mother, described by her daughter as "strong, instructing" and "charting" the steps of her future, breaks, unmediated, into Brooke's narrative: "*—Brooke, you've got to lose five pounds.*" and "*—Brooke, you can't go ice skating with the kids because you can't afford to break your ankle.*" Her mother's voice, narrates Brooke, "like a major theme returning in a symphony," intrudes into her "consciousness again." "*You want me to be proud of you, Brooke, don't you? You're going to be a star, Brooke*" (56).

Brooke's voice is split in the text as she openly expresses her love for her mother and her desire to please her but also voices her resistance to her mother's plans for her to be a star. Heard in her voice is a disassociation from self as she suppresses her own wishes: "What if I shouldn't become a star while my mother was here to enjoy it. Would I really want it for ME? Thump. A divider came down, closing me off from any feeling"(56). Brooke describes the voice in which she does articulate her own desires as "inner," "frightened," or "little." The dialogic pattern used in the Zindels' novel is characteristic of patterns of dominance, submission, and resistance between daughters and mothers in novels in which daughters are attempting to free themselves from the controlling and invasive voices of their mothers. Whereas, Apter argues that daughters define their differences through a "good fighting relationship," daughters in *A Star for the Latecomer* and Nixon's *Star Baby*, for example, are described as repressing their anger against their mothers—unwilling or afraid to risk disloyalty to their mothers by being openly rebellious until the closure of the novel or until after a mother has died.[5]

It is certainly tempting to draw analogies between some of the fictional accounts of the dynamics of teenage girls' relationships with their mothers described above with some of the descriptions of female adolescence by Brown and Gilligan in *Meeting at the Crossroads*. Research studies suggest that adolescent girls and women "silence themselves or are silenced in relationships" rather than risk open conflict and disagreement that might lead to isolation or violence (3).

Freeing a Daughter's Voice

In the Zindels' *A Star for the Latecomer*, Brooke looks into a mirror after her mother's death and says her "first truthful words in years." She now can voice her wish that she does not "want to dance," and "it was as though a curse had been broken." She "could feel the blood of Life beginning to flow inside of [her] again" (182). Her:

> childhood, my youth, my own voice that had once been loud and clear had slowly been murdered in my closet. It had all been lost when my mother had convinced herself that I should become a dancer. It seemed ironic to me that the closet—where I had always gone to hide, to share my deepest feelings, my most precious secrets of self—had been so totally invaded. I remembered it had been the only place I could stand naked (179–80).

This is one of the most powerful passages in any daughter–mother story that gives voice to a daughter's anger and resentment against a mother's invasiveness. The rhetoric and imagery—"murder" and "curse"—encode fantasies of death and the threat of a mother to the life and womanhood of a daughter. Reproduced is a rhetoric of death and aggression and sexuality that accords with the rhetoric used in psychological explanations of fantasies of the unconscious in narratives about mothers and motherhood—a rhetoric that has also been used in narratives of adolescent development in relation to the fantasy of replacing parents. At the beginning of *A Star for the Latecomer*, as in other novels in which a mother's controlling voice has been absented from text, a daughter's voice is freed to narrate her story of their relationship and to give voice to her anger against her mother.

If the closure of the generic novel is the locus at which contradictory scripts are resolved, then the closure of the Zindels' daughter–mother narrative is surely significant. Brooke places her dancing shoes in her mother's coffin as she says her final good-bye (184). A few passages later, she observes her father at the door and goes to stand by him. Her father "had been so shadowed by her mother," Brooke comments, that she "hardly knew him. . . ." Now she wants to get to know him and sees that her father also needs her (185). This novel would seem to encode a linear narrative that is analogous to oedipal versions of female development in which a daughter's mother, who has attempted to control her daughter's future, is absented from the plot leaving a daughter free to take her place at her father's side.

Hirsch argues that in Freudian narratives maturity for daughters can only be attained through a daughter's aligning herself with the paternal while breaking with hostility from her mother. A daughter's strong love for her mother turns to anger; it is this anger that "underlies the sequence of individual maturation; it makes that linear narrative possible" (168). Certainly, the Zindels' text, grounded as it is in the psychological dynamics of relationship between a daughter and her mother, can be discussed in the context of this interpretation of female development. The text is an exemplar of how conflict is linked with a daughter's wish for autonomy in selected young adult novels.

A Mother's Betrayal

The metaphor of the "wall" has also been used in reference to the wall of patriarchy against which girls collide especially during adolescence. In Colman's *Forgotten Girl* and Greene's *Summer of My German Soldier*, stories are told of adolescent girls' anger and disappointment with their mothers who betray them by acting in collusion with sexist practices that, in a very literal way, harm their daughters. In *Forgotten Girl*, Colman describes how conflict between an adolescent daughter and her mother is set in the context of a family relationship in which a mother favors her son—against whom she constantly negates her daughter. "Why aren't you a normal girl like other people," asks her mother. "Why can't you be like your brother?" (30). Kelly narrates that her mother is never going to see that she is "as good" and "as smart, as reliable, as *everything* in my mother's eyes" (10). Colman uses a sexist discourse that, according to Paula Caplan, continues to be generated through "male superiority" myths and through actual practices of mothering in which boys are treated differently from girls (99).[6] Statements such as "the boy belonged to the mother and the girl to the father"—used in the context of story to show how a mother has erred in the treatment of her daughter—illustrate, nevertheless, how Freudian descriptions of family relationships inform popular culture and contribute to a social reality of gender relationships in the nuclear family. Kelly's mother's reason for giving more attention and love to her son is that Kelly's father paid "too much attention" to Kelly (128).

Daughter–mother conflict is resolved in *The Forgotten Girl* by the unmasking of a son as a reprobate and the revaluing of a daughter by her mother. A mother's preference for a son is brought up as a subject of complaint by daughters in other novels. In Shreve's *Revolution of Mary Leary* and Rita Garcia-William's *Like Sisters on the Homefront*, however, daughters, who feel themselves too much the object of their mothers' critical attention, gaze crossly and enviously at their brothers who lie idly on couches—seemingly left to do as they please. In Marian Bray's short story, "The Pale Mare," Consuela is expected to give up her dreams to go to astronomy camp in order to help her parents with the family business. It is unthinkable to her parents that Consuela's brother, their "only son," should give up his football practice. They are "banishing" her "to the dark," Consuela narrates, but she cannot let that happen (101). Her mother tells her that they only want her happiness that involves settling down with a "nice boy" and having a family and silently implores Consuela that she stop struggling against her place in life (102). Made visible in this and other stories is the mother's complicity in her daughter's subordination.

In *Summer of My German Soldier*, Greene tells of a daughter's betrayal by her mother, who is represented as mildly protesting when her husband abuses her daughter in public, but assents through her silence when she is beaten in private.[7] Set in Arkansas during World War II, the alienated relationship between Patti and her mother is shown by Greene to be produced through divisions of class, race, and gender (362). Through Patti's first-person narrative, a story is told of an angry and embittered father from a Jewish family "considered the poorest of the poor" who marries the daughter of the wealthy Fried family. Refused a place in S. Fried & Sons, he was given money by his wife's family to set up his own business (25–26). Dialogue between Patti's parents: "Don't you dare contradict me! Think you're gonna treat me the way your God damn mother treats her husband?" shows the kind of relationship that is constructed between Patti's mother and father (83). Her mother complains that she has not been treated as well as her brothers:

> 'Papa, you *are* the company!' said my mother. . . . 'And you've always done that, given everything to your precious boys. Don't I count for anything? Don't I deserve something nice too?'
> My grandmother's chin lifted as though it had been struck by an uppercut. 'That's foolish talk, Pearl. Foolish! The difference between you and your brothers is that they've always liked whatever they were given, but you, Pearl, never liked anything once it was yours' (38).

Patti's mother's relationship with her own mother is represented as a less than harmonious relationship. The daughter–mother relationship, one of the bleakest in any novel included in this study, is represented as occupying a marginal position in the nuclear family. Violence is done to a daughter's body and spirit within its bounds. It fits a description of daughter–mother relationships in which it is said that mothers pass on to their daughters their own frustrations and lack of fulfillment, and also those descriptions that construct the generational story of mothers and daughters as a cycle of betrayal and loss. In *Summer of My German Soldier*, a mother is shown not to be there for her daughter when Patti is sent to reformatory school for sheltering Anton—an escaped German prisoner-of-war—as she neither defends nor supports her daughter or visits her. Ruth—the "colored" maid formerly employed by the Bergens—is represented as a surrogate mother figure in Greene's novel. It is she who visits Patty and whose voice empowers the young girl. The relationship between Ruth and Patti is used to bridge racial and class differences. Ruth tells Patti: "I've cared for chillun white and I've cared for chillun black. I've loved every single one of them, but nary a one as much as you, Patty Babe. Nary a single one" (220).

The negative psychological effects on a daughter's psyche and self-esteem caused by a mother's betrayal are made very clear in stories in which girls are abused. In *Forgotten Girl*, Kelly describes herself as an "outsider" and a "leper," who, in response to her mother's criticism and coldness, asks why her mother just doesn't "get rid of her" (Colman 46). At one point Kelly comments that there is "such a wall between us it was hard for me to imagine she had actually given birth to me" (127). There are, reports Kelly, no "bruises" on her "white and healthy body" to signify the emotional abuse that she receives from her mother (32). In *Summer of My German Soldier*, Patti narrates that her mother, a "beautiful woman . . . has an ugly baby girl. Me. A wave of shame flooded over me followed by another of full-grown anger. Shame and anger, anger and shame mingled together, taking on something beyond the power of both" (Greene 75). On another occasion just before her mother rebuffs her affection, Patti conjectures that the problem between her mother and herself to be her fault: "I've never been what she wanted, never done what she asked. Always making my own little changes and additions. Why do I do it? Why can't I be better? More obedient? More loving?" Her mother's sharp comment that she wished Patti would not bother her serves to reinforce Patti's focalization of their relationship (28).

Sex and Sexuality: Conflict and Divisions between Daughters and Mothers

As discussed in a later chapter, the relationships between daughters and mother are molded by the cultural ideologies of the societies in which women are situated. Novels such as those by Colman and Greene show how a girl's growth into sexual maturity is a time of risk within the family setting itself as girls cross the boundaries between childhood and womanhood. While Katherine Dalsimer has noted that a girl's welcoming of her "newly awakened sexuality" has been one of the most serious omissions from traditional psychoanalytic theory about female adolescence, issues constructed around sexual maturation, the body, and gender identity are, of course, inseparable from the cultural construction of female adolescents in young adult novels.[8] What is not so often examined in young adult novels is how these issues are shown to impinge upon a teenage daughter's relationship with her mother, although this aspect of the relationship is certainly addressed in writings about mothers and daughters.

Apter writes, for example, about the "split" that a girl experiences between recognizing herself as becoming sexually mature and her position as girl/daughter to her parents (131). In Adler's *The Shell Lady's Daughter*, for example, Kelly narrates that she can no longer share her "dreams" with her mother since they:

> were full of boys being devastated by me, adoring boys to whom I granted all sorts of liberties with my body, and then, and then . . . getting excited lying in bed and touching myself. I couldn't tell my mother that. Even as close as we were, I hid my curiosity about sex. I wasn't the sweet little girl Mother had called her best friend anymore (75).

In Adler's novel a girl's growing awareness of her sexuality and her newly found interest in boys is shown to be the cause of a disruption of her close relationship with her mother. Brown and Gilligan have written of the way in which girls can become disassociated from their mothers, other women, and themselves during adolescence as they move toward being women "which means being with men." [9] The adage that a daughter's sexuality is the root cause of much conflict between an adolescent daughter and her mother as the relationship becomes one of competition is reproduced in *My Mother/My Self* by Nancy Friday. This is, of course, a familiar daughter–mother theme immortalized in the Snow White tale and its variations. According to Friday, if daughters do not acknowledge that they are in "sexual competition" with their mothers their growth is thwarted, and there is the danger of "merging" with a mother and becoming "latency girls" (191).

The theme of sexual competition between a teenage daughter and her mother is only dealt with at any length in two of the novels included in this book. In Colman's *Sometimes I Don't Love My Mother* and Hadley Irwin's *What about Grandma?* daughters are described as feeling threatened, temporarily, by their attractive mothers whom they suspect of taking an interest in the same young men they are interested in dating. In Colman's novel, it fleetingly crosses seventeen-year-old Dallas's mind that her lonely, widowed mother might have fallen for her boyfriend, Victor. The "thought made her sick. . . ." (69). The theme is treated more extensively in Irwin's novel, in which sixteen-year-old Rhys sees her forty-two-year-old mother as her competitor for the attentions of twenty-six-year-old Lew. On one of Lew's visits, Rhys tears upstairs to put on her brief red bikini as she notices how attractive her mother appears and wonders why her mother couldn't "be ugly like June Rose Cronk's mother? Or stupid? Or grow warts? Or anything that would make Lew stop looking at her" (71).

The assumption that motherhood and sexuality are incompatible has been one of the fantasies surrounding the images of mothers.[10] This fantasy fits well with the representation of mothers and motherhood in books for younger children preserving, as it does, images of sexless (innocent) woman/motherhood but is belied in representations of mothers in some of the young adult novels included in this book. Teenage daughters' friendships and sexual experiences with young men are set against the background of their mothers' experiences with sexual relationships in several novels. The infidelity of mothers in L'Engle's *Camilla* and Nixon's *Star Baby* and Rainbow's mother's affair with Burke in Childress's *Rainbow Jordan*, for example, serve to show the negative effects of mothers' inappropriate behaviors on their relationships with their daughters.

Joan Merrill Gerber's novel, *Please Don't Kiss Me Now*, contains one of the most open acknowledgments of a mother's sexuality. Focalized by fifteen-year-old Leslie, her mother June's "sexuality was always just under the surface, in the clothes she wore, her stance, her hair, her makeup, and in her whole approach to men. It embarrassed Leslie, it was so obvious" (75). Much of the conflict is centered on issues of sex and sexuality in a plot in which mother and daughter's dating behavior are paralleled. "Try and see what you're doing with your life," Leslie admonishes her mother. "You're wasting it on creeps, crummy guys like Eric. You float around acting young and available and this is what you pick up" (103). June is described by her daughter as a selfish, uncaring, and "rotten" mother as she plans to go away with her boyfriend, thereby missing the opening night of Leslie's concert. Leslie is shown to have some justification when one of June's boyfriends makes a sexual pass at her. In a scene after Leslie is discovered in her boyfriend's van by her mother, late at night, out on the driveway, Leslie is described as:

> battling her mother, the same mother she used to love so desperately. How could they look at each other with so much hatred? Their bodies were ready for physical combat; they could have slapped each other, torn out each other's hair (101–2).

A similar pattern of criticism and countercriticism between daughter and mother is found in Klause's fantasy/horror novel, *Blood and Chocolate*, in which sixteen-year-old werewolf Vivian is also critical of and embarrassed by her mother's obvious sexual passion for twenty-four-year-old Gabriel—a year after her husband's death (27). Her mother, in turn, wishes to forbid Vivian's friendship with the human—"meat-boy"—Adrian. While these kinds of daughter–mother exchanges reproduce a popular daughter–mother repartee found in young adult novels, they do break the taboo of silence around sex and sexuality that, according to Shere Hite, has been constructed between mothers and their young daughters.[11]

One of the angriest scenes between an adolescent daughter and her mother is found in Levitin's *Beyond Another Door* when Daria challenges her mother's stories about her husband and marriage. "It's a lie," she accuses her mother, Peg, when she tells Daria that she was "twenty" when she married. Peg strikes her daughter when Daria continues: "You were never married to him. I'm just a bastard. And that makes you a —" (94). Mothers are represented in stories as trying to protect their daughters from the kind of mistakes they themselves made. They also are described as enforcing rules and setting limits—all of which lead to arguments and conflict.

In Shreve's *The Revolution of Mary Leary*, the story of conflict and love between Mary and her "smothering" mother is written with humor and a light touch. Mary, for example, reports on her unsatisfactory date with Jack Richards who had refused to kiss her despite her provocative poses (63). Her mother tells her later that she had had a "nice talk" with Jack Richards. Mary's brother, overhearing this talk, tells Mary more. Jack had been asked to take "good care" of Mary since she had not been on a date before. Her mother had gripped Jack's hands "as though the armies of Dionysus" were going to "strip" her daughter "naked in Dumbarton Oaks" (64).

Whose Body Is This Anyway?

A daughter's body is frequently made the site of contention between daughters and mothers. Reproduced through the voices of mothers in young adult novels are those familiar scripts that are used by mothers and others to shape their daughters into culturally prescribed ideals of behavior and appearance (Debold, Wilson, and Malave 207). Mothers are represented as criticizing their daughters' appearance, eating habits, dating behavior, and general behavior. Fourteen-year-old Jaimie, for example, complains of her mother's "straighten-ups" that include directives to straighten-up her back, her room, and her grades (Snyder *Leave* 76). "Remember to suck in your stomach, learn to smile without that toothy grin," a mother tells her daughter in Greenberg's *The Pig-Out Blues* (41). "Three full days," thirteen-year-old Cornelia exults in First's *Look Who's Beautiful!*, "plus almost two more . . . when I wouldn't hear one, 'Why don't you try combing your hair differently?' or 'What's the matter with wearing your yellow blouse for a change?' or 'That's enough potatoes, Connie,' or all three." Her father does not nag her, Cornelia adds (First 21). Her mother, Cornelia narrates, has "this old-fashioned obsession that if you're not a living doll, you're lost." She continues: "For myself that hurts. You see, I'm no beauty and I'm no sylph. I don't like to think that good looks is what makes a person a person." Her mother, however, makes her feel like a "whale" (2).

Rosalind Coward's *Female Desires* and Naomi Wolf's *The Beauty Myth* have drawn attention to how women and girls are seduced into cultivating the ideal body image that is prescribed through the beauty and fashion industries. Greenberg's *The Pig-Out Blues* particularly draws attention to the "beauty myth" that is constructed through the media and popular magazines for women. Fifteen-year-old Jodie is constantly criticized by her mother for not having the body image and other attributes that she thinks are necessary for her daughter to succeed. Jody narrates how her mother and friend watch the *Phil Donahue* show—admiring career women who are "beautiful and sexy" and who "earned over $100,000 per annum. For some reason," Jodie narrates, "Mother and Myrna identified with these women" (16). She describes how they pore over *Women's Wear Daily* looking and envying fashionably dressed women going to social parties (17).[12]

The critical voice of a daughter is used to show how women can be sucked into the association, constructed in the mass media, between beauty and success—the "professional beauty qualification" that defined beauty "as a legitimate and necessary qualification for a women's rise in power" (Wolf 28). Greenberg's novel, published well before Wolf's *The Beauty Myth*, illuminates well Coward's observations of how gender ideology works as women are addressed through their pleasures—an "ideal body," for example, as they pore through magazine advertisements (13).

Jodie's mother is represented as a problem to her daughter as she attempts to control her daughter's weight and body image. "She'll dissect all my bodily parts, performing verbal surgery," Jodie comments. "Whose body is this anyway?" she wanted to shout at her mother and Jodie knows her mother's answer: "I'm in charge of your body . . . and don't you forget it" (42). Her constant criticism is shown to contribute towards Jodie's low-esteem and eating binges. Jodie focalizes herself, for example, as an unattractive "fat, ugly wad," whose mother finds her repugnant (69). Jodie, in fact, only solves her eating problem in her mother's absence when she stays with a boyfriend's family whose mother cooks healthy and appetizing meals. As discussed in a later chapter, the convention of using alternative mothers to show a more ideal way of mothering is a frequent convention of the daughter–mother narrative in young adult texts.

Greenberg, however, makes clear how a working-class mother's attitudes are shaped by socioeconomic circumstances. When her mother objects to her part-time job as a waitress, Jodie comments: "So that was it! A job at Mr. Wheatley's Health Food Store symbolized everything she hated. Food equaled fat; a job as a waitress equaled social inferiority" (59). "'You better win something,' her mother had screamed at Jodie: 'That will show them.' *Them*—an ambiguous term for all the people in High Ridge who shopped at Trumbells and treated my mother like a lowly salesclerk" (37). Later, as Jodie and her mother work out their differences, her mother later tells her that she sometimes takes her frustrations out on Jodie and that she, too, is responsible for their fights. "It's just that I don't want you to make the mistakes I did and find yourself wondering if it's too late when you hit forty," her mother explains (96). Jodie's mother, to whom her daughter refers as the "Medusa of Main Street" at the beginning of the novel, is focalized by her daughter towards closure as "small, not the looming hawk-like figure" she had previously imagined (117).

Criticizing Mother: Equalizing a Power Relationship

Statements by adolescent daughters interviewed by S. Rich link the recognition of a mother as a "person" with "faults" to the establishment of a more equal relationship and to better ways of relating to their mothers. S. Rich reports that daughters' "descriptions of mothers' mistakes and instances of being wrong pervade the interviews." Daughters' statements of differences, disagreements, criticisms, and complaints against mothers are interpreted as part of the process of daughters differentiating, rather than separating from their mothers as daughters come to "voice their own views in the relationship" (263–65). According to Apter, it is a daughter's "high expectations of her mother" that lead in turn to "high demands" and thus to criticism when her expectations are not met (109).

The establishment of a relationship in which a daughter gains power in relationship to her mother is an aspect of many fictional accounts of daughter–mother relationships. Mothers' voices may be heard criticizing, justifying, apologizing, and explaining to daughters, but in the foreground are daughters' voices criticizing the imperfections and values of their mothers. Daughters' voices are constantly heard challenging the voices of mothers and their mothers' judgments and opinions in daughter–mother narratives. Unfailingly, daughters are represented as standing back and seeing their mothers through different and critical eyes. A daughter's superior vision to that of her mother's is quite often constructed through metaphors of seeing and blindness, a conventional figure of speech that is used, cross-culturally, to construct comparisons between teenage daughters and their mothers and which places value on a daughter's critical focalization of her mother. Mothers are frequently focalized by their daughters as being "blind" to their daughters' needs. In Gerber's *Please Don't Kiss Me Now*, Leslie critically focalizes her mother as "running blind" after her divorce and "blind" to her daughter's needs (178). She describes her recently divorced mother, June, as one of those women who, "terrified of being lonely the rest of her life," regresses "to some teenage ideal of dating, of running around so they don't have to think" (123).

Arguments between daughters and mothers are the forum for debates and the comparison of different values over career choices, lifestyles, attitudes, and values in different social and cultural contexts. At the site where the voices of daughters and mothers meet, contradictory values and attitudes are debated and resolved. A mother's voice is frequently that of a devil's advocate against whom the voices of daughters often carry the more liberal and "right" values. Conflict is often resolved as a daughter proves to her mother that she is right. Thirteen-year-old Cornelia, for example, in *Look Who's Beautiful!* confronts her mother's prejudice over elderly people when she asks permission to work for an elderly woman in an apartment complex nearby. "Is the place clean?" her mother asks. "Oh, Mom, why are you like that?" Cornelia says to herself (First 59). Thirteen-year-old Annie in Margaret Rostkowski's *After the Dancing Days*, set in 1919, deliberately disobeys her mother in order to visit a badly burned young man returned from the Great War. Her mother had not wished her to be exposed to all that "ugliness" (83). Through her friendship with Andrew, Annie literally learns to look with honesty at the brutal scars of war. She shows, like her father, that she has compassion and understanding for the wounded men—the unsung heroes of the war—setting an example for her mother.

Gerber's *Please Don't Kiss Me Now*, published in 1981, is one of a group of novels published around the late 1970s and early 1980s in which daughter–mother narratives give voice to feminist issues that serve as consciousness raisers. Again, it is through daughters' voices that these concerns are heard. In Gerber's novel, Leslie criticizes her mother, June, and a friend's mother, who had, according to Leslie, "just given up their personal development as soon as they got married." Leslie "could not imagine counting on some man for her definition as a person. A man should complement a woman not absorb her into his identity" (Gerber 17). It may be significant that Gerber's novel and others published during this era were the years that the struggle for ratification of the Equal Rights Amendment was at its height.

Transforming Relationships: Connecting across Difference

In Greenberg's *The Pig-Out Blues*, the relationship between Jodie and her mother during "noisy, angry years" is described as going through a process of change. "Out of the wall that was between us," narrates teenage Jodie, "came one brick at a time" (121). As pointed out at the beginning of the chapter, conflict between adolescent girls and their mothers can also be understood as a way of maintaining relationship between daughters and mothers. Gilligan has described the problem for adolescent girls as "making connection in the face of difference" (Preface 10). This can be read as striving for connections in a society that expects a daughter to develop as a mature, independent individual through exclusion of self and others; yet can also be particularized to a daughter's relationship with her mother. Many of the fictional accounts of the conflict between daughters and mothers bear resemblance to those described in Apter's research in which she found that adolescent girls and their mothers fight through differences towards a more loving and reciprocal relationship. Daughters are said by Apter to generally criticize, fight, and argue with their mothers in order to get them to recognize and trust in their independence (75).

There are, however, a number of conditions that must be satisfied, in story, before conflict is resolved or a move made towards reciprocity: open conflict; a recognition of a mother's voice and needs as legitimate and as "other"; a mother's "seeing" and meeting a daughter's needs; an acknowledgment of a daughter's growing maturity; and, finally, expressions of love and approval between daughter and mother. Gilligan writes that when daughters' voices express a "willingness to speak and to risk disagreement" relationships are constructed that make "it possible to reweave attachment" and in which "the distinction between true and false relationships" is made.[13] In those daughter–mother narratives in which conflict is structured through a dialogue between the voices of daughter and mother, a more equal and open relationship exists between daughters and mothers. Value is placed on the need for honest communication. Mothers are shown up in texts for lying to their daughters. There is also less covert criticism and interpretation of a mother's voice by a daughter than in those texts structured mainly through monologue passages in which a daughter voices her feelings about her mother in an inner voice—constructed so as only to be heard from a reader's position.

A daughter is shown to be a limited observer of her mother in the texts of many novels. A mother's voice has the authority and conviction to correct her daughter's perception of her behavior in Gerber's *Please Don't Kiss Me Now*. Leslie's mother's voice is legitimized through the use of dialogue in which she is heard strongly defending herself against her daughter when Leslie finds about the "early" pregnancy: "Funny you got pregnant so early in life if you were so sexless," Leslie had shot out at her mother (75). June tells her daughter that she is not taking this "holier-than-thou crap." She is not going to "apologize for the feelings" she and Leslie's father "had for each other then" (50).

A narrator's voice or alternative voices in a text may reinforce a daughter's critical focalization of her mother, but they may also be used in a text to decenter a daughter's dominant focalization. The convention of using secondary focalizations of characters in addition to a daughter's focalization can contribute towards constructing a more positive representation of mothers in texts. In Gerber's novel, Leslie is asked if she is being "fair" in the way she thinks about her mother (177). She is also told "not to be too harsh in judging" her mother, and to "be kind" to her mother (123). June "is a very fine woman," who has done much to help other people, Leslie is told by Kesey, the teacher who becomes Leslie's stepfather—a voice in the text shown to be respected by Leslie (57).

This same authorization of a mother is made in Greenberg's *Exercises of the Heart*. Roxie's mother is represented as having a speech disability. It causes, narrates Roxie, a "communication problem" that "goes beyond the generation gap for reasons that have nothing to do with typical mother–daughter stuff" (6). Reassurances are made to fifteen-year-old Roxie that it is "normal to fight" with her mother in adolescence: "What do you want to do, walk around your whole life feeling horrible because sometimes—like everyone in the world who has a mother, handicapped or normal—you fight with her?" (130). The move is made in the novel from a daughter's disparagement and criticism of a mother whose disability embarrasses her to a relationship in which an adolescent girl is described as feeling proud of her mother (6). As her mother is shown to be a strong woman in dealing with a situation in which Roxie's teenage friends are arrested in a drunk driving incident, Roxie narrates that "for the first time I'm right in her corner, rooting for her, proud of the way she's handling this." She is focalized by her daughter as "dignified—and wonderful" as she struggles "to find the right words" (124).

Roxie's revaluation of her mother is reinforced by secondary voices in the text that contradict Roxie's perception of her mother. A doctor—a voice of authority—comments that she is a "wonderful woman" (62). A friend tells Roxie that her "mother's really neat" and that she "shouldn't be so hard on her" (51). The harmonics of a relation change from one characterized by discord to a relationship in which the voices of a teenage girl and her mother are beginning to connect. "I know that this time we've opened that stubborn door," Roxie comments (131). In this text, and others that use similar practices, a mother's subjectivity is constructed from a number of different positions in the text that serve to liberate her from being understood only from her daughter's side of story.

In texts in which the daughter–mother relationship is described in terms of reciprocity and a loving relationship at the closure of the novel, a mother is represented as acknowledging her daughter's needs and showing love for her daughter. In Colman's *Forgotten Girl*, Kelly's mother hugs her and hopes that her daughter "can learn to love" her (153). Metaphors of "blindness" revert to those of "seeing" as Leslie's mother in Gerber's *Please Don't Kiss Me Now* is represented as seeing the damage done to her daughter by her regressive behavior. She is described as "beginning to see herself" and "beginning to see" her daughter (178). Representative of other daughter–mother narratives, a mother is shown in Gerber's text to acknowledge and pay attention to her daughter's needs.

Gerber's novel closes with a scene in which love and approval are expressed between daughter and mother as Leslie and her mother hug each other "till both of them could hardly breathe," and Leslie's mother recognizes her daughter's gain in stature: "Would you believe it?" she asks. "My daughter is taller than I am!" (218). Acknowledging a daughter's increased stature in relationship to her mother is a recurring motif in daughter–mother stories. As in similar scenes of reconciliation, value is placed on the importance of the daughter–mother relationship in a girl's life at the closure of story.

The personal dynamics of daughter–mother relationships are frequently described through scripts of conflict and love and approval that are stitched, contrapuntally, throughout a text. Phrases that describe a daughter's feelings of difference and anger with a mother, for example, are frequently stitched, contrapuntally, with expressions of needing a mother's approval.[14] Cassie, for example, tells her mother Abby that it "was important" to her that her mother was "proud" of her achievement as her daughter: "In spite of rebelling against you, I really wanted to please you" (Nixon *Encore* 193). In Greenberg's *The Pig-Out Blues,* Jodie wants to believe that she and her mother can get along and that she can please her mother: "But I knew that I had to keep a part of myself separate, that I had to be myself. That realization allowed me to take her hand" (121).

Love and Hate: An Ambivalent Relationship

"Sometimes I don't love my mother, I think. Sometimes I even hate her, Dallas thought, frightened by the vehemence she felt" (Colman *Sometimes* 54). One of the most popular psychological explanations of the mother–daughter relationship used in the psychoanalytic literature is that it is an ambivalent relationship. Caplan writes, for example, that the majority of mother–daughter relationships "involve a great deal of ambivalence" in a chapter entitled "Such Love, Such Rage" (18–19).[15] The understanding that ambiguity is a recognized explanation of mother–daughter relationships is reproduced in the title of Colman's *Sometimes I Don't Love My Mother.* The concept of ambiguity structures the relationship between teen daughter Dallas and her mother. Dallas's mother comments, for example, that: "She had read enough to know that the love between a mother and a daughter had a lot of ambiguities" (Colman *Sometimes* 167). Colman's daughter–mother narrative is representative of many others in young adult novels in which daughters are described as expressing love for their mothers on one page and hating them on the next page, as it were.

In *Overnight Sensation*, sixteen-year-old Cassie and her mother act out the tension and anger in their own relationship in a televised skit—a "knockdown dragged-out daughter–mother battle"—that mirrors the relationship in front of a live television audience (171). The other side of the relationship—the "loving daughter approach"—is constructed through the photographs that Cassie takes of her mother for a magazine (142). Nixon tells three different kinds of stories in her trilogy about daughters and mothers (*Star Baby, Overnight Sensation,* and *Encore*). In each novel she deals with the basic themes that generate conflict between daughters and mothers in young adult texts: independence, self-identity, and the establishment of a daughter's differences and boundaries from her mother.

Conflict: From the Personal to the Political

Conflict, changes, and tension between adolescent girls and their mothers are described as a normal aspect of their relationship across different racial, cultural, and socioeconomic contexts in the novels included in this book. The daughter–mother relationship is socially constructed as a site of contention as daughters question, renegotiate, and equalize power relationships between themselves and their mothers—or as is sometimes the case, more than balance the inequities between them. Psychological descriptions and explanations of conflict are dominant but stories also show how conflicts between adolescent girls and their mothers are produced through divisions of class, race, and sexism.

In *Mother Daughter Revolution*, Debold, Wilson, and Malave move the discussion of the daughter–mother relationship from the personal to the political. In this discourse, the authors speak of the empowerment of daughters by asking: that the voices of daughters and mothers make connections across differences; that mothers empower their daughters; and that women's voices join together across difference in a public speaking "that resists cultural systems of separation and dominance" (249). Miller has also written of the need for women to "reclaim" conflict in a positive sense that moves away from old models of conflict that work through domination and subordination.[16] Mothers are being asked to authorize and validate the voices of their daughters against the sexism that has divided women and mothers and daughters:

> Authorizing in mother–daughter relationships is a two-part harmony between the daughter's young soprano and the mother's more forceful alto. Authorizing goes further than validating. Not only does an authorizing mother validate

her daughter's reality, but she adds her authority as a mother, as a woman who has experience in this culture, to amplify and harmonize with her daughter (Debold, Wilson, and Malave 129).

Apter has argued that a new model of adolescent development is needed "that makes sense of the continued love between child and parent, and one that makes sense of the continued support an adolescent seeks from her parent" (3). In the following chapter, I discuss another side to the daughter–mother relationship that forms an important element of daughter–mother narratives—the love, attachment, and identity between adolescent daughters and their mothers.

NOTES

1. See, for example, Hammer; Rothchild.
2. For a similar explanation of the conflict between adolescent girls and their mothers, see Youniss and Smollar 45.
3. See, for example, Greenberg, Siegel, and Leitch; Josselson; Youniss and Smollar.
4. See Scheper-Hughes 362.
5. See Apter 97.
6. Freud stated that the mother's relation to the son "is altogether the most perfect, the most free from ambivalence of all human relationships." See "Femininity" 133.
7. See also Casey; Staples; and Woodson *I Hadn't Meant to Tell You This.* For a prose poem that deals with incest in young adult novels, see "Oh Mom, What Am I Made Of?" Anonymous.
8. See Dalsimer 140
9. See Brown and Gilligan 216.
10. See, for example, Chodorow and Contratto 91.
11. See M. Hite 96.
12. For an explanation of the social construction of a beauty myth in which the "working woman was told she had to think about beauty in a way that undermined, step for step, the way she had begun to think as a result of the successes of the women's movement," see Wolf 28.
13. See Gilligan "Remapping" 17.
14. I have borrowed and adapted the term "contrapuntal" to describe how contradictory scripts encoding ways of understanding the relationship between adolescent daughter and their mothers, for example, conflict and expressions of love and approval for a mother, are placed in relation (contrapuntally) to each other in specific phrases or in a text. See Gilligan et al. "Epilogue" 315–328.

15. In Freudian psychology, "ambivalence," notes Flax, "is always present in love relationships." See *Thinking* 50 and 54.

16. See Miller 125–40.

Six

Loving and Needing Mother

What remains unwritten is the story about how connection between mother and daughter, and indeed between child and parent, remains a strength, not an immaturity.

—Apter

Feminist accounts of female adolescence and women's psychology have stressed the centrality of relationships in the lives of adolescent girls and women. Feminists argue that this aspect of development has been devalued in narratives of traditional psychology and contemporary North American culture. In *Toward a New Psychology of Women*, however, Miller not only argues that women's development is centered around relationships but that individual development for men and women "proceeds only by means of connection" (83). According to Chodorow, a girl develops a lasting relationship and identity with her mother from the early primary tie that exists between them (*The Reproduction* 175). Apter argues in *Altered Loves* that there has been a conflation in traditional psychodynamic literature between defining separation as individuation and definitions of separation that imply that young people break off affectionate relationships with parents. In listening to the voices of girls talking about their relationship with their mothers, Apter and others have documented the importance and value of mothers to their teenage daughters. They write of relationships in which girls voice their love, need, and dependence on their mothers while seeking their mothers' acknowledgment and approval as they move toward maturity and independence.[1]

Fictional texts are multidimensional—certainly more so than the psycho-analytical narratives of adolescent development. The stories discussed in this chapter emphasize the *relationship* between a daughter and mother—placing value and meaning on the other side of a dominant narrative. As M. Hite points out:

> even though conventions governing the selection of narrator, protagonist, and especially plot restrict the kind of literary production that count as stories in a given society and historical period, changes in emphasis and value can articulate the "other side" of a culturally mandated story, exposing the limits it inscribes in the process of affirming a dominant ideology (4).

What is so visible in so many young adult novels included in this book is the writing in of a daughter's love and need for her mother and her disappointment, anger, and feelings of rejection when her mother is not available to meet these needs. Intertextually and cross-culturally, it is one of the most powerful aspects of the daughter–mother relationship written into story. Focusing on stories set in white, Western contexts, examples from young adult texts show how fictional accounts of daughter–mother relationships give voice to the value of this relationship and to the loving connections forged between teen daughters and their mothers. The daughter–mother narratives discussed in this chapter are partly produced through a maternal discourse that foregrounds the maternal body and fleshly links between daughters and their mothers. A daughter's need to identify with her mother is also a pervasive theme. Reproduced in these stories are fantasies of idealized love and relationships between daughters and their mothers.

DAUGHTERS, MOTHERS, AND SELF-ESTEEM

The topic of self-esteem has been central in recent discourses on female adolescence. While there has been disagreement on the definition of this term and its importance, attention has been drawn to adolescent girls' feelings of loss of esteem because of gender inequity in schools and the culture in which young people grow up.[2] Apter defines self-esteem as a complex concept that involves having a set of expectations about self and about meeting the expectations of others. Daughters, she explains, receive much of their self-esteem from mothers through their various daughter–mother interactions (139).

Apter found from interviews with teen daughters and their mothers that daughters look to their mothers for approval and validation during adolescence (61). This seeking of a mother's approval is an especially visible element of the daughter–mother narrative in many young adult texts. In Nixon's *Encore,* for example, teenage-daughter Erin tells her mother: "These past four years, I've wanted you to see me, see how good I really am" (193). First's *Look Who's Beautiful!* is representative of daughter–mother narratives in which young teen daughters are described as needing a mother's love and approval. Some of these fictional accounts accord with Apter's descriptions of the daughter–mother relationship in midadolescence. While this is the time girls are supposed to be in the thick of conflict with their mothers, girls in Apter's study spoke of their mother as being the person they were most close to and the "person who offered them the greatest support" (71).

Thirteen-year-old Cornelia in *Look Who's Beautiful!* defines herself as less than perfect in comparison to her "svelte" mother "who was born without a blemish"(6). Whereas, Cornelia wears a cervical refractor, her mother, narrates Cornelia, has "perfect teeth that never needed braces to get them in that condition" (6). Through her representation of Cornelia, also known as Connie, First highlights the sensitivity of young teen girls to their appearance and links this to Connie's desperate need for her mother's approval. To Cornelia, it seems as though her mother looks at her as if she has "leprosy" (3). She wishes that her mother would look at her lovingly no matter how ugly her skin got with allergies. She would like to be her mother's "most-loved object" (7). The moral built into story is, however, that it is not beauty on the outside that is important. Cornelia wishes that her mother would see how she really is—"beautiful on the inside" (103).

Cornelia wins her mother's approval via her selfless behavior in giving up a school class trip to Washington, D.C., in order to spend time with an elderly woman, whom Cornelia befriends, who has injured herself during a fall. "Connie, I'm so proud of you," her mother tells her. "I never thought you'd . . . do . . . a . . . thing like that" (103). Reproduced in First's novel are the values of selflessness and niceness that are traditionally associated with being a good, nice girl. Cornelia's perception of self is shown to change now that she has her mother's approval. She knows she is beautiful because her mother's look had told her so. "Beautiful on the inside, I mean, and I knew she saw it that way. Then I knew. What I was feeling now had to win over everything else that had ever happened to me" (103). Cornelia is described as "warm with the glow" of her mother's "approval" that made her "feel like Cinderella when the prince put the glass slipper on her foot" (104).

SEXUAL IDENTITY

Sexual identity, Coward writes, is formed in response to male- and female-gendered roles in the context of the family and through the meanings attached to the body through early experiences with sexual roles and behavior.[3] Stories featuring teenage-daughter protagonists who are the illegitimate daughters of teenage mothers particularly address how mothers' sexual behavior influences their daughters' feelings about sexuality and sexual identity. In Rodowsky's *Julie's Daughter*, for example, seventeen-year-old Slug tells how thinking about her mother, Julie, who did not know just who Slug's father was and who had abandoned Slug when a baby, makes her "feel dirty." It sullies her memories of her own relationship with a boy so that she feels "dirty in retrospect." If her mother "was what she was," Slug continues, "what does that make her?" (31).

In this particular novel, a mother takes up a subject position through her first-person narration and speaks openly about her sexuality—although she does not directly address her daughter. She was like "a dog in heat," she tells a dying elder woman. She "flaunted it. Gave it away." She was known as "loose. An easy lay. And I was pregnant by the time I was seventeen" (96). Through displacing the experience of being a teen mother onto a teen-daughter's mother, Rodowsky is able to set up different subject positions in the text so that more than one side to story can be told. Importantly, Julie, as a teenage mother, is not censured.

Pat Calvert also writes about teenage pregnancy in the context of a daughter–mother story in *Yesterday's Daughter*. Leenie, left by her mother, Mary Alice, to be brought up by her grandparents is full of resentment against a mother who had abandoned her and was the cause of her being labeled "illegitimate." She also resents her mother's returning home after seventeen years and decides that she will hide away in the Sawmill Swamp until Mary Alice's departure; she will "bail out" on Mary Alice just as Mary Alice had "bailed out" on her daughter (17). Leenie defines herself as a "tomboy"—denying her maturing body—so that she "won't ever have to worry about ending up like" her mother. Leenie reasons it is: "Easier not to be a girl, easier to ignore the fact you'd wakened one morning in a body that didn't belong to you" (95).

Through her own romantic and sexual feelings for the photographer, Alex, who stays at Leenie's grandfather's motel in order to do a feature on the swamp that Leenie loves so much, Leenie comes to understand and identify with her mother's sexual experiences. It was she who had "come on" to Alex, Leenie realizes. "His lips had tasted so good, his body against her own had felt so dear, so *right*" (106). "'Is this what'd happened to Mary Alice sixteen years ago?' she wondered numbly. 'Had it been as sweet and easy for her to do what I almost did, might've done too, if Alex hadn't had more brains than me?'" (107).

Her mother, Leenie is told, "was a nice girl who made a mistake" (28). In Calvert's text, as in other novels selected for this book, a female adolescent's growth toward sexual maturity is celebrated together with lessons on the responsibility that sexual maturity carries with it. The theme of moral responsibility is presented in Calvert's text, as in Rodowsky's novel, through the voice of a daughter who has suffered hurt and pain because of her mother's behavior. Leenie, who had refused to open her mother's gifts sent to her for birthdays and Easter, is not able to openly acknowledge to her mother that she forgives her. She is only able to mouth the words, "*I think I love you, too*" through the glass window of the bus when her mother returns to Boston (132).

A BINDING LOVE

While Calvert describes the relationship between Leenie and her mother as a tentative beginning, other novels convey the belief that daughters and birth mothers are naturally attached to one another because of the biological link between their bodies. Diane Eyer has argued that the relationship between mother and child has been invested with a hefty set of beliefs and values based on the concepts of instinctual love and mother–child bonding. These have been used in social and political agendas to control and influence mothers and attitudes towards child care and mothering.[4] In terms of the writings about the mother–daughter relationship the ideology of bonding has found expression in the script "loving" and "letting go" that Walters documents as emerging in "popular culture with a vengeance" during the 1980s (193).

Hall's novel, *Letting Go*, is one of the clearest examples of how this script is employed in a young adult novel. In the context of a narrative plot in which Casey and her mother share an interest in showing dogs, Hall uses an understanding of maternal love that is derived from bonding and attachment theories associated with instinctual animal behavior heard in such statements: "But the mothering instinct, there really isn't any logic behind that. It is just pure instinct. Survival of the species" (83).[5] Letting go of a daughter—a mother's task during adolescence—is analogous to the "weaning" of puppies:

> The dogs do it so well, don't they? They take care of their puppies, they play
> with them, enjoy them, teach them, and when the time comes, they give them
> a swift few bites on the muzzle and presto, they're weaned (53).

A number of other assumptions are conceptually together in the script of bonding and letting go: the overinvestment of a mother's love that is "hard to live up to"; the fear of a daughter's "unescapable closeness" to a mother; the idea that mothers have to let go; and the empty nest syndrome. Casey's mother asks, for example, what happens to the "mothering urge" and mothers "when there's nobody left who needs it or wants it? Do you hang on to your kids till they genuinely start to hate you? . . . Why doesn't the *urge* go away when the kids do? Why does there have to be this empty feeling, as though I'm going to cease to exist, somehow, if I don't have somebody to take care of?" (83). Eyer argues that the research on bonding undertaken taken by the medical profession in the 1970s was "a last gasp of the ideology regarding the all-powerful maternal sculptress"—at a time when a third of mothers were working and only thirteen percent of American families fit the description of the ideal family of two parents in which the man worked and the woman stayed at home.[6] Casey's mother's statement that women are there to "Serve the husband and be sheltered and cared for in return. Serve the baby and be loved in return" is an example of how ideologies of mothering and gender intersect, and how this view of the traditional nuclear family become part of a story script (Hall 82).

The following passage in *Bound by Love*, a general text about the mother–daughter relationship, can aptly be applied to the description of the relationship between a teen daughter and her mother in *Letting Go:*

> Since we become so symbiotically identified with our daughters, we are likely
> to have a hard time letting them go, or letting them define their own bound-
> aries, when they need to. We can't let them go because we're not through
> with them—we still need them (Gilbert and Webster 33).

Identical language is used in an adolescent psychology text on the daughter–mother relationship. The relationship is described as "a unique bond" and daughters and parents, it is stated, both have "trouble letting go."[7]

FLESH OF MY FLESH

"Flesh of my flesh, blood of my blood" is how Mary Leary "imagines her mother thinks to herself" about their relationship (Shreve 40). The mediation of the primary love between mothers and daughters by imagery of the maternal body is prevalent (cross-culturally) in the literature of the mother–daughter relationship in feminist writings, in poetry, and fiction.[8] A. Rich, for example, writes of the "flow of energies between two biologically alike bodies, one that has lain in amniotic bliss inside the other, one of which has labored to give birth to the other" (225–26). The concept and use of the term "bloodmother" in African American literature, for example, emphasizes the elemental relationship of "flesh and blood." Writing the maternal body into the text through an imagery of flesh and blood to emphasize the primary physical bond between a daughter and mother is a pervasive textual practice in the daughter–mother narratives in young adult novels that are written by women. Examples can also be found in passages in young adult novels. In *Notes for Another Life* by Sue Bridgers, for example, teenage daughter Wren thinks how she had once been:

> inside that body, had been attached, connected to that will. You will be, the pulsing cord had said to her. I am making you, linking you to me forever because we are closer than you will ever be to anyone. I am your first dream, your first memory, your first pain (168).

What is evident is the extent to which love and identity between an adolescent daughter and her mother are mediated by somatic imagery and constructs from a psychological discourse on mother–child relationships. The relationship between mother and child is conceptualized in psychological object theories, for example, as a symbiotic union that is described in terms of a merging and fusion and that emphasizes the presence of the mother.[9] Biological imagery is especially used to mediate attachment and identity between daughters and mothers in stories set in the context of emotional and ideological debates around the issues of adoption versus abortion and pro-life versus pro-choice.

In Shreve's *The Revolution of Mary Leary* the writing in of the maternal body is used to emphasize the primary connections between a teenage daughter and her mother. Set within the religious and political context of the debates on the "right to life," Shreve's novel endorses the political and moral choice of pro-life through the representation of Mary Leary's mother who is a staunch Catholic and campaigner for "Life Chance" and the "rhythm method" of birth control.[10] In her mini-rebellion, Mary takes flight from her mother to the alternative home of pro-choice Sally Page, where she helps with the household and baby-sits young Albert Page, places the daughter–mother narrative within the context of two opposing value systems. Mary's home is contrasted, with humor and not a little irony, with the disorderly and neglected household of the Pages—the setting for Reverend Page's "Death Group" meetings.

Shreve uses the conventional imagery of boundaries to set up a story in which Mary is determined to place difference and space between herself and her mother—even if the Page's home is only "about a mile" from her own home (21). The strong presence of Mary's mother (literally a "large woman") in her daughter's life is reproduced through a somatic language and imagery that emphasizes the maternal body, voice, and the fleshly links between a daughter and her mother. Her mother is said to arrive "in the flesh" in Mary's room, for example (45). A daughter's identity is constructed through her physical resemblance to her mother—even to the calves of her legs (23). Mary is leaving home and her mother because she wants to "avoid any further imitative tendencies on [her] part" (11).

Shreve's text is a good example of how discursive strategies can be used to give voice to cultural stereotypes and the attitudes they encode, while dissipating much of the bias against stereotyping a mother through the use of hyperbole and humor. Her "lungs," narrates Mary, "are probably one eighth the normal size of teenage lungs" because of her "mother's smothering" (43). Her mother, she narrates, is a "powerful woman" who could "steamroller a choir of angels if they were on the wrong course" (42). She is kept at a distance, partly through Mary's first-person narration— shown to be limited in perspective—and partly through plotted events of story in which some physical and psychic space is placed between daughter and mother. Mary's reaction to her mother is described as operating "entirely according to the rules of opposites" (41).

Despite Mary's protests and complaints, she is really close to her mother and is homesick at the Pages' home. Shreve's novel is representative of those in which adolescent girls are described as staying in relationship with their mothers although adolescence continues to be presented as a time when a daughter questions her relationship with her mother and as a time when there is tension between them. Mary's mother continues to be a role model for her daughter. Mary's subsequent revelation—"Boom. The Word in a cloud of smoke"—is that she understands her mother. Her mother, she narrates, is "a saint of a woman" and a "good woman" (179). The first-person narration of Mary (with which readers are invited to identify) is now shown to be in unison with her mother's voice. This works, of course, to place emphasis on the preferred value system in the text.

> Suddenly I understand her Serious Discussions and her pressure to make a Wonderful Family, her chocolate chip cookies and macaroons, and her pre-occupations with God and with the Virgin Mary. Even Life Chance.
>
> I see her looking like me—a bit older, rocking babies and changing them, cleaning floors, burning dinners—but mostly I see myself, sitting on her lap as Albert (179–80).

The mirroring of Mary and her mother works to stress their sameness rather than difference. Mary, as does her mother, believes "in the chance for life" (180).

The above passage is a good example of how the daughter–mother narrative is constructed through a discourse of mothering interconnected with discourses that place value on the maternal body and maternity that are spoken from a specific ideological standpoint. Shreve brings into contiguity motherhood, the Virgin Mary, the Word, and the Flesh—a religious discourse that Julia Kristeva argues has covered and controlled the semiotics of the maternal body and maternity.[11] The representation of the body has been problematic in feminist theories. The identification of women with the concept of the maternal and with their biological bodies has, as Hirsch points out, been avoided in some feminist analyses that have stressed the cultural representation of women's bodies and maternity to avoid essentialist positions (166). The text of *The Revolution of Mary Leary* acts as a reminder that young adult novels construct and purvey social, religious, and political ideologies within their texts as a part of story—stories that contribute to political debates and agendas that have crucial outcomes for young women. Shreve, however, does foreground, rather than obscure, the ideological stance of the novel.

The concept of bonding and the symbiotic relationship of child and mother are particularly used in Elfman's *A House for Jonnie O* in order to partly rationalize an unmarried sixteen-year-old teenager's decision to keep her baby daughter. It is an example of a text that stresses the value of the maternal body through the literal biological connections between mothers and daughters in order to inscribe a particular ideological viewpoint. Emphasis is placed on the fact that Jonnie's unborn baby is "her own flesh and blood child." Elfman uses a persuasive, emotive language and imagery of merging that erases boundaries and difference between mother and child.

Jonnie's unborn baby is described and focalized by Jonnie (through the agency of an anonymous narrator) "like a growing seed inside her, not a separate thing to be kept or given away, like an object, but part of her own *self.*" Jonnie and her baby "were an entity" and "the baby was the luck part of her, that her luck had been missing and had been restored with the baby" (63). Jonnie's daughter "would be a permanent bond with her, no matter what happened, no matter what transient angers. Forever linked to her" (163). The flesh and blood imagery is used to reproduce the continuity of connections between Jonnie, her own mother, and Jonnie's newly born daughter, Lark. Observing her newly born daughter, Jonnie "could see little veins that carried Lark's blood, and Jonnie's blood, and her mother's blood, like a roadmap of the generations" (162).

Through the birth of Lark, the rupture between Jonnie and her own mother is healed over. At the closure of the novel, Jonnie is said to be: "sixteen, and alive, and a mother, and a mother's daughter—and she had made choices" (164). The daughter–mother narrative is produced through a discourse of maternity and biology that carries with it a strong ideological message about abortion and adoption. As one sixteen-year-old daughter puts it in *I'm Still Me,* if her mother had had an abortion, she would not *be*—"I might have been an abortion" (Lifton 168). Seeing her mother's name on a birth certificate made teenage-adopted daughter, Lori, realize that she "had not just magically appeared in this earth, but had come from a real flesh-and-blood mother" (Lifton 55).[12]

The maternal body is invested with different meanings and values in the daughter–mother narrative in young adult novels. It is signified as possessing the power to abuse or impede, to "suffocate," and conversely, the "will" to procreate. It is mediated by images in which it invades a daughter's boundaries and also by sensual language and imagery in which daughters fantasize dissolving boundaries between themselves and the maternal. The maternal body signifies the body that a daughter fears becoming; as a mirror, it connotes love and approval or, conversely, disapproval for a daughter.

LOVE AND NEEDS/ABSENCE AND LOSS

In Bridgers's *Notes for Another Life,* Wren comments that she "didn't want to make demands, knowing how uncomfortably they could be met. It was better to let her mother be" (15). The daughter–mother narrative in young adult novels is partly composed of a Freudian discourse of love and needs that constructs teen daughters as blaming mothers for never being able to provide them with enough attention; that holds mothers of adolescent daughters responsible for providing an endless supply of love and nurturance.[13] "If you loved me, you'd want to be with me," a daughter tells her mother in Nixon's novel, *Encore* (171). The love and need for a mother that is inscribed in these daughter–mother narratives would seem, however, to signify beyond a prescriptive social construction of mothering in which mothers are expected to be available in all situations and contexts. What is striking is the emotional intensity evoked throughout texts: a mother's absence is shown to count. In Bridgers's *Notes for Another Life,* for example, the meaning of a mother's absence to her daughter is described in the passage below:

> What Karen was doing out of their sight in Atlanta always mattered. Her absence counted; it was a minus, a subtraction from the sum of their lives because it meant, that no matter how they struggled to deny it, that she didn't need them enough, want them enough, love them enough (16).

In Colman's *Rich and Famous Like My Mom* Cassandra is resentful that her rock star mother, Phillipa, is so frequently away from home and comments that her mother's presents do not compensate for her absence. When Phillipa was gone, she comments, "there was nothing" (45).

One of the most poignant scenes signifying the loss of maternal love is in Suzanne Freeman's novel, *The Cuckoo's Child,* in which Mia climbs the water tower in Iona, Tennessee, only to realize that she could never catch a glimpse of the Ionian sea where her parents had disappeared a week before. As her mother's sister rushes toward her, Mia thinks it is her mother then realizes it is her Aunt Kit. "I didn't want her looking like my mom now, like an imitation. I wanted her to go away" (17). Mia's tears, anger, the taboos and rules she sets up that must not be broken until the return of her parents—especially her mother—are sympathetically conveyed by Freeman.

THE DEATH OF A MOTHER

The articulation of anger, blame, pain, and loss is intensely written into stories in which daughters experience the death of a mother. In Deaver's *You Bet Your Life,* seventeen-year-old Beth writes letters addressed to her mother (after her mother's suicide) in which she blames her mother for leaving her while also writing how much she loves and misses her.

> The thing is, I know it was an illness. I know that. But what about me? How could you destroy what we had between us? I mean, what did you think would

happen to me after you were gone? Or did you even stop to think of that at all? These are thoughts I can't push away any longer. These are things I need answers to. I need to know (193).

The deep emotional pain and grief of losing a mother invoked in Oneal's *A Formal Feeling* are mediated through a language of love, anger, guilt, and pain. In a text rich in imagery, Oneal uses Emily Dickinson's lines: "As Freezing persons, recollect the Snow—/First—Chill—then Stupor—then the letting go—" as a metaphor for Anne's grief that is extended by Oneal through the ice-cold and snowy setting of the novel.[14] One of the most emotive passages in which a daughter gives voice to her grief for her dead mother is found in Hathorn's novel, *Thunderwith:*

It was not so much a word as a terrible cry from the heart.
    'Mother!' she screamed. The wind tore the word from her throat and carried it off and away across the fields and into the dark forest. 'Mo-o-o-ther!' she called again so that her throat swelled with the sound and rasped with pain at the intensity of the prolonged cry. It seemed that every fiber of her strength went into the world issuing from her blue cold lips.
    And again, 'Mo-o-ther!' her voice rose up louder than any summer-shrieking cicada shrill.
    'Mother, oh Mother,' a lamentation, an incantation. Over and over again she chanted the name (185).

Adolescence continues to be imagined in many young adult texts as a time when a daughter must bid goodbye to a close attachment to her maternal mother—a time of grief, mourning, and renunciation. Lara's cry, however, with other daughters' voices, is a call from the heart giving sound to the reality of pain, loss, and grief that comes with a mother's death.

If the "shadow" of a mother's power is represented as looming tall over her daughter in Freudian psychodynamic narratives, the dissolution of this power is represented through an imagery that describes the maternal body as "fading" and "crumbling" away. In some novels, this imagery is used to symbolize the "death" of maternal beneficence. In Smith's fantasy novel, *Snow-Eyes,* for example, a mother is associated with the ice, snow, and "frost" of winter. Her "gaze" to Snow-Eyes "seemed harder than silver, more chill than the ice on the black stone" (37). She had attempted to "trade" her daughter's life for that of her dead husband's. "Did you know that Death would take me in Paudan's stead?" Snow-Eyes asks her mother (190). In her mother's silence she hears an answer "that made her colder than any winter's frost" (191). Beya Rete is a "nightmare" to her daughter—

a mother who had failed to tutor and empower her (43). Associated with death, Beya Rete is represented as specter at the closure of Smith's novel: "Beya was as transparent as the icicles that had grown upon the twisted columns and roof; she seemed like an ice sculpture, carved atop the stone" (214). Her "phantom's hand" is described as "fluttering lightly over" her daughter's cheek. "Little by little, she lost substance, then disappeared and was gone" (220).

The death of a mother is dramatically illustrated in selected texts through the literal silencing of her voice and descriptions of the dissolution of the maternal body. It is only when this kind of imagery is accumulated from passages in a number of texts that attention is drawn to the grotesque and macabre way in which the death of the maternal body is described. It would seem to go beyond the reality of physical illness and death. Examples include descriptions of Bent's dying mother as a "frail body that felt like cotton wrapped around a stick" (Fosburgh 12). After her mother's death, Bent is described as running her hand across the sheet on the bed where her mother had lain. "If she pressed down on it, maybe she would feel a frail lump beneath, a shred of clothing, a shard of bone and body" (104). Brooke Hillary's dying mother in *A Star for the Latecomer* by the Zindels is described as "a ghost"—"a shell of what she had once been" (173).

When Meg learns, in Holland's *Of Love and Death and Other Journeys,* that her mother is going to die, she experiences a "chill like a thousand ages of blackness and ice . . ." (107). In Holland's text there is a striking use of a macabre death imagery that is directly associated with setting. Meg's mother's death takes place in Perugia in which "skeletons and blackened bodies of saints" were of "no great rarity" (122). Through Meg's vision, her mother's body is seen as one of Perugia's relics:

> The skeleton lay there in the half-open glass case, a dried-up garland of what were still identifiable as flowers sagging rakishly over the skull, wisps and rags of disintegrated silk lying around him (her?)—definitely, I thought with the garland, her (122).

This description is placed directly in contiguity with an image of Meg's mother as the skeleton becomes "a body that had once worn flesh and walked upright and had eyes and a mouth and laughed, like my mother, who sometimes, when we were on picnics, picked flowers and leaves and made garlands of them for her head" (122). A similar use of imagery of the grotesque is repeated later after the death of Meg's mother. Meg describes her mother's body as a "very dead, yellow white husk" (123). Her mother, "didn't look like Mother. She looked old and yellow and shrunken and disgusting and dead . . ." (140).

The final image of Meg's mother is a portrait received after her death: "She had on the yellow dress, and the tall reeds of broom waved around her shoulders where she sat, the flowers yellow against the blue of the sky. Her floppy hat was on the back of her head, and her hazel green eyes sparkled with mischief and laughter and love and . . . ." It was "joy," her father tells her (158). The representation of the maternal body in Holland's text well illustrates the binary oppositions of idealized and deidealized images through which the maternal body is fantasized in the daughter–mother narrative in young adult novels. The maternal body is mediated in texts by a language and imagery associating it with death and the macabre, and conversely, with joy, life, and love.

One of the most fascinating novels dealing with the death of a teenage-daughter's mother is Klause's fantasy/horror novel, *The Silver Kiss*, in which seventeen-year-old Zöe meets the beautiful vampire, Simon, as her mother lies dying from cancer. In a genre in which the unnatural invades reality, the conventions of the vampire story are used to show that Zöe's mother's death is a natural release from pain in comparison to the "horror" of Simon's enslavement to an unnatural life. "They make a strange pair: the dying and the undead," Zöe thinks when she takes Simon with her to visit her mother in hospital (142). The play on the word "horror" and the oppositions of natural and unnatural are made throughout the text. Zöe's suggestion that, maybe, Simon could "change" her mother so that she could be sustained by the blood of others is rejected by Simon with "horror." The change was "unnatural," and her mother would always be in pain (143). "Death would be better than living" the way that Simon had to live, Zöe reasons at closure. "Sometimes there was a time for death," Zöe then thinks about her mother. "Perhaps there was always a good reason even if you couldn't see it, and it was a crime against nature to deny change" (193). Zöe's assistance in helping Simon willingly give himself to a joyful death is made as her mother is shown to wish for her own release. Through the story of Simon's younger evil vampire brother, Christopher who kills his mother, Klause deftly uses a vampire story to show that the real horror is not the fact of a mother's natural death from cancer but the killing of the mother—the deliberate, unnatural act of matricide through the sucking away of a mother's life blood. Klause's text, thus, encodes references to a discourse that has given voice to the dark side of cultural beliefs and fantasies about mothers and mothering.[15]

"Pale as the milk of death, thin and sharp like pain," is the way Simon describes Zöe (19). The identification of a daughter with her mother is made in Klause's novel through a death imagery that evokes the beauty of a daughter who is as "thin as her mother," and who asks herself: "Wouldn't it be ironic if she died, too, fading out suddenly when her look-alike went" (2). The contrasting images of her mother conform with other descriptions of dying mothers—"so transparent and small . . ." that fits, too, with the reality of death (72). The daughter–mother narrative is also composed of those very human aspects of relationship that are found in other novels: Zöe's feelings of anger at being kept from visiting her mother, her anger at her mother's leaving her, and a mother's trying to shield her daughter from the reality of death and the pain of loss. Klause's story like so many of the stories discussed in this chapter tells a story about a daughter's acceptance and working through her mother's death.

LOVING MEMORIES:
EMBEDDED DAUGHTER–MOTHER NARRATIVES

Elizabeth Abel has identified patterns of narrative plotting in women's fiction in which female bonding and the daughter–mother narrative were frequently "relegated" to the background of the dominant linear narrative of a heterosexual romance plot. Abel associates these recessed plots of love and attachment to Freudian descriptions of pre-Oedipal development—"a female-centered natural world" that precede and lie "behind" a male-dominated society (163). Just as Bent explains in Fosburgh's *The Wrong Way Home* how her love for her mother is embedded in the walls of the apartment in which they had lived together, so in selected texts is the love and relationship that daughters have shared with their mothers embedded in linear narrative plots of daughter–mother separation (145). These embedded narratives, encoding a belief in the continuing psychic importance of the love of the primary bond between daughters and mothers, are written in the form of vignettes, dream fantasies, and sometimes even letters—all encompassing a going-back in time and memory that interrupt the time-frame of a dominant linear narrative.[16]

"My love for you Lara Meredith Ritchie is big as all the universe—you'd better believe it!" Lara's mother writes in a letter for her daughter to read after her death (168). Hathorn's *Thunderwith* is representative of texts in which fantasies of ideal love between a young daughter and her mother are embedded in a dominant linear plot. Lara, unhappy and treated as the

outsider by her stepmother at her father's farm, remembers back to the
happy times she had shared with her now-dead mother: "Mom lying on the
bed reading to her . . ." (49).

> Mom hugging her. Mom telling her over and over how wonderful it was, the
> two of them together as they were. Mom talking softly, seriously to her when
> she told her some of her worries at school. Mom singing and dancing and
> being crazy. Mom, noisy and embarrassing at some of the get-togethers they'd
> had at Idle Hours (50).

The dog, Thunderwith, befriended by Lara, comes to stand in for her
mother—a literal object of substitution. When she was with Thunderwith,
Lara "found peace. She didn't think about Mom anymore when she was
with the dog. She seemed so far away, so remote now" (89). An aboriginal
storyteller tells Lara that: "She sent the dog to you, to look out for you all
those long months when you couldn't see her. She sent Thunderwith just
as you thought, she sent something real to be with you" (200). When
Thunderwith is shot, Lara sees the "image of" her mother's face, "clear and
bright and close" (189). "It seemed to Lara that through the dreadful events
that had happened on the hill this evening, she had finally summoned her
mother. Cheryl had come out of the storm. And Cheryl was here now, be-
side her daughter" (188). The daughter–mother relationship is, thus, fantasized and conceptualized in Hathorn's novel as a continuing emotional
bond. Lara "thought of Mom as she often did now. But not in the blaming
way she used to think about her. . . . She knew Mom was here now. Somewhere, forever, very close by" (214).

In Martha Brooks's *Two Moons in August,* set in Canada in the 1950s,
an embedded daughter–mother narrative of love and connections is constructed from sixteen-year-old Sidonie's memories and dream fantasies of
her dead mother, Eugenie, who died from heart failure on Sidonie's fifteenth
birthday. Her mother's death, the previous August, had changed her world,
she narrates. There had been the "almost full" moon when her mother was
alive and at the end, "a big full cheater moon . . . that looked down so beautifully on the world when everything was awful and changed and never
would be the same again" (76).

Brooks also writes about a daughter who is working through her mother's
death. In recurrent dreams filled with images of her mother (associated with
roses), water, and drowning, Sidonie's past and present life become merged
with two central events in her life: the death of her mother and her near
drowning in rescuing her friend, Kieran. As in Hathorn's text and others,

images of a mother swim into view: "It's Mom—smiling at me, smelling of roses, her dark hair in a French roll. She pulls out the pins, and the wind catches it, blowing it out behind her like an immense Chinese fan" (45). On the morning of her mother's death, Sidonie narrates, she had combed her mother's hair—hair that was black like her own (3).

There are other passages in Brooks's text in which the celebration of the emotional and physical bond between a daughter and her mother are mediated by imagery that evokes the literal presence of the maternal body. Sidonie, for example, remembers the warm, physical contact she had with her mother—the feel of her mother's arms around her, her mother bathing her and teaching her to swim. She remembers how she and her sister, Roberta, on a trip to Florida with their parents, had taken turns in climbing over the car seat to be with their mother—playing "with her hair, her earrings, the gold cross on the gold chain that always hung around her neck" (95). In another passage, Sidonie narrates:

> My hands are like Mom's. Last summer we used to put them together out on the lawn cart overlooking the ravine. I'd smooth out her garden-roughened fingers, make her palms go flat and place mine on top. Then I'd dance my fingers up and down like a spider on a mirror (13).

The use of biological imagery evoking the presence of the maternal body is striking in this passage and others in daughter–mother narratives in young adult novels. In another passage, Sidonie narrates that: "A pelican flew over our heads, its neck stretched, its wings rustling like the sound my mother's dress used to make when she would cross the carpet from her closet to her makeup table" (Brooks 16). The prevalence of this use of imagery in daughter–mother narratives written by women certainly raises questions about the difference of women's writing and maternal texts.[17]

The closeness between a daughter and mother is mediated by an imagery of the maternal body and imagery associated with nature in Sharon Creech's *Walk Two Moons*. Salamanca's mother, who has left home shortly after a miscarriage on a journey from which she does not return, sends her daughter a postcard on which she has written: "Salamanca is my left arm. I miss my left arm" (144). Salamanca, missing her dead mother, narrates that when she tried to write about all the things that she liked finally wrote about her mother because "everything was connected to her" (121). Salamanca's telling of the "blackberry kiss" story illustrates her point. One day, she had watched her mother, after plucking and eating some blackberries, fling her arms around the sugar maple tree that grew on their farm and kiss it. Salamanca, later that day, also kisses the bark of the tree and tastes blackberries on her lips (122). From that day forward, Salamanca confesses in her journal, she had "kissed all different kinds of trees" and although each tree had its own distinctive taste, the taste of blackberries was always mixed in (122–23). The taste of blackberries is also in the kisses she exchanges with Ben in whose presence her blood "romped around as if it were percolating" (234).

Feminist writings about the mother–daughter relationship are also characterized by imagery and metaphors that emphasize relationship and interconnectedness. Chodorow, for example, writes of the fluidity and continuity of the boundaries between mothers and daughters (*The Reproduction*). Gilligan uses images of web and hierarchy, respectively, to describe the differences between experiencing self as interconnected with others and the understanding of self as isolated and independent.[18] The passages quoted above from Brooks's *Two Moons in August* and Creech's *Walk Two Moons* are examples of how much daughters' fantasies of being physically close to their mothers are part of daughter–mother narratives in young adult texts. In Brooks's novel, Sidonie comments that she could feel her mother's "arms very tight around" her "just by wishing it"(17). It is the fantasy of being close to the maternal body that is now absent that seems so strong in some of these passages—the longing for a physical connection with her mother that is no longer available for a daughter.

SEARCHING FOR MOTHER

Much of the outpouring of writings about the mother–daughter relationship since the publication of A. Rich's *Of Woman Born* has been an attempt to write in, or uncover, daughter–mother narratives and plots—an endeavor by "daughter–scholars" to "search for the stranger who has been our mother."[19] One can at least raise the question here about the relation of selected daughter–mother narratives in young adult novels to autobiographical narratives. Do women writers, at some level of consciousness, seek through story to reconstruct their self-identity with their mothers and to revisit the daughter–mother relationship in adolescence from another subject position? A daughter's actual search for her mother informs daughter–mother narrative plots in several novels published in the 1990s including Caroline Macdonald's *Speaking to Miranda* and Harry Mazer's *Someone's Mother Is Missing* (already discussed in chapter four). This search for one's mother is a dominant theme, of course, in stories in which adoptive daughters search for their birth mothers.[20] While all these stories *are* very different in kind and encode different aspects of the daughter–mother relationship, the retracing of a mother's steps and the going back and discovering a mother's past and whereabouts are presented in story as a mystery to be solved. At the heart of these stories is a girl's quest for her identity— a perennial theme in stories of adolescence. A girl's primary tie to her mother is shown to be important, in selected novels, in enabling a daughter to establish her own sense of self. As Ruby comments about her mother in Caroline Macdonald's *Speaking to Miranda*: "I resent her determination to obscure her past and leave me floating, nameless and unclaimed if it hadn't been for Rob" (70).

Speaking to Miranda is set in Australia and New Zealand. Eighteen-year-old Ruby has lived with her architect stepfather, Rob, since her mother, Emma, accidentally drowned when Ruby was two years old. Her mother, however, as Rob tells Ruby, when she insists she has a right to know who her mother was and where she came from, is a "mystery woman" (68). He had picked her up as she was hitchhiking with Ruby, taken her home, fallen in love with her, and taken her to meet his parents in Melbourne. The main portion of Macdonald's story is Ruby's search to uncover the mystery of her mother. This takes her from Melbourne to Waihi in New Zealand where she meets Sonny David Manuata and his mother and sees the "Emma Blake" house that had been her mother's family home. Emma was really Magda, Ruby discovers—a "kiwi" who had been married to Sonny but ran away when Sonny was in Vietnam. The daughter–mother narrative plot includes Ruby's retracing of her mother's journey so that initially Ruby partly identifies with her mother: "I'm like Emma all those years ago in Australia. The only difference is I don't have a baby in my arms" (187).

The play and mystery surrounding the identity of daughter and mother in Macdonald's story continue as Ruby's true identity is revealed. Ruby discovers that she is, in fact, Miranda—the name of the imaginary friend— "spirit"—with whom she constantly talked when small and whom she had consulted when older (94). Ruby is dead, Mum Manuata tells Miranda. She had died while her "trashy mother was out making you in the backseat of some pakeha's car" (206). The perjorative "trashy" does not, however, sum up the mother of Miranda and Ruby. Miranda realizes that her mother, a potential swimming champion, was a person who had many selves: "Emma/ Magna was extraordinary. She's left a strong image with everyone who knew her, but the images are all in different shades, flickering, changing, and I wonder if I'll ever be able to distill the essential Magda" (251). Miranda, in fact, comes to realize that her search for a self-identity has resulted in finding that her sense of self is composed of not one, but many identities. This realization is evident in her statement: "Magda—Ruby—Emma—Miranda. I'm losing grip on who I am" (207).

Macdonald builds connections between the genealogy of women in Miranda's family as Miranda decides to stay on in the house that had been in her mother's family since the days of her great-great-great grandmother, Emma Blake. Here Miranda finds clothes, records, and photos that belonged to her mother. Miranda's search for her mother, however, is encapsulated in a story that tells about her relationship with the man who has been father to her since her mother disappeared. At the closure of Macdonald's novel, Rob, who has broken off yet another affair with a woman friend, appears at the Emma Blake home. It is difficult, it seems, to write "other" than the Oedipal narrative so firmly ensconced in young adult novels as a narrative plot form.

A daughter's needs to establish her roots and identity are central themes, of course, in novels about teenage girls who are adopted. "I want to find my *mother*," narrates adopted teenage daughter, Natalie, in Lois Lowry's *Find a Stranger, Say Goodbye*. "I want to find out what happened, why I was born, why she gave me away. Who she was. Who she is" (16). Similar statements are made by adopted daughters in Betty Jean Lifton's *I'm Still Me* and in Okimoto's *Molly By Any Other Name*. Issues of identity and connections are approached differently in novels in which value is placed on the relationship between an adopted daughter and her mother. Elfman's *A House for Jonnie O* and Lowry's *Find a Stranger, Say Goodbye*, for example, are produced through contradictory discourses that encode ideological positions on teenage pregnancy and adoption that impinge so directly on teenage girls today. Natalie's father, for example, tells her that "what a person *is* has nothing to do with where they came from, not with what *body* they came from" (Lowry 16).

Feminist Sara Ruddick, in critiquing the concept of mother–child bonding, has argued that the biological function of a mother in giving birth should be separated from the maternal function of mothering: "Adoptive or stepmothers are no less qualified maternal workers because they have not given birth. Nor is giving birth sufficient grounds for undertaking maternal work or doing it effectively" (48). All mothers, states Ruddick, are "adoptive" in that they commit to sustaining a child (51).

In *Find a Stranger, Say Goodbye*, Lowry writes of fifteen-year-old Natalie's journey to Simmon's Mill to find her birth mother. As in other novels in which a daughter sets out to search for her mother, the search takes the form of a mystery as Natalie follows up the clues she has been given in letters retained and finally given to her by her adoptive parents—as "a gift." Julie Jeffries, her birth mother, Natalie discovers, became pregnant at fifteen years of age, and after giving up her baby for adoption, went on to boarding school and went on to became a successful model. Natalie finally finds Julie living in New York. She is married and the mother of two small boys. Through the comparisons made between the beautiful model, Julie Jeffries, and Kay Armstrong (Natalie's adoptive mother), Lowry places value on Kay. The representation of the creative, energetic, fun-loving Kay Armstrong falls into one of those wife/mother/homemaker figures that are held up to daughters in young adult texts as role models. Julie, however, in her first meeting with Natalie, is represented as a vain, controlling mother who immediately wishes to remake Natalie (who has Julie's "facial bones" and eyes) into her own image—a successful model—even to changing her name despite Natalie's insistence that she wishes to be a doctor. Lowry uses the perfect setting of Julie's home, her somewhat distant relationship to her sons, and the way Natalie feels a "tacky awkwardness" in the company of her birth mother to contrast with the warmth and free-and-easy style of living in Kay Armstrong's home.

More importantly, perhaps, Lowry creates positions in the text from which a daughter (and a potential reader) can compare the voices of her two mothers. In a diary given to Natalie by Julie one can hear the adolescent voice of an immature girl. After reading Julie's diary, Natalie narrates that her birth mother had loved her:

> It was a little-girl, selfish kind of love, the same kind of thing I used to feel for my favorite toys, so that I wouldn't share them with Nancy [birth daughter of Natalie's adoptive parents]; or like what I felt for that kitten I had once. I was jealous when it purred and butted against someone else, wanting to be petted; it seemed so important that it be only mine. But Julie *did* love me (153–54).

The simile of the kitten has the effect of diminishing Julie's love in comparison with the love that Kay Armstrong holds for her adopted daughter. Natalie states that her adoptive parents' love was different. The mature voice of Kay Armstrong is contrasted to that of Julie's in letters Kay has written to Tallie (Natalie's future grandmother) as Kay waits to receive her new daughter. Natalie "will be her own person," Kay had written (154). A reader is invited to share Natalie's comparison of her adoptive parents' unselfish love with the attitudes and behavior of Julie. Certainly, Lowry reconnects a daughter's voice with that of her birth mother, but she shows that Natalie's sense of self is more firmly grounded in the relationships she has with Kay and Alden Armstrong and with her grandmother, Tallie. At the closure of the novel, Natalie states that: "you have to relinquish things" and rumples up a picture of her birth mother and throws it in the trash (183). The connection made to Natalie's past that is really valued are Natalie's warm feelings toward her grandfather, Dr. Therrian, whose son, Terry (Natalie's biological father), had been killed in an accident. He had persuaded Julie to give away his grandchild for adoption despite his own pain.

Emphasis is placed on the need for daughters to be loved and nurtured in all daughter–mother narratives in young adult novels. There is a harking back to a familiar script of bonding as mothers assure adopted daughters that they are loved in the same way as if they were their daughters' actual birth mothers. "Oh Lori, we loved you immediately," her adoptive mother tells her daughter in *I'm Still Me* (Lifton 216). In *Find a Stranger, Say Goodbye*, teenage daughter Natalie narrates: "And my parents loved me then, even on that first day when they drove that long road to a strange place to bring me home" (Lowry 156).

At the heart of daughter–mother narratives are issues about mothers and motherhood that are so pertinent to today's daughters. Encoded in these narratives are different ideological positions on just what a mother should be for her daughter in her role *as* mother. Chapter seven discusses the ways in which the daughter–mother relationship is produced through a social construction of mothering.

NOTES

1. See, for example, Apter 69; S. Rich, 259.
2. See, for example, AAUW; Bank & Hall; Orenstein.
3. See Coward "Writing the Body" 367–68.
4. See Eyer *Mother-Infant Bonding* 127; Scheper-Hughes 409.
5. For the analogy made between the "child's tie to his mother" and animal behavior, see Bowlby Vol I, 183.
6. See Eyer *Mother-Infant Bonding* 127.
7. See Eagle and Colman 23.
8. See, for example, poetry in Bell-Scott et al.
9. For further descriptions and explanations of object relations theories, see Chodorow *The Reproduction* 61; Sprengnether 183.
10. For background to the abortion issue in the 1970s and 1980s, see Faludi 412–53; Davis 434–35.
11. See Kristeva "Stabat" 163.

12. The importance of knowing one's "biological origins" for a "sense of identity" is made by a nineteen-year-old woman, who asserts the right for donor children to know their biological parents. See Margaret E. Brown 12.

13. Freud spoke of the "reproach" daughters level at their mothers for their "lack of love." See "Femininity" 122; for an explanation of a social construction of mothering in which mothers and daughters are depicted as having "unmeetable needs for affection," see Caplan 107.

14. Verse lines are quoted from Emily Dickinson's "After great pain."

15. For a discussion of the sexual connotation of the vampire's blood-sucking practices, see Cranny-Francis 95.

16. Apter points out that a mother's "simple" and "strong love" for her daughter is missing from accounts of traditional adolescent development, 135.

17. For discussion and critique of the supposition that women's biological differences are a source of a specifically female writing—a writing from the body—see Jones; Showalter.

18. See Gilligan *In a Different Voice* 62.

19. See, for example, Davidson and Broner, eds. xiii.

20. See Lifton; Lowry; Okimoto.

Seven

Stories about Mothers and Lessons for Daughters

Maybe Mary Alice had a baby sixteen years ago . . . but that never really made her a mother. I mean, a mother is a person who sticks around, right?

—Calvert

The daughter–mother narratives in young adult novels encode social and cultural values about mothers and mothering. At issue in so many stories is just what a "real" mother should be for her daughter. The texts of young adult novels contribute toward a larger social and political discourse about women and careers versus the responsibilities of motherhood—issues that have been at the center of feminist debates and the Women's Movement.[1] Incorporated within stories set in different racial, social, and cultural contexts are lessons about the practice of mothering and about the gender socialization of girls that are pertinent to daughters whose own choices and decisions will be made in the context of economic pressures and societal values.

Aspects of a social discourse of mothering reproduced in daughter–mother narratives include cultural expectations of what it takes to be a good mother, the moral and social responsibility of mothering, and mother blame. Identified in texts are issues that have been raised and addressed by feminists and the Women's Movement including societal expectations that women are responsible for mothering, the conflicting demands made on mothers who wish to both engage in a career and raise a family, the "biological clock," the "fast track," absent fathers, and single parenting.

This chapter demonstrates through specific examples the different ways a cultural discourse of mothering informs daughter–mother narratives. Ini-

147

tially, the focus will be on how certain elements of a social construction of mothering inform the daughter–mother narrative in selected novels—fantasies of the ideal mother, the responsibility of mothering, and mother blame. I then discuss how contemporary debates about women's traditional role in the home and women's right to pursue their own careers inform the discourse on mothering in daughter–mother narratives. Intertextually, these issues are framed and debated from differing ideological viewpoints. Notwithstanding the different ways these compromises are resolved in texts, it is important to note that young adult texts are producing these issues as dilemmas for daughters in texts and for daughters positioned as readers of texts. The selection of texts has been limited to representations of daughter–mother relationships in the context of white American families situated in differing socioeconomic contexts. Novels were selected that best highlight different ideological assumptions about mothers and mothering in regard to the representation of the daughter–mother relationship.

A "GOOD ENOUGH" MOTHER:
A SOCIAL CONSTRUCTION OF MOTHERING

In Mazer's *Someone's Mother Is Missing,* a daughter, Lisa, asks: "Why did all mothers have to be perfect? Her mother wasn't perfect. Or her grandmother. No mother could hold the world together for her children. Nobody could smooth the pain away forever" (164). Mazer's text draws attention to a prevalent cultural assumption that mothers are expected to be perfect—an ideology of mothering that Chodorow and Contratto have found in nineteenth-century cultural ideologies about mothering in post-Freudian cultural ideologies about motherhood, and which they have also traced in feminist writings on mothering.[2] The message inscribed in this discourse is "not only that mothers can be perfect but also that the child's needs . . . are necessarily legitimate and must be met" (82). The theoretical formulations of child development and the discourse of mothers and mothering are embedded in a "culturally child-centered perspective," argue the authors, which limits and oppresses women and constrains accounts of mothering (95–96). Psychoanalytic theorists have particularly been responsible for developing the concept of the mother who is ever available and anticipates her child's needs—the "good-enough" mother.[3] In her study of the historical and social construction of motherhood, Thurer writes of the myth that prevails in American culture today—that of a loving devoted mother who is held entirely responsible for the well being of her child (xvi). We have cultural scripts for motherhood, writes Ann Willard, that tell us about the "right" way to be a mother (225). These cultural scripts also inform stories in young adult novels.

Why can't her mother be "like other mothers," twelve-year-old Henley asks her mother, Patti, in Rodowsky's *H. My Name Is Henley* (55). "Okay— okay. It's other-mothers you want," said Patti, mincing around a display table with her shoulder bag hooked over her arm. "I'm the other-mothers going to a committee meeting. Other-mothers playing bridge at the country club. Other—mothers—other—mothers-other—mothers. . . ." Patti hears her mother's voice "stretch to a taut flat line" (55). The expectations that daughters have of their mothers are heard through the voices of daughters as they criticize or blame their mothers for being "blind" to their needs, or ask why their mothers fall short of what they expect a mother to be for them. In selected novels in which mothers have walked out on their daughters and families, or abandoned their daughter at birth, mothers are, in effect, called to task by their daughters to give explanations and justifications for their behavior.

If mothers fail to meet societal expectations, then blaming the mother for when she makes mistakes also becomes acceptable. As Paula Caplan writes, this blaming has become part of a cultural dialogue about mothers and daughters that has affected the way we talk and think about the mother– daughter relationship (39).[4] The way in which the ideologies of the perfect mother and blaming work together can be heard through the voice of Kelly's father in *The Shell Lady's Daughter.* He tells his daughter that if her suicidal mother admitted to taking the pills on purpose, it would have been a "terrible way to fail as a wife and a mother" (Adler 111).

A daughter's voice can be said to collude, in selected texts, with a psychoanalytic child-centered perspective of mothering. Heard in some stories, for example, are the voices of daughters who feel that their mothers have failed them. In A. E. Cannon's *Amazing Gracie*, Gracie blames her suicidal mother for not caring enough about the family (158). Merle states, with a tone of bitterness, that her mentally ill mother had provided her with "nothing" in Riley's *Crazy Quilt* (133). In Rodowsky's *H. My Name Is Henley*, the failure of twelve-year-old Henley's mother, Patti, to mother her daughter responsibly is pointed out by her friend who tells her:

> That it isn't always fair to Henley, yanking her from one place to the next. Kids need a place to live that isn't always moving out from under them like some kind of damn escalator, and a school that's more than a way station, and friends to grow up with (84).

The idea that mothers are morally and socially responsible for bringing up their daughters is one of the most pervasive mothering scripts of the daughter–mother narrative in young adult novels. A prescriptive message about the practice of mothering is built into selected texts in which mothers are represented as failing their daughters as mothers. *Hannah in Between* is another of Rodowsky's novels that focuses in on how a mother's irresponsible behavior can harm her daughter. Twelve-year-old Hannah tells of her discovery that her mother is a secret drinker and her realization that her parents are denying the problem. Set in the context of a middle-class family, Hannah reports finding empty bottles, driving with her drunk mother, and her embarrassment at inviting friends home. All this contributes to a heavily laden message about alcoholism that is combined with lessons about the responsibilities of being a mother. Hannah's relationship with her mother is also shown to be affected by her mother's behavior. Hannah tells about the time when her mother lets her down over a promised day together in Ocean City: "*Remember* and say it, how this was going to be our special day, just for the two of us, the day you said it'd be. The way you promised. *Remember. Remember*" (21).

Clear-sighted, responsible daughter protagonists are represented, not surprisingly, perhaps, in view of the potential audience, as absolute paragons of virtue. Although they are models of reliance in comparison with their irresponsible mothers, their own vulnerability is also acknowledged and, importantly, their need too for responsible mothering. When twelve-year-old Freedom Jo Avery in June Wood's *A Share of Freedom* tries to discourage her alcoholic mother from drinking at the fairgrounds, Mary Margaret scolds back at her daughter: "Don't 'but Mama' with me. I don't want to hear it. Nag, nag, nag. That's all you do." She is, her mother continues: "Perfectly capable of making decisions" on her own and she doesn't "need a nosy old social worker and big-shot whiz kid to keep me in line" (19). When Mary Margaret is found unconscious the next day, she is taken to hospital and then to a rehabilitation center. Rather than be taken into foster care, Freedom runs away with her younger brother, Jackie, but is forced to call Miss Hambaugh, the social worker when a tornado leaves them without shelter. Freedom, despite her self-reliance, is still shown to be in need of a responsible and loving family.

Stitched seamlessly into selected texts are vignettes of the good mother—a beaming representative of the "Angel in the house"—a convention used in the telling of stories of daughters and mothers in novels published into the 1980s and 1990s.[5] This better mother is, not surprisingly, often the mother of a teenage-daughter's friend. The contradiction between the idea of the perfect mother and the impossibility of mothers attaining that ideal is made most apparent in those novels in which the mother is placed in a socioeconomic context in which she is simply unable to mother or provide for her daughter. In *H. My Name Is Henley* Henley opts to stay to live with Aunt Mercy, the woman doctor whom her mother had briefly visited some years before. Fantasized by Henley as a "sort of combination Madame Curie and the Bionic Woman" from listening to her mother's stories, Aunt Mercy—as her name and profession suggest—is represented as being able to give Henley the stable home and responsible mothering that she needs (120).

In contemporary American society in which divorces and remarriages are ubiquitous, conventions used in fairy tales such as absenting the "real" mother and the employment of the split images of the good and bad mother continue to find a congruity with cultural discourses about daughters and mothers. However, perhaps because of the influence of Freudianism, the practice of writing about "real" mothers who are seen as harmful to their daughters' development has been acceptable in contemporary times. Mother-blame is laid squarely—if not fairly—at the door of mothers in many young adult novels rather than transferred to the wicked stepmother figure of fairy tale. Fantasies of ideal mothers in the guise of other mothers continue to haunt texts for young people. They are perhaps part of a deeply ingrained desire for perfect mothering that surfaces differently in story according to sociohistorical views about mothers and mothering in different times and contexts.

In *The Pig-Out Blues*, Greenberg makes visible how the fantasy of the perfect mother pervades American culture. Jodie stays with her friend David Simms's family while her mother is away. Here, Jodie gets a taste of ideal mothering in the context of the ideal family unit. As Jodie comments: "For a girl to whom paper plates, plastic flowers, and TV dinners were a way of life, a sit-down meal with flowered china, crystal goblets, and sterling silverware on lace doilies was not only 'wondrous strange' as Mr. Shakespeare said, but awe inspiring" (89). There is an ironic awareness in Greenberg's text that this vision of mothering is, indeed, a "wondrous" fantasy—particularly since David subsequently runs away from home. Presented through the figure of Mrs. Simms is the "ghost of the mythical 1950s television mother," that Chira reports, continues to haunt working mothers who still search and worry about what, in reality, is being a "good mother" for her children (32). Greenberg shows in her novel how the Mrs. Simmses of the world and what they represent also haunt Jodie's single mother who has to bring her daughter up in limited circumstances.

A CROSSROADS FOR MOTHERS

The AAUW Report: How Schools Shortchange Girls drew attention to the contradictions and conflicting demands made on female adolescents due to divisions that have been constructed between the public sphere of work and careers (13). Divisions set up between women's responsibilities as mothers and women's abilities to succeed in the public sphere are made highly visible in selected stories set in the context of white, middle-class America.[6] Mothers are represented in these stories as being situated at a crossroads as they attempt to meet the demands of their daughters while trying to develop their own skills and talents. The mothering scripts encoded in the novels Snyder's *Leave Me Alone, Ma!*, Mary Anderson's *Step on a Crack*, Kristi Holl's *Patchwork Summer*, and Corinne Gerson's *How I Put My Mother Through College* would seem to be analogous to those cultural scripts identified by Willard that construct the self-development of a mother in opposition to the development of her child—scripts in which a mother is asked either to sacrifice her own desires or the desires of her child (241).

Snyder's *Leave Me Alone, Ma!* is one of a group of novels that shore up the view that motherhood and a full-time career are incompatible. This story of a middle-class mother who agrees to give up her full-time career in order to spend more time with her daughter was published in 1987—just around the time the media was awash with reports of women leaving the fast track, of trying to balance home and career and the directives to women of "—go home or crack up" (Faludi 89). Described in Snyder's text is the image of the working mother in the 1980s who, notes Flora Davis, was "driven to desperation by the competing demands of job and family" (473).

The stance taken in the text on the inadvisability of mothers working full-time is reinforced by the lesson that Jaimie learns in school "that with more women working, increased numbers of them were having heart problems" (110). The bonds of family are stressed over a mother's career and ambition. Her family, narrates Jaimie: "had every*thing* except each other" and she feels "rotten" (105). The critical voice of Jaimie is joined by that of Jaimie's grandmother. "Where are you going in such a hurry?" she asks her daughter. "Up the ladder of success and right over the top with a crash" (143). On another occasion, she admonishes Jamie's mother: "You can't be in two places at once. You're not perfect and you don't have to be" (53). She tells Jaimie's mother that it is "important" that she does her work and is happy: "But enough *mishegas* already, enough craziness. Settle down. Compromise" (144).

Fourteen-year-old Jaimie describes, through her first-person narration, how she is getting increasingly angry and upset by her parents' "'long-distance marriage' and 'creative parenting'" (4). Her anger is shown to be directed more particularly at her mother, who once worked part-time but is now described as working as a full-time Wall Street banker. Once she had been able to get home before her daughter came home from school. Now her mother, Jaimie comments, was not home until six o'clock and sometimes later (22). When her mother gives her a diary, Jaimie comments that she had "felt like saying, 'You made your choices—a career and time with Daddy. I don't want to write my life down in any diary, so you won't feel guilty'" (18). Jaimie makes clear, through her informal, chatty style of address, that she wants to spend more quality time with her mother and wants more of her mother's attention "—a chance to talk" (3). She tells her mother: "When I say 'Leave me alone, Ma,' I don't really mean that I don't want you to care or spend time with me. I need you to be around to talk to, because even though Amanda [a friend] and Grandma are important, I need you, too" (142). Clearly articulated is the choice a mother should make between being available for her daughter and a career on the fast track. Jaimie's mother finally agrees to give up her full-time job. She tells her daughter that perhaps she can work part-time; that she had not realized how much she missed her daughter (141).

Anderson's *Step On a Crack* is an exemplar of how the contradictions between motherhood and career are made through a series of hierarchical oppositions in the text: motherhood and artistic creation, family and career, the selfless, ideal mother, and the selfish mother. As the story unfolds, it is revealed that fifteen-year-old Sarah Carpenter's "Mother" is the sister of Sarah's birth mother, Katrin—an artist. Sarah had been adopted by Katrin's sister and her husband as a small child after she had been physically and emotionally abused by Katrin who had attempted to bring up her small, illegitimate daughter while working and also spending time developing her potential as an artist.

Sarah tells in the novel how she suffers from traumatic nightmares and spells of kleptomania, the source of which is eventually traced to the abusive treatment meted out to her by her birth mother. The novel contains one of the strongest fantasies of blame and revenge against a mother found in any of the novels in this book. In the dream re-enactment of her punishment, Sarah describes the reversal of roles as her mother is trapped behind the iron bars:

> I took my jump rope, snapped it around her waist and tied her to the bars. I never saw Mother's face, but I heard her let out a terrifying scream. Her body slumped down onto the gravestone, her face buried in a puddle of blood (5).

In a later version of the dream, Sarah tells a friend: "I wrap my rope around, strangling her until she's dead. I never see her face, though" (101). The old skipping-rope rhyme, sung by Sarah as part of this recurring nightmare is, itself, evident of a long-standing cultural fear and indictment of mothers—"step on a crack, break your mother's back, step on a line, break your mother's spine." Confronting Katrin after fifteen years and discovering her real identity, Sarah asks her: "How could you do such *awful* things to me?" (166).

Anderson uses the narrative convention of splitting the representations of the mother figure: Katrin is the "wild gypsy artist in long skirts" (34) who could not nurture and protect while "Mother" is described as "the homebody type, the nest builder" (10). Sarah describes her adoptive mother as being "super at all sorts of things. She cooks beautifully, does all her own housework, embroidery, decorating and gardening" (4). She is represented as the epitome of the textbook mother who, when not "tending the children," should "be an amateur interior decorator, chef, mender, home nurse, retail buyer, and member of the local parent–teacher association" (Eyer 124).[7] Katrin and Mother represent the selfish and selfless mother respectively. Katrin—later represented as a successful artist—asks her fifteen-year-old daughter to understand her position and her feelings that she would "sacrifice *anything*!" at the times she succeeded in achieving her goals (57). Sarah narrates, however, that Mother had given up a promising career as a concert pianist and had given that all up for "the joys of motherhood" (4). She had told Sarah that she preferred being a wife and mother to having a career in music (32).

Anderson's text is not quite seamless. Alternate focalizations by Sarah's adoptive mother and the narrated voice of Katrin add an extra dimension beyond the anger and focalization of a daughter who narrates events from her position as the neglected and abused daughter. Through Katrin's narrated voice (sympathetically slanted), the choices of a young unmarried girl who chose to keep her baby are placed in social and economic context. Also explained through Katrin's voice is the anger and frustration felt by a young mother struggling to make it on her own:

> Many unmarried girls have and keep their babies; society makes allowances. But it wasn't like that fifteen years ago. I honestly tried reserving a place for you in my life, but some people aren't meant to raise kids. It seemed you were always underfoot when I wanted to work. I had so many needs and frustrations locked inside, I guess anger all came out on you. Sometimes, I felt so *alone* (168).

In a story in which a daughter is described as burning mementos of her birth mother in a "funeral pyre," attending therapy sessions, and stating that she is not yet ready to forgive Katrin at the end of the novel, Katrin's reasons are not found sufficient to be entirely exculpated from blame.

> And is Mother right, are we all victims of victims, none of us villains? Should we share responsibility instead of placing blame? I don't accept that either, yet. Right now, my world's full of grays when I'd prefer black and white. Sifting through my past will be hard, but it's probably necessary groundwork for my future (180).

Daughters in Apron Strings

In *Patchwork Summer* by Holl, thirteen-year-old Randi also documents the harm done to herself and her younger sister by her mother who has left her home and family in order to write a novel. Randi tells how she has had to give up "the band and Girl Scouts and summer camp" because she "was needed at home" (79). Her mother, narrates Randi, "had had no right to think only of herself, to hurt them all when none of them deserved it" (37). A mother's success in having her work published is set against the hurt of a daughter, who is described as being on a regime of "antacids" to help her cope with the stress of her mother's return, and at the closure of the novel, is described as having to "forgive" her mother. Randi's father's voice legitimizes Randi's voice. "I know it's been hard on you. It's been hard for me, too. I can't even call home during the day anymore! I'm afraid I'll disturb her writing, or find out she's packed and gone again" (79). The blaming of a mother is reinforced by the authoritative voice of the family doctor who had warned Randi of the effect of the "shock" of her mother's leaving on her younger sister, Meggie. Meggie had "used up her reserves" so that she might find it difficult starting school (7). Faced by her daughter's accusations, her mother apologizes and wishes that she "could turn the calendar back and change things" because she has hurt her family more than she thought possible. She promises Randi that she will never do the same again (113).

In *Patchwork Summer* and Gerson's *How I Put My Mother Through College*, daughters are shown to be socialized into those same gender roles of motherhood that place constraints on their mothers. In Holl's novel, Randi is shackled to household duties as she takes the place of her absent mother. [8]

> The first months after her mom deserted them, Randi had been in shock, try-
> ing to cope with everything. Her dad wandered around in his own personal
> fog, barely speaking, working longer and longer hours at the store. So Randi
> had taught herself to cook simple meals and keep house while taking care of
> Meggie. The work wasn't hard—there was just so much to do! Finally, by
> drawing charts and making a written laundry schedule, she managed to guar-
> antee clean socks and underwear at least five days out of seven (Holl 14–15).

Randi is held up as an ideal mother as she takes care of her younger sister.
"You're going to be a terrific mother someday," the family doctor tells her.
"Meggie's lucky to have you" (7).

A similar story is told in Gerson's novel in which a daughter "at the ten-
der age of thirteen, became a mother" (6). Corinne is described as taking
on the household chores—"all the stuff mothers usually do" (19). The front
flap of the jacket of Gerson's novel, describing how thirteen-year-old Jessica becomes the all-supportive daughter of a mother who goes back to
college, shows how this narrative plot convention is designed to appeal to
a teen reader. "IT'S HARD to be thirteen and starting junior high," the blurb
begins. Jessica's problems are spelled out: a best friend who has moved
away and "a just-divorced mother who has decided to go back to college
and there becomes a typical teenage freshman instead of a mother." Jessica is placed in the position of mothering her mother, the blurb explains,
as her "mother asks for advice about college courses, about dating, asks
permission to go out at night, and asks how late she may stay?" Later in
the text, there is a vivid and humorous picture of Jessica's mother's transformation from mother to teenager:

> Mom paraded around the house in her new plaid shirt and her new jeans that
> were as stiff as a board so that she couldn't even sit down, and her new boots
> that were so hard she couldn't bend her legs. Her hair, which she had always
> worn up, was down now, flowing gorgeously over the back of her plaid shirt,
> and her eyes sparkled with pleasure as she posed for Nana and Gramps.
> Gramps kept shaking his head and saying, "Well, I don't know, going to col-
> lege is one thing, but do you have to become a *teenager*?" (10).

Jessica comments: "You could almost say we're growing up through these
difficult and changing years together, couldn't you?" (Gerson 27). Jessica
tells her worried mother: "I'm absolutely positive you're going to fit in just
like everyone else. You just have to give it a little time. After all, a person
doesn't adjust to big changes overnight. Give yourself a few weeks and—
you'll probably be the most popular student on campus" (17).

The narrative convention of representing the growing down of a mother to a teenager—a mother who is shown to ape the behavior of a teenage college freshman and to behave irresponsibly—has the effect, of course, of showing off the superior vision and maturity of a young teenage daughter in relation to a mother. The inappropriateness of Jessica's mother's behavior and the consequences of her abrogation of her role *as* mother are made quite clear. Jessica's younger brother, Ben, runs away from home because he is upset by his mother's behavior and his parents' divorce. Jessica narrates: "After I had put Mom through college, she'd just have to be on her own, because Ben was going to need me. If he ran away from home at ten, what would become of him as a *teenager*?" (120).

The value system in Gerson's text is made clear at the closure of the novel as relief is expressed by Jessica when her divorced mother begins to behave "the way she used to be when she was like a mother," and moreover, "wearing skirts and pretty shoes, the way she used to" (135–36). "I think her time has come to help me," Jessica narrates (136). Order is restored since her mother "only has two classes today, and she's going to spend the rest of the day cleaning the house and cooking, because Dr. Reynolds— Dante—is coming to dinner. He sounds nice and Ben and I are both curious to meet him" (136).

In the novels by Snyder, Anderson, Holl, and Gerson, set in middle-class contexts, women are shown to be placed at contradictory sites between the private and public division of family and work that have existed in American society. However, the contradiction is resolved at the closure of each novel so as to place importance on the traditional values of family and motherhood. While some recognition is given to the achievements of mothers in these novels, it would seem that the dominant values in these texts fit in with a conservative discourse on mothering. In these particular novels, when a mother chooses to take up a professional career or follow her ambitions, divisions are set up between daughters and mothers. Relationships between daughters and mothers are shown to be difficult until a mother is once more fully available to meet her daughter's needs.

The first-person narrative of a daughter (who is also the main focalizer of events) colludes, in these novels, with a daughter-centered perspective of mothering to show that a mother's rightful place is at home providing loving care and nurturance for her daughter. It is also important to note how the first-person character-bound narration in these novels invites readers to take up identification with the subject position of daughters who are blaming their mothers for not being good-enough mothers. This narrative practice strengthens the ideological viewpoints being presented in the text through story. The texts are, in effect, moral tales for daughters and mothers. In *Of Woman Born,* A. Rich argues that the:

> most important thing one woman can do for another is to illuminate and expand her sense of actual possibilities. For a mother, this means more than contending with the reductive images of females in children's books, movies, television, the schoolroom. It means that the mother herself is trying to expand the limits of her life. *To refuse to be a victim:* and then to go on from there (246).

While mothers are, indeed, represented as trying to extend their possibilities in these novels, one wonders how much the above texts, written by women, open up the idea of choice for young women. In terms of sociohistorical context the Snyder, Holl, and Gerson novels were written during the 1980s—years that Faludi documents as years of the backlash against the progress that women's rights activists had made. They contribute towards a discourse of mothering that has been noted by Christian-Smith in her sample of teen romance novels in which "motherhood is woman's destiny and that a woman's rightful place is at home" (2).

A MOTHER'S RIGHT TO LIFE

Intertextually, the daughter–mother narrative is produced through contradictory discourses on mothering. One also finds resistance to cultural scripts that ask women to sacrifice self in order to be mothers. For example, mothers in Bruce Brooks's *Midnight Hour Encores*, Stephanie Tolan's *The Liberation of Tansy Warner*, and Bridgers's *Notes for Another Life* are held up as alternative models for daughters as they claim a right to ways of life that give them independence and self-fulfillment. Reflected in these novels are some of the sociological trends such as the pursuit of individual desires, the resistance to authority, and a soaring divorce rate that also characterized the family scene in the 1970s and 1980s.[9]

In *Midnight Hour Encores*, Bruce Brooks tells how the mother of Sibilance, involved in her role of being a hippie, refused to mother her newly born daughter. Seventeen years later, her daughter, Sibilance refers to her mother as a "self-realized squaw" (94). "How convenient," Sibilance comments "that no, what you call it, *bonding* could take place for a couple of days. Makes it very easy to dump your kid, doesn't it? Not like you're really even in the kid's life yet, right?" (87). Connie explains to seventeen-year-old Sibilance, who had asked her father to drive her across the states to meet her mother for the first time since she was born, that:

> I didn't want to give you milk from my body; I wanted my body back for myself, after you had had it from inside for nine months. I wanted to drink brandy again. And coffee. I wanted to sleep until ten, sometimes. I wanted to sleep until ten with a *man* sometimes. When you cried, I didn't give a damn why—I wanted you to shut up (212).

It is one of the few passages in the texts in this book in which a mother's voice is heard so honestly resenting being a mother—regarding it as an intrusion and invasion of self. Brooks, through the representation of Sibilance's mother, deconstructs the ideological assumption made in theories of mother child bonding that mother love is instinctive and that "all women are inherently suited for motherhood" (Eyer *Mother-Infant* 1). Mothering is said to be, rather, "a matter of constitution, of personality . . ." (Brooks 213). Connie tells her daughter that she had not been ready to take on the role of motherhood. She had not been ready to "give" what she thought she "would have to give" (209).

Connie's choice is framed in Brooks's text as a choice between a mother's responsibility to self and responsibility to her daughter. Connie, a successful businesswoman, later tells her daughter that she gave up the responsibility for her daughter in order to take care of herself (232). The decision by a mother to not mother her daughter, handing over the responsibility to Sib's father, Taxi, was made, he explains to his daughter, in the 1960s, an era when the individual quest for self-fulfillment was seen as the important thing to do—when "one was *supposed* to think first about oneself" (93). Sib's mother's decision can also be discussed in the contemporary context of women's resistance to cultural scripts of mothering. In her interviews with daughters of feminists, for example, Glickman reports that these particular daughters were of the opinion that "caring for their babies is no longer a biological imperative. Roaming through the variations on how children should be cared for and by whom, the daughters never so much hint at feelings of guilt over not being the constant primary parent" (79).

In *The Liberation of Tansy Warner*, Tolan also constructs a mother's choices through scripts of responsibility to self and to others. The daughter–mother narrative in Tolan's novel is set in the context of a narrative plot in which Tansy's very existence is owed to her mother's refusal to have an abortion against the wishes of Tansy's father. When Tansy's mother, Joan, leaves her home and family, she particularly asks Tansy in a letter to understand why she has left Tansy, her older siblings, and her husband. She loves her family, she explains: "But my love isn't worth much unless I have some value in the world" (7). When Tansy eventually tracks down her mother, her mother asks, "Should I care for you and not for me? Do I have to go on forever being someone else's idea of me? Do I have to pack myself away with the macramé materials every year?" (123). She did not "just opt for [her] happiness and to hell with you all," she tells Tansy. She "will always be a mother," her mother continues: "Where I live doesn't change that. But I can't 'take care' of you right now. Right now I have to take care of myself" (125).

Joan Warner's friend confirms a mother's right to claim a subjectivity other than mother:

> Loving someone—even if you're a mother—doesn't mean you give up your own life. If you sacrifice everything you are for someone else, what is there of you for that person to love? If I weren't a person with a life of my own, what would your father have to relate to? And I have to believe that when you're older you'll be glad that the mother you had was a separate person (81).

These statements, together with phrases such as " 'Mother' isn't a person, Tansy, it's a *title*" (123) draw attention to how Tolan's text, through the voice of Joan Warner, contests a social construction of motherhood that, according to A. Rich, has spelled the " 'death' of the woman or girl who once had hopes, expectations, fantasies for *herself.* . . ." (166). Irigaray has also argued that the reason the mother-daughter relationship has been covered over and repressed in Western phallocentric discourses is that mothers have been thought about only in terms of their maternal function rather than provided with a personal identity and language (Irigaray 97). Mothers' personal names often seem to be buried in daughter–mother stories in young adult novels especially in those stories in which mothers do not claim subjectivity other than that given to them by the title "mother."

In Bridgers's novel, Wren's mother, Karen, also claims her right to be "other" than mother. In *Notes for Another Life*, Karen explains to her daughter why she stayed away from her husband and children in order to follow a full-time career. Even before her husband was sick, she had not felt satisfied, despite the fact that she had a good husband, a nice home, and two children. She just could not the stand the everyday life of being a housewife. She could not attach any value to it. She had "wanted to have a life that was uniquely" hers, she explains to her daughter. "I didn't realize what it would mean. I didn't know what I had to give up. It was as if there were two roads and one of them looked so familiar, so ordinary. I just had to take the other one. I had to" (169). She is "good at her job," she tells her daughter. She would not want to change her life (170).

Setting out Choices for Daughters

While the voices of mothers in the above novels by Brooks, Bridgers, and Tolan certainly claim the right to fulfill their own needs and desires, these texts are certainly open to discussion in regard to what extent they interrogate cultural scripts of mothering. Brooks's text, for example, despite the representation of Sibilance's mother as an independent, successful mother freed from the responsibilities of mothering her daughter for sixteen years, can arguably be said to encode a conservative view of mothering. One of five male writers represented in this book, Brooks deromanticizes a mother's instinctual bonding with a child only to replace it by another idealistic view of parenting—the fantasy of the ideal father. Taxi, as a single father, is described, in effect, as practicing mothering by taking upon himself the responsibility of caring for his baby daughter. Indeed, Taxi engages in the kind of maternal practice that Ruddick has defined as responding to "the reality of a biological child in a particular social world" (17).

Taxi's "response" to his baby daughter "was very fine," admits Sib's mother. "He read your little screaming mind. Within four or five hours he already knew what three different kinds of crying meant—what we should do to make you comfortable according to the way you expressed yourself" (212). This is a story, moreover, of a single father who proves that he can successfully balance a professional career with the rearing of a daughter with whom he invests a great deal of time and energy—the super father who could do it all. "Is it really impossible to pursue pursuits with a kid?" Sibilance asks her father. "*You* didn't find it impossible? *You* didn't give up everything did you?" (154). Taxi is the ideal father who was "*there* for twenty-four hours. Babies need you when they need you. For lots of things" (157).

The slant of the anonymous narrator is detectable in places in Brooks's text. There is a tone of smugness—in Taxi's assertion, for example, that he could not find any babysitters that would satisfy his requirements for looking after his daughter (160). A daughter, moreover, is shown in this story to have been given the kind of intellectual fostering that has contributed toward her developing into a cellist prodigy. When Sib chooses to return East with her father rather than stay with her mother, giving up the chance to study with a noted cellist, Taxi and his daughter repeat a journey they had made when Sib was a baby—back East—away from Connie. Brooks would seem to affirm the values placed on the kind of mothering that demands total investment with the child.

In *Notes for Another Life*—a more plural text—Bridgers clearly presents, through the voices of Wren and her mother, the kind of contradictions and difficult choices that daughters may have to face between career and family. Wren's mother lays out before Wren, already an accomplished pianist, the kind of decisions that Wren will have to make. "Before you know it, you'll have to be making decisions about your life, the kind of decisions I didn't know how to make," she tells her daughter (170). Wren takes up different positions on the issues that she will have to confront. At one point in the text, she says, for example, that: "She wouldn't be like Karen, giving up husband and children for a career. She wouldn't abandon infants, expecting them to love her anyway, in spite of all the emptiness left" (157). Later, she voices her right to do what seems "right" for herself whatever other people think (192). In reference to her mother's choices and her own future, Wren questions the either/or choices that are laid out before her. She had been very hurt, she tells her boyfriend, Sam, when she heard her mother: "tell how she made a choice between a career and me. It hurt so much. But what if I have to make a choice like that? I don't want to. It would be so much better to have everything. I want everything, Sam" (196).

Bridgers moves away from a daughter-centered narrative by presenting the complexities and difficulties of choices from the different narrated positions of a mother, her daughter, her son, and other family members. Left open are the compromises and contradictions that are shown to arise from the choices that society offers women. They are represented as very painful choices in Bridgers's novel in which a son attempts suicide, and the hurt of a daughter is articulated with intensity in the text. A daughter, however, is shown to be positively identified with a mother who values self, the work she does, and who is sure of her choices. Sam sees that Wren is as beautiful, confident, and as ambitious as her mother; Wren would take her music seriously (140).

Bridgers reinscribes a more traditional view of mothering in her story through the ever-present and loving mother figure of Bliss, the grandmother with whom Wren and her brother live—and without whom Karen, their mother, could not have left to pursue her career. Bridgers, indeed, in an interview, refers to Bliss (whose name has obvious symbolic value) as having a "traditional mother" role (Atkinson 314). Traditional views about mothering and concepts like bonding have depended, of course, on the retention of the nuclear family. Bridgers does place value on the traditional family through her representation of Wren's grandparents who provide a stable home for Wren and her brother. Bridgers's plural text, however, offers plenty of room for discussion with young people about the choices made by Wren's mother that can be related to the choices that other daughters will have to make.

In *The Liberation of Tansy Warner,* Tansy's mother discusses with Tansy the choices that Gwen, Tansy's older sister, will face including the issue of the "biological clock"—raised by Betty Friedan who reported, in the 1980s, that career women were now concerned that they were missing out on maternity and motherhood (*The Second* 22–33).

> I've watched her make her choices, feeling so sure of herself. But once she is the lawyer she's anxious to be, do you think the rest of her life is going to fall neatly into place? What about marriage? How many years will she want to be alone? And what will she do when she's getting close to thirty-five and there's not much time left for having children? She has that brain of hers, the grades, the scholarship offers, the trip to France. But does she know who she is? (123–24).

Gwen is described as getting a taste of the contradictions between housework and excelling at a career when her mother leaves home.

Tolan takes the more unequivocal stance on questions of gender, marriage, and mothering than either Brooks or Bridgers as she more openly questions the potential oppressiveness of the institution of marriage on the life and individual rights of women. The house she had left was a "symbol" Tansy's mother tells her daughter. It belonged to Tansy's "father. In name and spirit too." The apartment she lives in now despite the smallness, the dirt, and the cockroaches belongs to her—the first time she has had a home "that didn't belong to somebody else" (122). Tansy notes, significantly, that there are "the signs of Joan Warner" in her mother's drab apartment (Tolan 121). The term "liberation" takes on a double valence in the text as Tansy is also shown to stand up to the father who had so negated her.

SINGLE MOTHERS

The relationships between daughters and mothers in many of the young adult novels included in this book are also situated in familial structures that reflect the increased numbers of divorced and one-parent families in present day society, although the nuclear family remains a strong structuring paradigm. While the two-parent nuclear family is represented as the desirable family unit, in many novels mothers of adolescent daughters are represented as unmarried, divorced, or widowed. This pattern is representative of novels included in this book published in the 1970s, 1980s, and the 1990s.[10] One of the most positive representations of a single working mother is found in Sarah Ellis's *Pick-Up Sticks* in which thirteen-year-old Polly's mother is a glass lead designer who runs her own business and has stayed single by choice. The conflict between Polly and her mother is centered around Polly's anger at what she sees as her mother's failure to earn enough money to let them stay on in their apartment when the rent is increased and her mother's refusal to take on the job as manager of an apartment block. "Would it be such a big, hairy disaster to take that manager's job?" she asks her mother:

> Other people have real jobs. Other people make enough money. Other people get married. You're always so big on choosing. 'I chose to be an artist.' 'I chose to be a single mother.' I've heard about that enough times. Well, why did you choose it if you can't even do it right? (54–55).

Polly's views about her mother's job are shown, in the text, to be misguided. Value is place, rather, on her mother's voice and her choice of a career as an artist. "Do you think," Polly's mother says to her brother (Polly's uncle), that "I'd been making a living for seventeen years selling stained-glass mushrooms at craft fairs? Get real, Roger" (51). Polly grows to understand and accept her mother's values at the closure of the novel.

An aspect of mothering that is also addressed in daughter–mother narratives in young adult novels is the frustration, hopelessness, and sometimes anger of single mothers who cannot obtain for their daughters the advantages that they would claim for them. In Levitin's *Beyond Another Door,* for example, the desk that Daria's mother would like to buy for her daughter "was a symbol, Daria knew, for all the things her mother thought a girl ought to have, which she, Peg Peterson, ought to provide but couldn't" (15).

MATERNAL ANGER

Maternal anger has been theorized in feminist writing from both social constructivist and psychoanalytic approaches. A. Rich graphically describes the violence of maternal abuse in *Of Woman Born,* which she explains is the result of the "invisible violence of the institution of motherhood." that Rich views as a source of oppression for mothers (277). Published in 1991, Nancy Honeycutt's *Ask Me Something Easy* documents a recently divorced mother's anger and frustration in the context of a white, middle-class suburb. Addie describes the constant anger of her divorced mother, who struggles to maintain her home and the family's standard of living when her husband leaves her with their four children so that her elder daughter, Diane, represented as academically bright, "can have the life [she] never had" (32). Why, asks Addie "does everybody have to be so awful? So mean?" Diane explains: "Nobody's being mean. Mama's just very worried. We don't have enough money, and there are other things, too. Things about Daddy. We might not be able to stay in this house" (63–64).

Through her first-person narration, Addie describes the gendered relationships in her family in which she has defined self in relationship with her father while her elder sister is shown to be aligned with her mother. Addie's mother is represented as displacing her anger at her husband onto Addie. Accused of being "headed straight for trouble" and of being in danger of ending up like her father, Addie is ostracized and constantly berated and slapped by her mother. In scenes occasioned by Addie's mother's selling the new bicycle Addie had received from her father for her birthday, Honeycutt not only describes the hatred and violence between Addie and her mother but makes a strong social statement about family violence. Addie is described flinging and shattering the "silver-backed mirror" that was her mother's "pride and joy. Now Dinah's pride and joy."

Addie narrates: "Then I sat on my bed and just stared ahead and felt hatred. Pure hatred. Undiluted . . . and while I hated, something inside of me slowly turned to stone" (127). Honeycutt does not distance the scene in which her mother physically reacts to Addie's defensive statement that her mother had had "no right" to sell the bike her father had given her:

> I guess she went berserk, then, because she grabbed me by the shoulders and yelled some more, then shoved me up against the wall and shook me while my head banged against the plaster. Bang. Bang. Bang. Bang. Bang. And then the plaster cracked and I heard it. And some fell on the floor, and I heard that too. And then she stopped (128).

If, as it is argued, that "Mothers repeat the lessons they learned as girls to their daughters" (Debold, Wilson, and Malave 55), a powerful social message is being reiterated in texts that foreground maternal anger. The consequences of Addie's abuse are made eminently clear. A few days later, Addie walks into her twin sisters' room:

> What I remember of that moment is walking into their room and seeing a scene of utter carnage. The Barbie dolls were all dismembered. Torsos and limbs were scattered about, and the heads of two of them hung by their hair from the window shades (129).

Their dolls "were bad," Tiny, one of the twins, tells Addie. "We're punishing them," Bits, the other twin, tells her. "They have to be punished so they'll learn to behave." Addie narrates: *"They're only dolls.* I reminded myself of that. *After all, they're only dolls, and this is just pretend.* But something about it sent prickles down my spine" (129).

Representative of other novels, the experience of maternal anger is explained from a child–daughter perspective. A mother's voice is not heard in Honeycutt's voice giving more explanation for her anger; her side of story is suppressed from the daughter–mother narrative. *Ask Me Something Easy* is an example of a recent novel that explains and constructs maternal anger as a sociological rather than an inherently psychological phenomenon between daughters and mothers. Honeycutt, however, also writes into story the psychological effect of a mother's abuse of her daughter. For an art assignment in eighth grade, Addie represents herself as "half a person" in a self-portrait (122).

THE MORAL RESPONSIBILITY OF MOTHERING

Feminist writers have drawn attention to how girls grow up with the expectation that they will put aside their own needs in order to nurture others.[11] As Caplan states, the "'woman-as-nurture' myth is deeply ingrained in our notion of female identity" (78). Encoded in daughter–mother narratives in young adult novels are lessons for mothers and daughters on the social and moral responsibilities of mothering. Jane Agee has pointed out the presence of the "inherent socioideological contradiction between becoming a strong independent woman and becoming a 'good' daughter, wife, and mother" in two Newbery novels published nearly fifty years apart (182). What is so visible in the novels discussed in this chapter are the divisions that have been set up between the responsibilities of mothering and women's desires for self-fulfillment and for work. If, as Debold and her colleagues argue, girls are asked to make "painful compromises" between work and family (247), it is of interest to see how these issues are addressed and resolved in texts marketed for young people. It is important to note, too, that because these divisions and choices, produced through a discourse of mothering, are placed in the context of daughter–mother relationships, the relationship between a teenage daughter and her mother is, thus, represented as a locus of contradictions and conflict.

The emphasis in this chapter has been on daughter–mother narratives and a social construction of mothering. In her psychoanalytic approach to female development in *The Reproduction of Mothering,* Chodorow theorizes that daughters are psychologically prepared for mothering as a result of a sex–gender system in which women mother: "Women daughter–mothers who, when they become women, mother" (209). As a teenage daughter tells her mother in Nixon's *Overnight Sensation*: "Sometimes I may even have a daughter of my own, and then you can teach me about being a mother" (180). The relationship between a teenage daughter and her mother is frequently set in the context of a generational story. Chapter eight discusses the cyclical patterns and repetitive daughter–mother scripts that compose grandmother daughter–mother narratives in young adult novels.

NOTES

1. See, for example, Faludi.

2. The "fantasy" of the perfect mother is shown be a dominant ideology in picture books; see Kertzer 159–60.

3. For an explanation of the concept of the "good-enough" mother, see Winnicott 10–11; for criticism of psychoanalytic theories of motherhood, see Dally 87.

4. See Chodorow and Contratto; Thurer 292–93.

5. I argue that the ideal mother continues to exist as a fantasy that haunts mothers as well as being present in actual representations of mothers in novels from the 1980s and 1990s. For the view that the "too-good-true mother" has disappeared in young adult novels published from 1975-1992, see Maxwell 126.

6. For discussion and explanations of a sex–gender system in which sexual divisions are produced through divisions of labor in which mothers mother in the less valued and privileged spaces of the home while men possess and have access to sources of power and authority denied to women, see Flax *Thinking* 143; Chodorow *The Reproduction* 209; Debold, Wilson, and Malave 195, 247; AAUW 13.

7. Eyer quotes from Farnham 1.

8. For descriptions of 1980 TV shows in which disgruntled adolescent girls are left with the household duties as their mothers are represented as away "*fulfilling* their needs," see Faludi 155.

9. See, for example, Eyer *Motherguilt* 64.

10. This would seem to differ from the class and family structure patterns found in Christian-Smith's selection of young adult romance novels published between 1942 and 1981 in which the "dominant pattern" is "that of a white middle-class father, a working-class mother, and several children," see Christian-Smith 62.

11. See Hancock 188.

Eight

Grandmother Daughter–Mother Narratives

Here we are, three generations. There's Grand at the bottom, Lake in the middle, and me, whoever that might be, looking down at both of them. I wonder if there is any cosmic significance to this arrangement?

—B. Cannon

A story about a teen daughter and her mother is frequently told in the context of a generational story. The interrelationships between grandmother, mother, and adolescent daughter form a significant element of the daughter–mother narrative in different racial and cultural contexts. In texts in which the complexities of daughter–mother relationships are necessarily compressed into limited time spans, the grandmother daughter–mother narrative serves to provide a more extensive description and explanation of the daughter–mother relationship. The generational story also serves to place the relationship between a girl and her mother into a "historical" context. In this chapter, the texts of young adult novels, as a popular genre of mainstream culture, are shown to also inscribe within their texts popular scripts about the mother–daughter relationship in adulthood. The stories discussed are set in the context of white American family situations in varying socioeconomic contexts.

A HISTORY OF RELATIONSHIPS

Shreve's *The Revolution of Mary Leary* includes a chapter entitled "A Historical Perspective." Here, teenage daughter Mary Leary tells the story

169

of her mother's unhappy childhood caused by her mother's lack of interest in her and how this, in turn, had affected Mary's own mother's devotion to "creating a Wonderful Family" (43). Shreve's text draws attention to a prevalent assumption, made in many texts, that the relationship between an adolescent daughter and her mother is affected, in some way, by the mother's prior relationship with her own mother. In Nixon's *Overnight Sensation*, Cassie comments that her mother, Abby "rarely talked of her childhood or of her own mother. . . ." According to one of her mother's friends, Abby's mother, Gladys Baynes, had attempted to make-up for her thwarted ambitions to become an actress through her daughter Abby's achievements, but Abby had "disappointed her mother" by embarking on a career as a comic. Cassie attributes her mother's demand for constant attention to this daughter–mother history (11). In *Letting Go*, teenage-daughter Casey:

> felt herself a part of a living chain of cause and effects. Her grandmother had been an unloving woman; her mother, perhaps in reaction, was immensely loving. Thirty years from now Casey's daughter would be a product of the mother love that Casey, reacting to Pat, would have learned to give or to refrain from giving (101).

It is this explanation of the daughter–mother relationship as an ongoing "chain of cause and effects" that is seen so clearly in the cycles and patterns of relationships that are reproduced in generational stories of grandmothers, mothers, and teenage daughters.

"We are, none of us, 'either' mothers or daughters," A. Rich wrote, "To our amazement, confusion, and greater complexity, we are both" (253). The relationship between the mother of an adolescent daughter and her own mother is used to double the relationship that is foregrounded in the text between an adolescent daughter and her mother; it is used as an instructive foil in order to illustrate what a better relationship might be. A mother of a teenage daughter is positioned in a "double identity" as "mother" and as an adult daughter to her own mother. Depending on the narrative strategies used in a text to open up a position for a reader to identify with a teenage daughter or with her mother, this position of double identity has the potential to offer a reader a more multidimensional representation of the relationship. Grandmother daughter–mother narratives frequently serve to prescribe what kind of relationships there should be—or should not be—between daughters and mothers. Daughters, of course, are represented as keen observers of the relationship between their mothers and grandmothers as in the following passage from Bettie Cannon's *Begin the World Again:*

Lake thought about how Grand did so many things the way Selene did, how their gardens were alike, how they noticed colors and flowers. Even the work that Grand did on the Reynolds house seemed like something Selene would do—it was just that Grand was looking back and Selene forward (162).

A Repetitive Script

A repetitive script shown to be handed down from grandmother to mother to daughter is a frequent convention used in the grandmother daughter–mother narrative. In selected texts this script is used to instruct and reassure a teenage daughter that the difficult relationship that she is currently experiencing with her mother is "normal" during adolescence. In other texts repetitive patterns and subplots of the daughter–mother relationship are used to instruct and remind a mother of what it is like to be an adolescent daughter, so as to guide her to behave appropriately in relation to her teenage daughter. In either case, repetitive scripts reinforce particular ways of understanding the daughter–mother relationship, and therefore, reinforce a dominant set of values pertaining to this relationship.

Francine Pascal's *Hangin' Out with Cici* is one of the clearest examples of how a repetitive script and a doubling of plot work to reassure an adolescent daughter that conflict is normal between a daughter and mother during adolescence; to reinforce the values of independence and responsibility; and to construct understanding and connections between an adolescent daughter and her mother. In constant trouble with her mother over her irresponsible behavior, the relationship between thirteen-year-old Victoria and her mother is described as one of conflict. In her chatty, conversational tone, addressed directly to a reader, Victoria tells how her mother "seems to be all over her life." Unlike her father, her mother "ruins everything" for her with all her orders (20).

Pascal uses the narrative practice of displacing place and time in order to place Victoria as observer and participant in her mother's past. Victoria is transposed in time to 1944, where she meets and becomes friends with teenager Cici (her mother), who takes her to her home. Observing Cici's escapades, Victoria, who had previously stated that she could not believe that her mother had ever been her age and that she "must have been born a mother," now narrates that she and Cici "seem to have a million things in common." Cici, comments Victoria, is "always getting into trouble for the littlest, most unimportant things. Just like me" (47). The conflicts with mothers, Victoria discovers, however, do not change as she listens to the familiar "mother phrases" used now by her grandmother and listens to her mother and grandmother arguing over Cici's untidy room as though mother

and daughter were "reading from a script" (85). The expectation is, of
course, that readers will recognize and identify with this familiar daughter–mother talk.

Participating in her mother's escapades, Victoria now realizes that her
mother's behavior is irresponsible. The reiteration of a script of independence and responsibility is particularly reinforced at this point in story. Cici
as a teenager tells Victoria, after she has been persuaded to face up to her
wrongdoings:

> When you're little, there's always someone to take care of things like that,
> someone to tell you, no, don't do that. But when you get older, like us, you
> have to start taking the responsibility yourself. I was still acting like a kid. I
> guess I just didn't realize that it was time to stop being a kid and start grow-
> ing up (125–26).

After praising Cici for getting things together, Victoria narrates that she
feels closer to Cici and is sure that Cici feels the same about her. Responsibility changes one, Cici also tells Victoria (126). Hearing this from Cici
speaking as a friend rather than a mother, Victoria now applies what Cici
is telling her to her own situation at home. Pascal builds connections and
understanding between a teenage daughter and her mother in a story through
the strategy of mirroring their experiences as adolescent daughters—along
with a lesson on responsibility.

Reinforcing a Hegemonic Script

Feminist writers studying the mother–daughter relationship have drawn
attention to the cultural myth that daughters must separate from their mothers in order to be independent. Hancock writes of the "vast psychological
distance" that adult daughters are expected to place between themselves and
their mothers.[1] Not surprisingly, there are stories about mothers and adult
daughters in young adult novels in which adult daughters are also represented as dependent in some way because they have failed to establish their
own independence apart from their mothers. One has only to think of Patti's
childlike mother in Sachs's *Just Like Friends* to see how this cultural expectation is written into a daughter–mother narrative in a young adult novel.

One of the main functions of subtexts and subplots is to reinforce a dominant value system in the text. Colman's *Sometimes I Don't Love My Mother*
is the text that most obviously uses the subtext and subplot of a relationship between an adolescent daughter's mother and grandmother to show a

mother the inappropriateness of her relationship with her own daughter. Set in the context of a white middle-class family, recently widowed Ellen Davis is described as being dependent on her seventeen-year-old daughter, Dallas, for company and support in the absence of her husband. Dallas, however, who has delayed going to college so as to spend a year at home with her mother, is represented as resenting her mother's dependency on her and her friends and resists her mother's attempts to plan their lives together.

The arrival of the "imposing" figure of Ellen's mother who suggests that she and Ellen would now benefit from living together thus replicates the situation and issues set up between teenage daughter and mother. The doubling of a mother's identity as mother and adult daughter is constructed in Colman's text through a split narrative. In three chapters, the thoughts and feelings of Dallas's mother, as mother to her teenage daughter and as adult daughter, are articulated in narrated monologue as she focalizes her position between her own mother and daughter. For example: "My daughter doesn't approve of me. My mother never approved of me, and now my daughter doesn't" (95).

This narrative practice and a narrator's slant works to point out the inappropriateness of a mother's behavior. Dallas's earlier statement that she did not think that she could "bear living alone in that house with my mother" is echoed by her mother, Ellen (19). "No, she said determinedly to herself, I am not going to end up living with my mother" (166). Ellen is now shown to be self-critical as she thinks about the kind of relationship she has wished to have with Dallas. "She was as bad as her mother, worse. Her mother was trying to hold on to her, and she had desperately been clinging to Dallas" (174). She had, she continues, been "more the adolescent than" her daughter and she needed to "find" her "own way" (183).

This distance created between an adult mother and her mother is a consistent element of plot in grandmother daughter–mother narratives. In Hadley Irwin's novel, *What about Grandma?,* teenage-daughter Rhys observes the distance between her mother and her grandmother as they sit together in the car. "They were sitting only a foot or two apart, yet there didn't seem to be any closeness between them. I couldn't imagine them touching each other. I knew then it was going to be a long four weeks" (22).

BREAKING THE CHAINS THAT BIND

One of the cultural myths that has contributed toward the way the mother–daughter relationship has been written and talked about is the myth that women's power is dangerous—a gender-biased narrative that has served to see a mother's power as threatening.[2] In several novels discussed in this chapter, the figure of the grandmother is used to represent the maternal power that mothers are said to hold over their children. "Adult daughters," Caplan writes, "often react to their mothers as though they (the daughters) were still powerless: 'She makes me feel like I'm an adolescent again when I visit her!'" (120). The feeling of being positioned as a child again in relation to a powerful mother is heard through the voice of a mother in Colman's *Sometimes I Don't Love My Mother*. Dallas's mother comments that: "if she lived to be a hundred, she would still feel overshadowed by her mother" (162). Rhys's mother admits to her daughter that coming back home to where her mother lived made her "feel like a child again. All the old questions, the old doubts, the old expectations" (Irwin 43).

The understanding of the relationship between mothers and daughters as a cyclical pattern of negative relationships is frequently written about in texts about the mother–daughter relationship. Naomi Lowinsky, for example, in a book about reclaiming mother–daughter relationships, draws attention to negative grandmothers who are said to "bind and abuse their daughters' souls. In turn the daughters bind and abuse their daughters' souls. In turn the daughters bind and abuse their daughters" (118). Chodorow and Contratto write of the chain "of aggression that goes from mother to child, from child to mother, from mother-as-child to her own mother" that are produced in writings about mothers and motherhood (85).

Only My Mouth Is Smiling and its sequel, *Crazy Quilt* by Riley, and *Cages of Glass, Flowers of Time* by Culin are grandmother daughter–mother narratives shaped through pain, anger, and abuse. In all three stories, adult daughters are represented as still under the powerful control of their mothers represented as *grand*mothers. Elements of story include conflict, the transgression of personal boundaries, and the unsafe place that teenage daughters occupy between a fearful grandmother and disempowered mother. These are warnings enough about the need for daughters to develop independence, responsibility, and determination to make their lives different and separate from that of their mothers.

In all three stories, adult daughters are represented as attempting to break free from their adult mothers. In both the Culin and Riley novels, negative aspects of maternal power are displaced onto the figure of the grandmother. In *Crazy Quilt*, Merle frequently uses the adjectives "afraid" and "dangerous" in referring to her grandmother who attempts to deal with a mentally ill daughter while protecting her grandchildren. She is represented as somewhat of an ambiguous mother figure in Riley's text as she is also, at times, represented as a supportive grandmother. In Riley's *Only My Mouth Is Smiling*, Merle's mother, described as "crazy," attempts to get away from her mother's control as she takes Merle and her siblings to live in a tent on the shore of Lake Lune, Wisconsin. "Get out of my house," Merle's mother yells when her mother suddenly appears—"big as life"—at the tent entrance in order to bring the family food (56–57). Arguments over territory and control are described in other passages in which teenage daughter Merle is often described as placed in the uncomfortable, middle space between mother and grandmother. The relationship between adult daughter and mother is described as one of anger and "long-running fights" that erupt into physical violence when Merle's grandmother "kicked" her mother "as hard as she could. . . . Kick. Kick. Kick" (*Only My Mouth* 20). In *Crazy Quilt*, the convention of a repetitive subtext draws attention to a cycle of conflict between daughters and mothers through Merle's grandmother's acrimonious comment that "It's starting all over again," as she listens to the accusations and counteraccusations made in the interaction between Merle and her mother. Merle, she tells her daughter, Elaine, would soon be telling her mother that "she didn't ask to be born . . ." and she "laughed and laughed" (186).

The grandmother in Culin's novel is certainly the most vicious and nasty characterization of a grandmother represented in the novels selected for this book. Claire cannot go to her grandmother's for protection from her abusive mother because "*Grandma's worse. Grandma's worse*" (40). Fourteen-year-old Claire Burden is placed in the custody of her working-class, alcoholic mother after her father—an artist—who is also an alcoholic, has neglected and abandoned Claire. Claire is also neglected and physically abused by her mother who forbids her daughter to practice the artistic talent she has inherited from her father. "I told you!" she screamed. "I told you no drawin'! I told you I'd kill you for bringin' his dirty stuff here!" (11).

Using a plotting strategy in which the relationship between the mother of an adolescent daughter and her mother doubles the relationship between a mother and her adolescent daughter, Culin tells a story of two daughters bound by terrible mothers. Claire's mother tells Claire that her mother (grandmother Simmons) never leaves her alone: "She gets in my head! Yellin' at me. Hittin' at me! I can't get her out! I tried to stop drinkin'! I tried to!" (211). Claire later describes her mother's position as being "in jail all her life with Grandma!" (308). Claire's mother is represented as an adult daughter who continues to be physically abused by her own mother.

She comes home to Claire with her arms black and blue from beatings from Grandma Simmons (41).

The cycle of physical abuse is made clear as Grandma Simmons tells Claire: "I started beatin' your momma too late! I'm not makin' the same mistake with you! I'll beat sense into you if it's the last thing I do!" (31). The only meaning that Claire, heir to Galway Hall (her father's home), has for her maternal grandmother, who attempts to wrest Claire away from her mother, is money. The violence comes full circle in the most vicious, aggressive scenes enacted between mothers and daughters described in the novels included in this book. Coming home drunk after getting fired from her job and told to report to court to prove that she is a fit mother, Claire's mother beats Claire senseless when she discovers that Claire has been drawing. Claire revives enough to overhear Grandma Simmons battering her mother in turn: "Killed her . . . teach you . . . ruined my chances! Now I'll never get that money!" (270).

Cages of Glass, Flowers of Time is almost a case study of child abuse and neglect—the kind of novel that presumably led to the characterization of realistic young adult novels as problem novels. Of all the novels in the study, it comes closest to reproducing "the heart of maternal darkness" described by A. Rich in *Of Woman Born*. Certainly, it can be said that Culin's novel gives voice to those aspects of the mother–daughter relationship that Flax maintains are covered over and suppressed in accounts by feminists. These include, for example, the psychological and physical violence between mothers and daughters, and the desire by women for separation and autonomy.[3] The root cause for Claire's mother's and father's neglect and abuse is attributed, in Culin's novel, to their respective mothers, Grandmothers Burden and Simmons, who are represented as having bound and caged their adult children, refusing them the right to make their own lives. "It's strange," narrates Claire, "how much alike Daddy and Mom were, trying to do what their mothers wanted, even when it was wrong for them." No one, Claire asserts, is going to "make life a cage" for her again (315).

The divisions between mothers and daughters in Culin's novel are produced through divisions of class and gender. Claire's mother is also described as one of the most pitiful mothers in the daughter–mother stories in this study. Represented as socially castigated by the Burdens, Claire's mother was allowed to live at Galway Hall for three years with Claire's father but forbidden by Claire's grandmother to take care of or even "touch" her daughter. She was eventually given money to leave Galway Hall (185). Claire's mother tells her daughter that Mrs. Burden "learned you to hate me, too. Learned you to look right through me on the street like you didn't even know I was your momma" (185–86). Her mother, narrates Claire, had never had a chance. Her life had been ruined by her mother (306). *"Nobody ever cared about Mom. Nobody was ever gentle to her"* (279). The cycle of daughter–mother aggression is ended in Culin's novel by a young daughter caring enough about her mother to set her free. In order to save her mother from jail, Claire lies about her beating by displacing the blame on to her grandmother. Finally, Claire sells her father's portraits of her so that her mother will have a chance to have a home away from Grandmother Simmons.

As Debold, Wilson, and Malave have written in *Mother Daughter Revolution*, the real lessons that daughters learn are not about the formidable power of mothers but about women's lack of social and economic power. What is written uncritically into Culin's novel are the cycles of betrayal and loss between mothers and daughters (and the financial transactions that secure them) in a discourse that emanates from a sex–gender system that has normalized mother blame and the expectation of the separation of mothers and daughters in adolescence and adulthood.

RELATIONSHIPS IN PROCESS

The novels by Culin and Riley are produced through cultural scripts that emphasize the darker side of relationships between mothers and daughters. A lighter side to the relationship is produced through a popular psychological discourse in which mothers and daughters are said to be engaged in working out, repeating, or resolving the relationships between them.[4] The lacuna between adult mothers and their mothers continues, however, to be scripted into story. In *Begin the World Again*, Lake and her mother:

> had made up what they called a folding dance. They faced each other like partners in an old-fashioned minuet, then came together, holding the white sheet, and then danced apart as the sheet billowed out between them (18).

Daughters and mothers in B. Cannon's daughter–mother narrative come together and part again according to the pattern of the "folding dance." Selene, the mother of sixteen-year-old daughter Lake, leaves Lake at the commune, where she has lived with her husband and daughter, in order to go to Nashville where she has an opportunity to sing. She "wants something more. Something of her own," Selene's father tells her (86). Lake, heartbroken when Selene leaves her on the very day of her sixteenth birthday cries out to her father: "What about all that primal bonding she talks about? She said when you carry something around inside you for almost a year, you feel a lifetime attachment. But she lied" (87).

Lake finally makes the decision to leave herself and to go to her grandmother's home—partly because she wants to ensure her future by going to college—but mostly because she wants to learn more about Selene and her grandmother. Selene had left her own mother during the time of the Vietnam War in the 1960s (13). Lake is made welcome by Jeannette Grand Flemming Thurston, her grandmother, whom Lake will call "Grand" since Grand is a name that comes from one of her "maternal great-greats" (137). Lake is given her mother's old room where her mother's books, dresses, and shoes are still stored in the closets.

Encoded in Cannon's novel are familiar elements of a daughter–mother narrative plot: a daughter's going back to her mother's roots, the distance between daughters and mothers during adolescence, and the lacuna between an adult daughter and her mother. When Selene visits Lake at her grandmother's, Lake finds that the close relationship with her mother has changed, and Selene warns her about how things stand between herself and Lake's grandmother. Nothing changes, Selene tells Lake. She would see how things stand between Selene and her grandmother (164–65). Lake listens to the bitter exchange of her mother and grandmother over her mother's decision, as a young woman, to give up scholarships for a promising singing career. "Is she trying to live your life for you, too?" asks Lake's mother about her grandmother (164). Watching the pool sweeper as she swims, Lake:

> thought about how the long cord attached to the cleaner had proscribed for it the same circles over and over and how Selene upon seeing it must have wanted to dare, dare, double dare herself. Maybe it hadn't been politics and Vietnam and hair and music and blood families, after all, that drove Selene away. Maybe Selene had to leave because her whole life was planned out in places like Bay View, like Grand's, as orderly as a chord of music (181).

At the closure of the novel, as Selene leaves both her mother and Lake again—this time for California—the relationship between an adult daughter and her mother is represented as still unresolved. Selene tells Lake, "Every time I come here, I let myself be dragged back into all that old stuff, that garbage again. No more!" (174).

Cannon's novel is representative of how a social and psychological construction of the mother–daughter relationship dominates the representation of the relationship in texts ranging from self-help books for adults to fictional accounts of the relationship in novels for adults and young people. After Selene leaves Lake for the second time, a school friend of Lake's tell her that her mother had not spoken to her own mother until her mother had finished law school. Now, however, her mother and grandmother are "like twins," and her grandmother had also gone back to school (177). This contemporary discourse on mother–daughter relationships includes advice on how mothers and daughters can go about healing their relationships.

Healing Rifts

The mother–daughter relationship has certainly been socially constructed as a difficult or ambivalent relationship at best, judging from the number of texts now available that are addressed to daughters and mothers in adulthood on how to mend the rifts in their relationship. The "unhappy mother–daughter bond that remains unresolved threatens all our attachments," writes Victoria Secunda, whose entire book is devoted to this topic (15). The "coming to terms" with one's mother is vital, Secunda continues, since the:

> difficult mother–daughter relationship is a time bomb, set to go off in the next generation. It is inherited as surely as are blue eyes or brown. Curing it is painful; it means shedding light on the dark places of your history to discover where you can look for love and where you must give up looking for it (16).

This understanding of the mother–daughter relationship informs Kit Pearson's daughter–mother narrative in *A Handful of Time*. Pearson uses the narrative strategy of displacing time in order to shed light on the history of twelve-year-old Patricia's mother with her own mother as a teenager and to show how this antagonistic relationship between an adolescent daughter and a mother has continued—unresolved—into adulthood.

Patricia is staying with her grandmother and aunt's family while her mother and father go through divorce proceedings. Alienated by her cousins, Patricia takes refuge in the small guest cabin. The watch that Patricia finds under the floorboards that had belonged to her grandmother is the device used to send Patricia back in time where she observes her mother, Ruth, as an unhappy "alienated" teenager at odds with her brothers and especially with her mother. Patricia listens as her twelve-year-old mother is continually berated and negated by a mother described as "furious" and out-of-control. Back in "real" time, Patricia hears her grandmother continue to blame and criticize her mother. "What did" her mother "do to drive" her father "away?" she asks Patricia. "Too headstrong as usual, I suspect," her grandmother tells her (108).

Pearson uses the subplot and subtext of the relationship between grandmother and mother as a foil against which to construct the relationship between Patricia and her mother. Patricia identifies with her mother as Ruth takes and hides the watch that belongs to her mother in retaliation for the unfair treatment she has received. When the watch breaks and Patricia is no longer able to access her mother's past, she feels grief and longing for the girl, Ruth, with whom she had felt so close. "The adventure was over, and the person she had felt closest to in her life, troubled, rebellious, spirited Ruth, was gone" (140). The mending of Patricia's distant relationship with her mother is resolved when Ruth visits her daughter at her family's home. They finally speak of the love that they have for one another after Patricia has made it clear that she wishes to live with her mother after the divorce. Ruth tells Patricia that her own mother had not accepted her as she was. Looking into Patricia's eyes, she tells Patricia: "I guess I've done the same with you . . . not seen who you really are" (183).

Pearson's daughter–mother narrative is grounded in a mother–daughter discourse that emphasizes connections between mothers and daughters and a belief that relationships between mothers and daughters can be resolved. Ruth speaks of forgiving her mother: "Yes, Mother can be fierce. She's had a disappointing life in many ways and sometimes her anger about it erupts. But I guess at some point we have to forgive our parents." She and her mother, she explains, "have become so much used to not getting along that it's become a bad habit" (184). Even Patricia, despite her focalization of her grandmother as an angry woman "with a long crooked mouth," is ready to imagine that she and her mother and grandmother "could make a fresh start." "Sometimes," Patricia continues, "it might be best to forget the past. Or at least accept it, and then keep on going" (184).

The novel, *A Handful of Time,* is yet another example of just how much the representation of the daughter–mother relationship in young adult novels is constituted through a discourse popularly used in self-help books about the relationship. Rifts in daughter–mother relationships are also healed over in Nixon's generational daughter–mother narrative. At the closure of story in *Encore*, granddaughter Erin is described as "warmed" by her mother Cassie's decision to make a film together with herself and her mother, Abby. "It was no longer Abby and Erin against Cassie. It was the three of them together, all with the same goal" (187).

DAUGHTER–MOTHER TALK

Particularly heard in generational stories about mothers and daughters are the staple derogatory phrases and descriptions used in conversations, magazines, and other novels about the relationship including, for example, identifying mother as "smotherer," and "devourer." [5] They are heard, for example, in the dialogue and repartee of daughters and mothers in Irwin's *What About Grandma?* In the story in which Eve, accompanied by her teen daughter, Rhys, returns home to care for her mother who has been injured in a fall (and unknown to her daughter, has been given only a few months to live) Irwin would seem to cover every aspect and side of the mother–daughter relationship that is written about in popular texts. Rhys's mother tells her daughter, for example, that she is afraid she and her mother will "devour each other" if she and Rhys stay much longer (42). She also tells Rhys that she has "always tried to be as different from her as I could. Maybe every daughter does that. . . . Now I think I'm growing more like her every day" (11). The concerns voiced by Eve are representative of those found in discourses about the mother–daughter relationship: a daughter's perception of her mother as "perfect," whom "she couldn't imagine making a mistake"; a mother's concern that she did not want to "smother" a daughter or make her a "clone" of herself; and a daughter's feeling that she had needed more from her mother and had not "understood what" her mother "wanted" her "to be" (Irwin 37–38). Rhys observes and comments on the conversation between Rhys's grandmother and Eve that is typical daughter–mother talk. "You and David can't live my life for me or—she stopped as if searching for a right word—or . . . control my . . . future." Rhys comments at this point that her grandmother and mother were "tiptoeing around" each other rather than really talking to one another. Eve replies: "Mother, we have enough trouble living our own lives. We certainly don't want to interfere with yours." Her mother's voice was "getting higher," Rhys notes. Eve continues, "We're just trying to do what is right." Rhys narrates that her grandmother replies in matching tones: "Then stop treating me as if I'm your child!" There was a difference between wanting and needing her there, Rhys's grandmother tells Eve, but Eve had never learned the difference (88–89).

The language and imagery used to mediate the relationships between adult daughters and their mothers in *What About Grandma?* and B. Cannon's *Begin the World Again* are in accord with contemporary descriptions and explanations of the mother–daughter relationship. Rhys's mother in Irwin's novel, for example, comments to her daughter: "Here I am. Forty-two years old. I've spent all my life being a daughter and half my life being a mother. When do I get to *me*?" (42). Described is that space—no place—that is mediated through mirror imagery in Irigaray's essay:

> You look at yourself in the mirror. And already you see your own mother there. And soon your daughter, a mother. Between the two, what are you? What space is yours alone? . . .
>   You take off your face of a mother's daughter, of a daughter's mother. You lose your mirror reflection. You thaw. You melt. You flow out of self (63).

In B. Cannon's *Begin the World Again*, Lake's mother also focalizes her position in relation to her daughter and her mother: "Here we are, three generations. There's Grand at the bottom, Lake in the middle, and me, whoever that might be, looking down at both of them. I wonder if there is any cosmic significance to this arrangement?" (168).

In Irwin's novel as in so many of the generational stories, the lacunae in relationships are constructed between teenage daughters and their mothers, and between adult daughters and their mothers. Bridging these lacunae, however, are the voices of grandmothers and granddaughters. In Irwin's *What About Grandma?* Rhys describes how her voice is joined with that of her grandmother and mother:

> In their laughter I heard the backward echo of my own, Mom's strong and controlled, Grandma's weak and frail, and for the first time I understood that part of me would die with Grandma, but part of her would live in me (150–51).

When Rhys's grandmother dies, Rhys is at her bedside but her mother is absent. There is "a special bond between grandmothers and granddaughters," Rhys's mother tells her daughter, that is different from others (73).

A SPECIAL BOND

The special bond between grandmothers and granddaughters is a frequent element of story in grandmother daughter–mother narratives in young adult novels. Two main aspects of story have been identified in which the relationships between a grandmother and a granddaughter are a significant part of the daughter–mother narrative. First, the bond serves to connect a daughter to the women in her family by suturing over the differences and/or absences of a daughter's mother. Secondly, the bond may also serve to connect a granddaughter to a beneficent grandmother who empowers her grand-daughter in a way that her own mother cannot.

In Jeanette Ingold's *The Window*, fifteen-year-old Mandy makes connec-tions to her mother, grandmother and great-grandmother through learning about their past. A daughter's search for her mother is also embedded in Ingold's story. Mandy's mother, who had been brought up in a series of foster homes, had been searching for her roots when she was killed in a car accident. Mandy, blinded in the accident in which her mother was killed, goes to live with her great-Aunt Emma and Uncle Gabriel in Texas, where she learns to adjust to her blindness and makes friends at her new school.

Ingold is another writer who uses time displacement in a daughter–mother narrative in order to build connections and identity between a young girl and her maternal forebears. In dreamlike sequences, Mandy observes the young girl, Gwen, whom she discovers is her grandmother, playing with her brother Abe as she grows up. On other occasions she sees Gwen har-ried by her mother (Mandy's great-grandmother), and watches Gwen's meeting with the young man, Paul, with whom she elopes and marries at the age of fifteen. In a subsequent dream, Mandy is with Gwen just after she sees Paul fall from his plane to his death months before their child—Mandy's mother—was born.

The grandmother daughter–mother relationship is written as ongoing chain of cause and effects as Gwen's mother is seen by Mandy to rip up the letter that tells her where her daughter Gwen has gone with her hus-band. "One woman, and her meanness," narrates Mandy, "spoiled Gwen's life and my mother's life" (159). Her daughter-in-law, Aunt Emma, remarks that she didn't think Mandy's great-grandma knew "how to love." Aunt Emma and Mandy agree that it was as if there was a "coldness passed on" down to her from a generation of mothers before her (132).

Encoded in Ingold's daughter-mother narrative is a teen daughter's fantasy to feel close to her deceased mother. Mandy's memories of her mother and the time they spent with each other are an important part of this narrative. Ingold also emphasizes, however, the connections made be-tween a teenage girl and her grandmother in a generational story. "I've made room," Mandy narrates at closure, "for Gwen inside me, and for my mom, and maybe even for Gwen's mother. I know how to feel, and love, for us all" (181).

The Bequest

The motif of the bequest or "heirloom," encoding a form of maternal power that is handed down from grandmother to granddaughter, is a conventional plot motif. In Irwin's novel, for example, it takes the form of a "knowing" that Rhys's grandmother passes on to her sixteen-year-old granddaughter. She tells her own daughter: "It's a pity I couldn't pass the power on to you, Eve. Rhys has it, you know" (150). Levitin and Smith use the motif of the bequest in their respective novels, *Beyond Another Door* and *Snow-Eyes*. The similarity of the patterning of the grandmother daughter–mother narrative is quite striking—demonstrating the formalized patterning that so often constructs the generational story. Both authors use, appropriately enough, the element of fantasy to tell story: Levitin uses elements of the supernatural in a realistic novel, while Smith uses the device of a secondary world in her fantasy novel. The use of the supernatural by Levitin, for example, is certainly an appropriate medium for describing the fantasy of maternal power invested in the ghost figure of Daria's grandmother who is described as possessing a "special power" as a psychic medium (148).

Levitin's and Smith's uses of supernatural and fanciful elements of story collude with elements of narrative plots to reproduce Freudian psychological descriptions of childhood fantasies of the mother split into bipolarity of power and powerlessness, strength and weakness, and blindness and "insight" that associates the negative aspects of these oppositions with the place of a teenager's mother and the positive aspects with her grandmother. Maternal power, in both novels, is fantasized in the form of an insightful knowledge. As in the psychoanalytic narratives, it is associated with fear, for it is a "special power" that one has to learn how to control and be instructed in its use. The shaping of the grandmother mother granddaughter narrative is identical in each novel: maternal power associated with a grandmother; a teenage daughter's mother signifying absence or lack—a break in the chain of empowering connections between women; and the special bond between grandmother and granddaughter.

In *Beyond Another Door*, Daria's mother, Peg, is represented as the weak link in the chain of three generations of women. She is described as "not ready for matters of the spirit. Perhaps she would never be" (160). Peg is said to have "fought" against her mother's "special powers." She had:

> hated it and it scared her something terrible. And you know why she was so scared? I think inside herself, Peggy was more convinced than anybody of Mama's special power. I think that's why Peg was so dead set against it. Because somehow she thought Mama would use it to run her life, or that Mama would *make* things happen. And Peg was too spunky and independent and practical for that (140–41).

Mothers are criticized and blamed for not being able to hand down maternal power to their daughters. In *Snow-Eyes*, Beya Rete is described as failing to have tutored her daughter in the use of her gift of "insight." Her daughter, Snow-Eyes, thought of all that she had believed a mother to be: "You did not care for me when I was little, you did not stay to be with me, you were not there! Why should I care if you are my mother?" She goes on to say: "You teach me nothing. And . . . I don't want to learn anything from you, now" (143). In both novels, the bequest—an heirloom—is inherited by a granddaughter and becomes the means by which a daughter is able to overcome the disadvantages that are associated with her mother. Beya Rete narrates:

> I glimpsed a flash of your unawakened insight. I was shocked. You were powerful, and your anger hit me as a flame come straight from the sun. It terrified me to see such a thing in so small a child. How could I even begin to tutor that? I fled. In fright, I fled—and oh, yes in envy (Smith 217).

Levitin uses the convention of the fantasy of role reversal to show how a daughter fantasizes how her superior inner strength can be used to "rescue" her mother. In a dream fantasy, Daria rescues her mother in a car crash. Her mother had called her "Mother." A friend explains to Daria: "That means you had changed roles, in a way. You were the one in charge" (155).

Through the convention of the special bond, both Levitin and Smith encode into story familiar aspects of the generational story: establishing the special relationship between a grandmother and granddaughter and empowering an adolescent girl so that she not only gains stature in relation to her mother but surpasses her mother. Daria realizes that she "*was* the child of Rose Whittlesey, as much as she was the child of Peg Peterson." It was a bond her mother had dreaded—that her daughter would "become like the grandmother" (151). In a mirror scene, "Daria could see both her own reflection and her mother's, and beyond these, in the eye of her mind, she could see Rose Whittlesey, and she knew that something unmistakable in her own features showed in their bond" (159). Emphasis is placed in Levitin's novel on mending and resolving relationships. Daria is asked by the ghost of her grandmother to give her mother the love that her mother had not been able to accept (160).

GRANDMOTHERS' HOMES:
HAVENS FOR GRANDDAUGHTERS

In Bridgers' *Notes for Another Life*, B. Cannon's *Begin the World Again*, Cynthia Voigt's *Dicey's Song*, and Thesman's *The Rain Catcher*, the grandmother and granddaughter relationship is also represented as central to a young woman's development. Grandmothers are represented in these novels as nurturing figures and their homes described as havens of security for their granddaughters. In *Notes for Another Life*, teenage-daughter Wren's mother's home in Atlanta where she works "seemed to Wren an impossibly alien place" (Bridgers 26), whereas "everything that Wren owns" is "protected within those sturdy walls" of her grandmother's home (14).

In *Begin the World Again*, descriptions of Lake's grandmother's home and homemaking would seem to be straight from the equivalent of a Martha Stewart's guide to good living and make a stark contrast to Lake's experience of communal living. Lake drinks in the "lush richness of linen and golden candlelight" and listens to her grandmother's explanation of how she buys freshly made Alfredo sauce, freezes it, and then pops it into the microwave (B. Cannon 133). Her grandmother's garden, the fireplace with embroidered cushions in the chimney corner, and the roses on the china plates and wallpaper were the signs of the orderly and good life her mother had left behind. Yet Lake also observes that her mother had taken away with her some of her grandmother's ways of doing things: the layout of the flower and vegetable garden and the way they both skinned tomatoes. In Voigt's *Dicey's Song*, Gram's home lies at the end of Dicey's odyssey that was undertaken when her mother abandons her children in a supermarket parking lot. Gram's "shabby farmhouse" is "Home" with room for Dicey and her siblings, while Gram is the kind of person that they need.

In Grayling's grandmother's house in Thesman's *The Rain Catchers* live the women whom Grayling refers to as the "mothering circle" who "watch over one another" in a house "where we are safe, where the honeysuckle rain falls in the summer, where most stories have beginnings, middles, and ends" (12). Grayling compares her grandmother's haven (where she feels protected) to her mother's house in San Francisco in which there is "nothing alive. . . . All the plants are artificial. And she has no pets. There's nothing here that could ever need her attention" (100). Neither does Grayling feel safe and protected in her mother's house despite the iron grilles that protect the windows and doors and a burglar alarm system. At night, her mother's house "terrifies her." It is a place where she imagines her "nightmares might come true" (101).

It is during a stay with her mother, Norah, who had left Grayling as a small child with her grandmother after her husband's murder, that fourteen-year-old Grayling meets the dark, mysterious young man, "Dancer," who proves to be both alluring and dangerous. After Grayling deliberately seeks out Dancer a second time with the result that he visits their house late at night, her mother decides that they should immediately go to her apartment in San Diego. Her mother, comments Grayling, is "very good at running away" (137). Norah, unable to deal with a daughter who, as Grayling narrates, brings "chaos" into her mother's orderly life, sends Grayling back home to her grandmother.[6] While Grayling's mother believes that girls of Grayling's age should be stepping out alone, Thesman's story is also about how adolescent daughters continue to need protection and guidance. Although Grayling takes responsibility for her encounter with the Dancer, she comments that her mother was right to send her back. She, Grayling, needed a "whole house full of women to keep" her "from doing stupid things" (160).

Grayling's grandmother and the mothering circle gather every day at teatime to share their news and learn about their lives through story. Grayling, who has learned from her mother the reason why she had been left by her at her grandmother's, stands in the margin of the doorway of the story-telling room to tell her story about her visit to her mother and the "Dancer" (169). Grayling tells her story to women who have also made "mistakes" and have been "frightened and embarrassed at the results" (182). Thesman's story, thereby, gives voice to the feminist practice in which women learn to speak—to construct their own ways of knowing the world— in order to authorize their own experiences. Grayling learns the importance of having an authentic voice in her grandmother's home.[7]

However, as in so many other novels, the voice of a maternal mother is missing from the circle. Norah's voice is marginalized—the narrated subject of her daughter's story. In terms of the grandmother mother–daughter narrative, Grayling's mother represents a rift—a difficulty—in the relationship of mothers and daughters. Grayling may have connected briefly with her mother's voice but it is a voice full of fear and loneliness. Her mother, Grayling explains, is "filled with fear, secreted under layers of sophistication as thick as enamel" (101). Empowerment for Grayling comes from the connections with the women in her grandmother's home. At closure, Grayling and Colleen join the storytelling circle: "Here are the women to fill the empty chairs. . . . Just so the circle won't be broken" (179). They are represented as young women who grow toward maturity and responsibility through a model of mothering practiced in Grayling's grandmother's home in which value is placed on interdependence, care, and relationships.

Thesman's description of Grayling's grandmother's mothering circle accords with a perspective of mothering used in contemporary feminist discourses on mothering and the mother–daughter relationship. In *Mother Daughter Revolution* by Debold, Wilson and Malave, a "circle of mothers" is used to signify a group of mothers that join together in mutual support to empower daughters in a way that interweaves the political and the personal (241). A practice of mothering using other-mothers—a concept borrowed from African American mothering practices—is also part of mothering discourses in which nonbiological mothers voluntarily help mothers care for adolescent daughters. These women teach girls strategies of resistance to sexism and other power relations to which they are subjected (237).

Thesman's story draws attention to the sexism practiced against adolescent girls in today's contemporary society through the story of Colleen, who is sexually harassed by her stepmother's brother. Colleen's father is described as "mean to Colleen. Really mean" (5). He has told his daughter that he will send her mother, who attempted suicide and from whom he is now divorced, to the asylum again if Colleen attempts to see her mother (31). Grayling's grandmother fights for Colleen's custody despite the threat by Colleen's father that he would look into the circumstances of the death of Olivia, a member of the circle who has recently died from cancer. At her grandmother's home, Grayling is thus provided with models of resistance against sexism and the kind of fear that keeps her mother living alone in her "fortress"—afraid, still, of meeting the man who had murdered her husband. In contrast to the dangerous encounters with Dancer, Grayling's friendship and romance with Aaron develops within the safe environment of her grandmother's home.

The bond between grandmothers and granddaughters is a significant element in daughter–mother narratives in other cultures. Discussions of the grandmother daughter–mother narrative in Nancy Farmer's *A Girl Named Disaster*, Mori's novels, and in African American novels for young adults are included in subsequent chapters. The next chapter focuses on the daughter–mother narrative in other cultural contexts.

NOTES

1. See Hancock 183.
2. For further commentary, see Caplan.
3. See Flax *Thinking* 174.
4. See, for example, Freud's essay, "Femininity," in which he comments on the "preliminary attachment to the mother" that being "so rich in content and so long-lasting . . . could leave behind so many opportunities for fixations and dispositions" (129).
5. For examples, see Secunda; for the deconstruction of these and other epithets describing mothers and daughter–mother relationships, see Caplan.

6. Adrienne Kertzer has interpreted Thesman's novel as a maternal pretext in the context of a Red-Riding Hood narrative. I would argue, however, that Thesman's novel also has to be read in the context of narratives of contemporary adolescent psychology and other stories in young adult novels in which the absent mother is a convention of story. See Kertzer "Reclaiming."

7. For a discussion of feminist practices and women's voices, see Belenky 134; Debold, Wilson, and Malave 240.

Nine

Making Connections Across Differences: Cross-Cultural Narratives

I saw her with American eyes: saw the little woman with the funny skin and the odd eyes.

—Yep *The Star Fisher*

The theories of adolescent psychology that have informed our understanding of adolescence in North America have not only denied the centrality of the daughter–mother relationship in the lives of girls and women but have also not taken into account how this relationship is experienced in different social and cultural contexts. Recent studies of female adolescence by Gilligan and others include the voices of girls from various different ethnic, racial, and socioeconomic backgrounds, although the actual numbers of girls studied have, as yet, been small.[1] In *Between Voice and Silence*, the authors report that there are "greater differences in the way black, white, Portuguese, and Hispanic girls describe their relationship with their mothers than in the way they describe other aspects of their lives that were covered" in their research (Taylor, Gilligan, and Sullivan 70). Black feminists have particularly emphasized the importance of examining the mother-daughter relationship in racial, social, and cultural contexts. They stress that white Western psychological interpretations and analyses of the mother-daughter relationship are inappropriate to studying the black daughter-mother relationship.[2]

There has been a significant increase in the number of young adult novels in which there are descriptions of relationships between adolescent girls and their mothers that are either positioned across cross-cultural ethnicities

191

within the United States, or are set within racial and ethnic contexts other than North America.

This chapter discusses issues of culture, ethnicity, class, and gender in relation to a cross-cultural daughter–mother narrative that emerges from stories about teenage daughters and their mothers who have been brought up in different cultures. These issues are also discussed in relation to the representation of daughter–mother relationships in selected novels set in the Middle East and Asia. A discussion of the African American daughter–mother narrative is deferred until the next chapter.

MAKING CONNECTIONS ACROSS DIFFERENCES: A CROSS-CULTURAL NARRATIVE

The daughter–mother narratives in novels by Casey, Mitali Perkins, and Laurence Yep are produced through themes that are commonly encoded in a discourse about daughter–mother relationships in adolescence including the understanding of adolescence as a time when daughters question their identity and their relationship with their mothers, and as a time when there is tension and conflict between teenage daughters and mothers. In the cross-cultural daughter–mother narrative discussed in this chapter, these themes are integrated with issues of cross-cultural differences and racial discrimination. Particularly foregrounded are issues of identity as daughters construct for themselves a plural and shifting sense of self as they identify with mothers whose own upbringing took place in different cultures or ethnic backgrounds than those in which their daughters are growing up.

Taylor, Gilligan, and Sullivan have observed that "Tension and conflict about being bicultural or multicultural are perhaps most apparent in mother–daughter relationships" (70). Discussed below are novels in which conflicts and feelings of alienation between teenage daughters and their mothers are set within the context of differences caused by a daughter's growing up in a different racial or ethnic, and often social, milieu from the kind of world that had shaped her mother's cultural values and beliefs. Born in England, where she lives with her family, fourteen-year-old Mary in Casey's *Over the Water* touches upon the heart of these stories as she asks herself in regard to her homesick Irish-born mother: "Will I be able to help her in England? Or am I a stranger to her, this daughter of hers who was born in a foreign land?" (238). Through Mary's first-person narration, a reader is potentially able to identify with Mary and to experience how the relationship between an adolescent daughter and her mother is affected by the intersection of ideologies of gender, nationality, religion, and social class.

The story of Mary's contentious relationship with her mother, Bridie, is told during Mary's family's annual return home to her grandmother's farm in Ireland in the summer. Mary's Irish mother is described as attempting to impose on her daughter, brought up in England, cultural beliefs about womanhood and femininity formed through her own upbringing as an Irish Catholic in Ireland. Her mother, narrates Mary, is either avoiding her, hitting her or telling her to pray (Casey 172). Mary describes her feelings of separateness from a mother who constantly berates her about clothes and appropriate behavior using such language as "Pull down your skirt and cover your knees, you bold hussy" (86)

Casey deals forthrightly in this feminist coming-of-age story with issues of sexism and religion showing how religious and cultural mores are the cause of silencing and prohibitions constructed around Mary's sexual maturation. In a compelling scene, Casey makes visible how the Virgin Mary has been held up to women as a controlling image of virginity; and how a discourse constructed around the Virgin Mary constructs conflict and silence between a teenage daughter and her mother.[3] Ordered by her mother to kneel down and pray to the Virgin Mary for "purity" when she has her period, Mary narrates how she cannot repeat all the words of the Litany after her mother and asks: "Well, anyway, why do all those prayers keep going on about mothers being pure, and chaste and so on? And the mother of God being a virgin! Doesn't God think normal mothers are good enough, then?" (38–39). Her mother, narrates Mary, is unable to look into her eyes. "There is so much that she's not saying! And I'm desperate for her to speak to me" (41).

The silence built around Mary's sexuality extends to her father who is represented as feeling ill at ease with his daughter. Casey makes visible how the dynamics of power and gender work in Mary's Irish family. The story of Mary's grandfather's fight to rebuild the family farm after a brutal attack by the English illustrates the need for family men to be strong but, as Casey shows, this same power can be used against mothers and daughters. Beaten by her father, Bridie, in turn, has let her husband beat his children with "bamboo sticks" (126). When Mary is blamed for her brother's injury, she is severely beaten by her father. Mary narrates how her mother attempts to save her from the worst of her father's blows ("Not her head! Mind her head!"), but as Mary comments, her mother is an accomplice—she hands her husband the switch with which he continues to whip the rest of her body

(141–42). Attention is drawn in Casey's daughter–mother narrative, as in others, to the way mothers so easily become betrayers of their daughters by allying with fathers who use their power as titular head of the household to dominate women.

Ideologies of ethnicity and class are also shown to affect the relationship between Mary and her mother. As Mary explains to Nuala, England is a "foreign country for Mammy" but it is the country where she, Mary, has always lived and where she has gone to school (102). Mary's English way of speaking—associated in Ireland with privilege and dominance—makes her feel alienated and apart in Ireland (73 and 88). In England, however, she is embarrassed about her friends hearing her mother "talking Irish" (124). The differences between home and school culture that are found to cause tension between daughters and mothers situated in bicultural contexts also cause conflict between Mary and her mother who attempts to hold her daughter to her own standards and traditions.[4] The girls at school, Mary explains, think she is "weird for being Irish." She is not able to get to know them because her mother has curtailed her activities in England to the extent that she cannot "*ever*" go out with school friends on weekends, so that she is forced to lie to them about her activities (125).

Heard in *Over the Water*, as in so many other stories about adolescent daughters and their mothers, is the desperate longing of a daughter for her mother's love and understanding. "Who is Mammy? I realize with a shock that I'm looking for a *person* inside Mammy, a person I can talk to. And I'm too shy to say so" (41). Casey writes about the reconciliation and acceptance between an adolescent daughter and her mother as Nuala helps Mary to understand the difficulties faced by her mother in bringing up a daughter in a foreign country where she has no idea of how people "bring up their kids" and is fearful that she will be accused in Ireland of bringing her daughter "up mannerless and heathen" (126).

An aspect of the relationship that appears central to cross-cultural daughter–mother narratives is that a daughter comes to appreciate and understand her mother's personal history and culture and how these have shaped her mother's outlook and attitudes. Bridie tells her daughter the story of her necessary and heartbreaking decision to leave the home she loved and how she struggled in England alone to make the money that would help her family in Ireland. At the closure of the novel, Mary is able to say that she is "finding a friend in her mammy" (219). Emphasized in Casey's story are values that speak to the strength of family love and ties, the love and appreciation of Irish life and culture—"something to be proud of . . ." (236).

In his novel, *The Star Fisher,* Yep tells of the difficulties that beset fifteen-year-old Joan Lee and her family when they move to Clarksburg, West Virginia, from Ohio in order to set up a Chinese laundry. Yep interrelates the conventional language that is frequently used to describe the relationship between an adolescent girl and her mother with themes of cross-cultural differences, racial prejudice, and discrimination. Conflict between Joan, born in America, and her Chinese mother, and Joan's feelings of being separate from her mother are reproduced, for example, through the narrative convention of seeing mother as "other."

> I always seemed to be reaching out my hand and getting it slapped. And those were the times when I sometimes looked at Mama and saw a stranger—not just someone who was unknown to me, but a real stranger. I saw her with American eyes: saw the little woman with the funny skin and the odd eyes (72).

Differences between Joan and her mother are set against differing cultural expectations regarding such issues as discipline and what a mother expects from her daughter in terms of deference, obedience, and helping with chores. Joan, her mother tells her, compares her to American parents and so thinks of her as "mean" (79). The convention of showing a daughter's growing maturity in relation to that of her mother's is demonstrated through Joan's ability to translate, for her Chinese speaking mother, the English language and American customs, and through a mother's reliance on her daughter to negotiate for her with the local storekeeper and their neighbor and landlady, Miss Lucy.

The difference between American and Chinese language through which the differing experiences of Joan and her mother are produced, and which are shown to affect their relationship, are literally made visible on the pages of the text. Yep explains that English conversations are italicized while Joan's first person narration and reported conversation with her mother in Chinese are produced in regular typeface (viii). Significance is placed, through the means of designating Chinese as the main sign system in the text, on Joan's Chinese heritage. Described are the strengths as well as the vulnerabilities of a Chinese mother, who is represented as bringing up her daughter according to values that she believes in, and who is described as the "practical" and business head of the family in contrast to her scholar husband (98–99). The theme of crossing barriers of language and cultures, however, is central to Yep's story. Joan's mother tells her daughter that she will "try harder to be more American" (101).

The popular discourse on parent–child relationships that evokes the fantasy of the all-powerful mother is also interrelated with a cross-cultural narrative in Yep's text as Joan describes how she sees her mother "for the first time, not as the all-powerful woman who could handle anything, but as a human being: a small, frightened, vulnerable woman alone in a strange land, except for her not-always-too-grateful family."[5] The knowledge that her mother does not have "magical powers," Joan narrates, makes her "feel grown-up and sad and angry all at once" (48).

Joan's growing ability to view her mother through "a double pair of eyes" is demonstrated again when Joan narrates: "And suddenly I realized that there wasn't another Chinese woman for probably a hundred miles or more. All Mama had was me and Emily, and we were half-alien to her. In her own way, Mama must have felt as cut off as the star fisher" (99). One way of reading the legend of the star fisher that Yep uses throughout the text is to read it as metaphor for the relationship between Joan and her mother. Joan tells her younger sister, Emily, the story of the star fisher mother who returns to earth to claim her earth-born daughter. Changing into a golden-feathered bird like her mother, the daughter, who has been marked as a star fisher by her mother's sisters, could still be seen some nights as she skimmed "up the stars like a kingfisher" (45).

In relating this legend to her own situation, Joan identifies herself with the star fisher's daughter and her mother with the star fisher. Joan's mother, for example, talks about going back to China, and Joan wonders how the star fisher's daughter "had felt when the star fisher told her they were going back to the sky—back to that strange land that was their birthright and yet was so mysterious and frightening" (100). As in the legend a daughter, marked with the blood of her mother, constructs self in identity with her mother. Joan tells her mother: "We may talk and dress and act like Americans, but in our hearts we'll always be Chinese" (146). In identifying with mothers across cultural and ethnic boundaries, adolescent girls appreciate that they do not have one fixed identity but are able to construct self from a number of different identities—analogous to the star fisher's daughter who identifies with both the earth where she was born and the sky where she lives with her mother.

Daughters and mothers are described as being caught between contemporary American and traditional Indian cultures in Mitali Perkins's novel, *The Sunita Experiment*. Described in Perkins's grandmother daughter–mother narrative are the cross-cultural differences over dress, food, and accepted social behavior that cause tensions between daughters and mothers when thirteen-year-old Sunita's grandparents arrive in California from

India. Her mother, narrates Sunita, "had stopped being her mother and had changed into being their daughter right in front of [her] eyes" (10).

Sunita describes her embarrassment when her mother begins wearing the customary saree, red stripe in her hair (to show she is married), and the red dot on her forehead, and the difficulties encountered when she is told she may no longer be allowed to invite boys to her home or sleepover at her friends' homes. In the following exchange between Sunita and her mother, cultural differences are shown to cause conflict between a daughter and a mother when a daughter constructs herself in relation to a culture differently from the way her mother identifies self with a set of cultural traditions. Sunita shouts that her "name is not BONTU!" but "SUNITA." She continues: "I'll never wear one of those long sheets in public. If YOU want to be elected Indian woman of the year or something, just go right ahead, but LEAVE ME OUT OF IT!" (117).

The authors of *Between Voice and Silence* write that in "educating girls to simultaneously 'fit in' and 'be themselves' [mothers] may revisit their own development and face their own relationship to culture in an intensely personal and often conflicted way" (Taylor, Gilligan, and Sullivan 70). Mothers of teenage girls are described in stories by Casey, Yep, and Perkins as occupying shifting positions between two cultures and two generations. In Perkins's text, this transition is characterized by uncertainty and ambiguity. Sunita's mother, for example, is shown trying to placate her own mother while trying to please her daughter. "Sunita hates to see me in sarees. But my mother would faint if she saw me in slacks" (151). She explains to a friend that while she stills feels she has "enough Indian" in her to make her parents "happy," she is "not the same obedient daughter that left India all those years ago" (151).

Sunita's mother's decision to give up her college teaching during her parents' visit illustrates how the image of the "perfect Indian woman" who "would never neglect the care of her family for a full-time job" can still be a dominant cultural fantasy for a working Indian mother. It is made clear through Sunita's grandparents' encouragement and pride in their daughter's achievements that this particular social construction of motherhood had changed and need no longer prevent Sunita's mother from following an ambitious career particularly in the context of California in the 1990s (155).[6]

In his novel, *Thief of Hearts*, Yep again sets the differences between a daughter and her mother in the context of Chinese American cross-cultural differences, alienation, and racial discrimination. Teenage-daughter Stacey learns how her Chinese mother, Casey, was her age when she had moved to America; that her mother had felt like a "real outsider" and had had "to adjust" in making the transition from Chinese to American culture is "news" to Stacey (125).[7] She had not, Stacey narrates, realized how difficult it had been and how much hard work it had taken her mother (a college professor) "to get where she was" (124).

The issue of cultural identity is raised through Stacey's recognition of her own prejudice as she introduces a newly arrived Chinese girl, Hong Ch'un, to the predominantly white school that she attends and confronts, for the first time, the knowledge that she, herself, can be subjected to being identified as a "half-breed." When Hong Ch'un is missing, Stacey takes a literal journey into her mother's past with her mother and her grandmother, Tai-Paw, as they search the streets and homes of San Francisco's Chinatown for the girl. Through this experience, Stacey gains a sense of pride in her cultural and family roots and is able to identify with her mother's successful transition across cultures.

Emphasis is placed in stories by Casey, Perkins, and Yep on a process of reconciliation and acculturation in which teenage daughters come to understand their mothers and to identify with them through learning about the different historical contexts and cultural heritages that have shaped their mothers' thinking and lives. The daughter–mother narratives in these novels are produced from a number of common elements. Teenage girls are described, at closure of story, as accepting rather than resisting their mothers' heritages. They are shown attempting to find ways of balancing those things that hold value for them from their mothers' traditions with the beliefs and value systems of the cultures in which they, themselves, are growing up as young women. At the closure of Perkins's novel, Sunita is answering to her Indian name "Bontu" and is trying on sarees with her friends (172 and 178). Reproduced in these daughter–mother narratives is a version of female development in which a girl constructs self through multiple identities across different cultures and ethnicities and in which self-development takes place in relationship with a mother.

The ability to see from multiple perspectives is shown to be important in these stories as, akin to Stacey in Yep's *Thief of Hearts*, adolescent daughters are represented as "borrowing" their mother's eyes as they look from the outside of their mother's lives to the inside (126). The connection made across differences described in daughter–mother relationships in these stories can also be read on another level. Encoded in this cross-cultural daughter–mother narrative are lessons addressed to young people about the need to acknowledge, validate, and respect cultural roots and traditions in the plural and multicultural society in which daughters of today are growing up.

POWER AND DIFFERENCE:
DAUGHTERS AND MOTHERS IN OTHER CULTURES

The daughter–mother narratives in Staples's *Shabanu: Daughter of the Wind* and *Haveli,* Kim's *The Long Season of Rain,* and Sook Choi's *Echoes of the White Giraffe* are set, respectively, in the Cholistan Desert, Pakistan, and South Korea. Made visible in these daughter coming-of-age stories are how gendered relations in particular cultural and historical contexts affect the positions of daughters and mothers relative to the status given to sons and fathers. In these fictional accounts, mothers teach daughters to fit into their proper place in family and society. Described is the extent to which daughters and mothers resist or find space for themselves within the boundaries of patriarchal cultures.

In *Shabanu: Daughter of the Wind,* Staples writes about daughters growing to womanhood in the Muslim nomad culture of Cholistan, Pakistan. In "Writing About the Islamic World," Staples explains how her story grew from her time spent in the Cholistan Desert listening to the stories told to her by the women of the desert community: "Every scene and chapter," Staples writes, "was based on a story told" to her "by a real person" (19). Staples makes it clear, however, that the setting and cultural context for her story of Shabanu is particularized to the Cholistan Desert.[8] In *Shabanu,* Staples describes a culture in which women have been regarded as objects of exchange through the institution of arranged marriages, and in which the daughter–mother relationship has not been valued as a relationship of social, economic, or political importance. This is made clear through Shabanu's first person narration: "As Muslim girls, we are brought up knowing our childhood homes are temporary. Our real homes are the ones we go to when we marry" (21).

Staples describes how Shabanu does, indeed, become an object of exchange. Shabanu's marriage to the wealthy Rahim-*sahib* is arranged to ensure protection for Shabanu's elder sister, Phulan, and her betrothed because Rahim's brother, Nazir Mohammad, had attempted to kidnap Phulan. Described by Staples in this novel and the sequel novel, *Haveli,* is a male-dominated society in which important decisions regarding women's lives, including marriage, are made by men. In *Shabanu,* the subordinated position of mothers and daughters in a culture where sons are valued over daughters is shown to be enforced through the religious and social institutions of Cholistan culture. Shabanu's family travel to the desert shrine at Channon Pir "where women pray for sons and good marriages for their daughters" (91).[9]

In patriarchal cultures, daughters learn that power resides within that public sphere defined as a man's world. In Helen Kim's *The Long Season of Rain,* set in contemporary Korea, a daughter hears her father tell her mother that she should not "involve" herself with the "men's world" when she asks where her husband goes at night. It was, her husband tells her: "nothing to do with her" (247). How daughters and mothers and their relationships are marginalized in a culture that has also traditionally valued sons and the patrilinear family is made visible in Kim's feminist daughter–mother narrative.

Eleven-year-old Junhee tells her mother's story—the story that lies at the heart of Kim's novel—during the summer that her mother wishes to adopt the boy, Pyungsoo. Indeed, Junhee's narrative can especially said to be dominated by the subjectivity of a mother since Junhee is an acute observer and reporter of her mother's actions and words (that dominate the text) as she comes to understand her mother's position within the family. In explaining why she wishes to adopt Pyungsoo, Junhee's mother tells her daughters how it is: "In years to come, when you are a stranger in someone else's house and you have no one to speak with, you will understand that even your daughters are not your own. That you have no one." To emphasize her point, she bites her eldest daughter's fingers, one by one to demonstrate the pain she feels. She cannot "bear," she tells her daughters, that "all" her "fingers will be cut away from" her "someday" (151).

Junhee is a sympathetic and sensitive observer of her mother as she notes her mother's subordination in a household run by her husband's mother from whom she must ask for permission and money for the upbringing of her daughters. She sees the outward signs of her mother's unhappiness: the cuts on her mother's fingers (146), and the scar left from teeth marks on the back of her mother's hand (148). Heard in Kim's novel are the desperate cries of a mother oppressed by a gender ideology that places value on the mothers of sons: "Don't I have any feelings? Aren't daughters-in-law human beings?" In reference to her mother-in-law, she asks: "Are my feelings her feelings? Does she know what's best for me? Sixteen years in the household and not once did she know what I felt, not once did she ask me what I wanted, not once did I get to say what I wanted" (232).

Throughout her narrative, Junhee reports on the pressures and stress experienced by her mother because she had not produced sons. Significantly given no personal name of her own, her mother is identified as Changee's mother—Changee being the name of her first-born daughter. There is a paradox in Kim's daughter–mother narrative. Junhee may take up the role of narrating her mother's story and be her mother's confidante, but she was given the name of a boy in the hope that she would be a son (9). How a girl's valuing of self, voice, and subjectivity is compromised through patriarchal ideologies of gender is made visible through her apology to her mother that she is not a boy. Her mother's reply shows that she continues to construct her daughter's value relative to that of a son when she tells Junhee that she is like a son to her—is "better than a son" (206).

Socializing a Daughter into Her Father's Culture

The daughter–mother narrative is produced in Kim's *The Long Season of Rain*, as in the novels by Staples and Choi, through a discourse of mothering in which mothers are concerned about bringing their daughters up in a proper manner by preparing them to fit into roles of womanhood that are deemed appropriate. Analogous to accounts in *Between Voice and Silence*, mothers are described in these novels as serving "as bearers and guardians of culture" (Taylor, Gilligan, and Sullivan 70). Junhee's mother, when angry with her daughters over some impoliteness or disobedience, tells them that she must have failed in her "duty as a mother"—that she "must be to blame" as she hits them with a switch (Kim 137–38). In *Shabanu*, Shabanu is asked to wear the *chadr*. In a Muslim society, the *chadr* signifies (among other social meanings) the veiling of women for purposes of modesty and concealment of sexual allure and also signifies the division between the private female sphere in which women are enclosed in the home (the *chardewari*) separated from the public sphere of men.[10] Shabanu's aunt's injunction that Shabanu wear the *chadr* since she was now a "young lady" who was "too old to act like a boy" is gently enforced by her mother who silently pleads with Shabanu to obey and places the *chadr* over her daughter. Privy to the exchange, her father, narrates Shabanu, seated on his camel nearby, "looks straight ahead" (Staples 33).

Shabanu's mother is described as having a crucial role in initiating her daughter into codes of conduct that demand her deference and obedience to a father, and in the not too distant future, also to her husband. The warm and easy relationship described between Sabanu and her father, who is represented as caring very much for his daughter, is shown to be dependent on Shabanu's obeying him without question. "Don't ever disobey me!" he tells his independently minded daughter, shaking her so that her head "snaps" back and forth (27). Shabanu is as "wild as the wind," her mother tells her. She "must learn to obey. Otherwise . . . I am afraid for you," her mother continues. The injunction is repeated. "You must learn to obey, even when you disagree" (28). When Shabanu shows signs of rebelling against marrying the wealthy and powerful Rahim-*sahib*—old enough, she narrates, to be her grandfather, her mother slaps her. Her mother's face is "harder" than Sabanu had ever seen it. Shabanu is to "say nothing more. It is done" (193). Learning to obey is shown to be a matter of survival, Shabanu learns, in a society where women are beaten, and even killed, for being disrespectful and disobedient.

Echoes of the White Giraffe by Choi is set in Korea in the 1950s. In Choi's story, despite the social upheavals due to the Korean War, young men and women are still expected to adhere to the social rules governing their behavior. Even though fifteen-year-old Sookan, her mother, and brother are refugees from Seoul, outsiders living in a shanty home way up on top of a mountain in Pusan, Sookan's mother is concerned to uphold social standards. When the young man Junho visits their home, Sookan knows that her mother is waiting for Junho to go:

> I knew what she must have been thinking. 'It isn't proper for him to stay now. What will people think? They will say that I am not raising my daughter properly because she has no father and no elder brothers around. Besides, I might give Sookan the wrong impression. She should know that it isn't proper for her to chat the whole afternoon away with a young man' (67).

"For once," Sookan narrates, she wishes her mother "would forget about tradition and the neighbors" and let her talk to Junho (67). Sookan's mother is described as being willing, on several occasions, to stretch protocol as far as possible for her daughter. At the same time it is clear that there are limits to how far rules can be bent. Sookan describes how she feels she has "betrayed" her mother when she goes beyond appropriate behavior in agreeing to have her photo taken with Junho alone—usually seen as a formal convention acknowledging an official engagement (80). "Our good son is ruined! Your daughter is bad news," Junho's mother tells Sookan's mother (85). Sookan's mother now tells her "daring child" that she "must behave like a proper young lady now" (87).

In "Loss of Voice in Women's Coming of Age Stories," Mary Lewis has drawn attention to female coming-of-age stories in a variety of different cultural contexts, including Staples's *Shabanu* in which girls are represented as being silenced, or shown to practice self-silencing, as they are forced to "modify their behavior, their words, and sometimes even their thoughts in an attempt to be desirable daughters, companions, or wives to others" (69).

In Choi's novel, a mother's role in restraining her daughter's voice can also be discussed in relation to the value that is placed on silence in Asian culture. When Sookan climbs to the top of the mountain to shout greetings to a poet on a neighboring hill, she is told that she should not shout "with such abandon." She is "a young lady now," her mother tells her. "You cannot afford to be so impulsive anymore. People are going to say you are growing up wild and without manners because you have no father and no older brothers. I expect you to behave like a proper young lady at all times. Do you understand?" (16).

Accounts of the gender socialization of girls in *Shabanu* and *Echoes of the White Giraffe* are produced through opposition of wildness/masculinity and domesticity/femininity—a set of conventional images and metaphors that are frequently used in fictional accounts of girls' socialization into their mothers' roles.[11] Eleven-year-old Shabanu narrates, for example, that she "can't abide anything that keeps me from the animals, from running free and climbing thorn trees." She has "no patience with housework" (Staples 29). Later, Shabanu is told by her father that it is time that she stayed at home with her mother and learned how to "look after a house"—an admonition reinforced by her mother (230).

Lessons in Resistance

Current feminist discourse about daughters and mothers in adolescence have stressed the importance of mothers supporting their daughters' resistance to the different forms of oppression and marginalization to which they are subjected. Daughters in these stories observe how their mothers or other women practice resistance in the face of patriarchal ideologies of gender and learn lessons on how to resist subjugation. In Kim's *The Long Season of Rain*, Junhee describes the secret, and sometimes open, acts of defiance that her mother engages in on behalf of her daughters. She enrolls her daughter Moonhee in art classes against her husband's and mother-in-law's wishes (149). Junhee notes that even her mother's cutting her hair, wearing a new dress—short, bright colors—and exchange of rebellious words with her friend, Mrs. Parks, are small signs of agency and defiance. Junhee's mother's final act of resistance is to leave her husband's home and her daughters to return to her mother's home. She tells Junhee that she would have left home a decade ago—after the birth of Changhee, her first daughter—if it had not been for her children (237). She writes a letter to her husband in which she states that she can no longer remain in the home that is a "prison" to her if he does not behave as a father to their daughters and if he does not treat her with "respect" (267). Junhee's mother, despite her position on the margins of authority in Junhee's family, does find courage and voice when it matters.

Debold, Wilson, and Malave write in *Mother Daughter Revolution* of how the family can become a "revolutionary cell" against the sexism to which daughters are subjugated (230). At the conclusion of Kim's novel, Junhee reports how her father takes his daughters to their Catholic Church in deference to his wife's religion and then to their maternal grandmother's in order to fetch his wife home. He tells them that their mother is a "good person, a good mother." If his daughters "could be half as good as her, I would be satisfied, proud," he continues. Identifying himself as not a "good father" or even "a good person," he tells his daughters that their mother "knows things that are good for" them and should be obeyed (269). Kim's novel, thus, ends on a more positive note as a father is forced to give voice, through his wife's action, to her value as a mother of daughters.

In *Shabanu*, Staples tells the story of Sharma (cousin to Shabanu's mother), who had escaped from the husband who beat both mother and daughter when Sharma had failed to produce sons. Now established as an independent woman with her own herds of sheep and goats, Sharma's daughter, sixteen-year-old Fatima, has the freedom to stay unmarried if she wishes (97). Alternative choices are also open to Shabanu, her aunt tells her, offering her sanctuary if she should ever decide that she wanted it (226). In Staples's sequel, *Haveli*, Shabanu allows Mumtaz to "wear her favorite old *shalwar kameez*" (a tunic), for she would have to "stay indoors and wear the *chadr*" soon enough (1).

In Pakistan, as in other cultures, the education of women has been viewed as a means of obtaining liberation in male-dominated societies.[12] In *Haveli*, Shabanu, enduring the life of a fourth wife in her husband's harem, takes advantage of the opportunity to learn to read herself and wishes her daughter, Mumtaz, to grow up knowing how to read so that she may have a vocation (Staples 71). As Choi makes visible through story in *Echoes of the White Giraffe*, education has also been, primarily, the domain of men. Sookan, determined to take the government examinations so that she might leave Korea to study in the United States, narrates how she walks into a "room full of men" some of whom "glared" at her as if "insulted" that a girl should be there. Later, the presence of her name, standing alone among the names of successful men, so stuns Sookan's brothers that they call to check no mistake has been made (125). Encoded into the daughter–mother narrative in all four texts by Staples, Kim, and Choi are the aspirations and hopes that daughters will have more freedom than their mothers. At the closure of *Haveli*, Shabanu has taken her daughter back to her own family in the Cholistan desert so that she may not be treated as a servant girl in the harem. In *Haveli,* it is the desert culture that, for now, represents freedom for Shabanu and Mumtaz (259).

Chodorow has argued that while women may be placed in a subordinate position in patriarchal and patrilocal societies in which there are rigid gender divisions, they may preserve a sense of their own worth in their separate domestic sphere in which daughters may identify and develop relationships with other women (*Feminism* 64). Certainly, in Shabanu, Staples writes about the loving connections that Shabanu, her sister, and her mother maintain with the strong, warm desert community of women relatives and other women who meet together at the shrine of Channon Pir and special family ceremonies. Staples's stories are also a reminder how women's relationships to each other are produced through the intersections of gender and social class. Shabanu narrates that she will always envy her elder sister's access to this "warm circle of our women" (216). As fourth wife to a man with seven sons, Shabanu will be "slave" to the other wives, who will never take a "desert girl into their circle" (205).

Daughters and their mothers may be positioned in patriarchal societies in the stories discussed in this chapter but have their voices connect in love and relationship. Feminist writers such as Casey and Kim, however, especially make visible the gender ideologies that shape daughter–mother relationships in their stories.

KYOKO MORI'S DAUGHTER–MOTHER NARRATIVES

In discussing Mori's work, I focus, primarily, on Mori's daughter–mother narratives in her young adult novels, *Shizuko's Daughter* and *One Bird,* set in Japan. However, I refer throughout this discussion to Mori's autobiographical daughter–mother narrative, *The Dream of Water,* and the way in which the memoirs of her mother are intertextualized with her novels to create, in effect, a maternal metanarrative that forcefully, and with beauty, speaks of a daughter's continuing love for her mother.[13]

In writing about women's autobiographies, Sidonie Smith defines a maternal text as a text in which a daughter in representing self discursively in text thinks back through her mother (57–58). Arguably, there are points of connection between fictional representations of the daughter–mother relationship written from a feminist perspective and an autobiographical maternal text. The relationship between Mori's daughter–mother narratives in her young adult novels, *Shizuko's Daughter* and *One Bird*, and her daughter–mother narrative in her autobiography, *The Dream of Water,* especially show how permeable the boundaries are between personal memoir and fictional narrative. Certainly, in reading Mori's autobiography and young adult novels, I felt I was involved in a reading experience in which each text illuminated another. Autobiography, as Smith points out, can be viewed as a " 'fictive' process in that the autobiographer constantly tells 'a' story rather than 'the' story, and tells it 'this' way rather than 'that' way" (46). In her essay, "Landscapes," Mori explains that she used details of her own childhood and adolescence in Japan including "the mother's suicide, Yuki's running, the father's and stepmother's concern about 'appearances,' Yuki's desire to leave home as soon as possible" (137).

Mori's daughter–mother narratives both begin in *The Dream of Water* and in *Shizuko's Daughter* with a mother's suicide. In *The Dream of Water*, Mori tells about the events of the days immediately after her mother's suicide: her father's unkindness and his accusing her mother's family of having "bad blood," and her reading of her mother's journal in which her mother had written out her unhappiness—her wish to die (1–9). In *Shizuko's Daughter*, the reader is invited into the dreams, feelings, and thoughts of Shizuko as she prepares to commit suicide before her daughter Yuki comes home. She has done this, she writes in her suicide note to Yuki, because she loves her. Yuki, she writes, is a strong person who will be able to go on after her death (6). Through her narrated monologue, Shizuko breaks the silence and lies that her husband, Hideki, constructs around her death. Hideki had told his daughter to say that her mother had died of cancer. If the truth were known about her suicide, she would be considered "mentally unstable" (75).

In her plural, nonlinear text of *Shizuko's Daughter*, Mori employs an effaced narrator to construct story from the different subject positions of Yuki's family: Shizuko, Hideki, her stepmother, Hanae, and her maternal grandparents, Masa and Takeo. While Mori's story is centered around Yuki as adolescent daughter protagonist, ten of fifteen chapters in her plural text are narrated from Yuki's subject position. While a daughter's narration is still dominant, Mori decenters a daughter's voice in the text in comparison with the way story is told in many young adult novels. The identities of Shizuko and her daughter Yuki are, therefore, constructed from multiple positions in the text.

Family Relationships

Elements of story in *Shizuko's Daughter* parallel the narratives in Mori's autobiography and *One Bird*, respectively. They include: a mother's decision to leave her family because of an unhappy marriage, an unfaithful husband who has a mistress, and an adolescent daughter left with a father who treats her badly. The telling of a story this way, and not that way, is particularly noticeable in comparing the narratives of *Shizuko's Daughter* and *The Dream of Water*. In *Shizuko's Daughter*, set mainly in Kobe and spanning the years from 1969 to 1976, the story is told of Yuki's unhappy and contentious relationships with her father and with her stepmother Hanae, her father's former mistress.

In the chapter in which Hideki's side of the story is heard, it is made clear how relationships between daughters and their mothers were positioned in a patriarchal Japanese culture in which matrilinear connections were subordinated to the patrilinear line of descent. Despite his being head-of-the-family, Hideki is also bound by a strict code of conduct. Divorce from Shizuko's mother would have been "disgraceful and impractical. Yuki would have been left with him since she was his only child" (164). Hideki is shown to be hedged in by a series of disgraces. He feels unable to intervene on Yuki's behalf with her stepmother, since he was afraid that Hanae would carry out her threat of running away if he fails to bring Yuki to task. He would "be expected to step down from his supervisory position. A man who had had two wives and could not control either of them was not fit to supervise other men" (165–66). Described is the distance between father and daughter. Hideki:

> could not remember a time when he had felt a strong bond with Yuki. Even before her mother's death, she was a strange, quiet child to him, though other people said she was cheerful and likeable. Most of the time, he wanted to have nothing to do with her. The thought of Yuki, as far as he could remember, brought him nothing but a useless sense of guilt—guilt for her mother's unhappiness, guilt for her eventual suicide, for which, Hideki knew, Yuki held him responsible (164–65).

A similar pattern of family relationships structures the daughter–mother relationship in *One Bird*. On the opening page, Megumi describes her mother's getting ready to leave her daughter and husband to return to her home village where she will live and work with her elderly father. "If I don't leave your father now," she tells Megumi, "I can't bear to live long enough to see you grow up" (8). Megumi is left with a father who spends most of his time in Hiroshima with his mistress and her father's mother who comes to care for the family. Grandmother Shimizu is described as a brusque, critical woman who finds it difficult to show affection for granddaughter and who, Megumi narrates, had always been critical of her mother (22). Megumi is told by her grandmother and father that she is not to see her mother as long as she lives in her father's home. "Seven years is almost half my life," Megumi comments. "My mother has left me, knowing that we will not see each other again till I am twenty-two" (23).

Yuki and Megumi are almost mirror images. Represented as excelling at school, they are also represented as rebelling against their fathers' authority. At her father's marriage to Hanae, for example, Yuki deliberately drops and shatters the bowl of ceremonial sake. In the chapter "Grievances," Hanae's narrated monologue, is an endless recycling of her resentment and anger against her stepdaughter, Yuki, whose long black hairs she is constantly having to sweep up from the bathroom floor—a sight that "sickened" her (*Shizuko's Daughter* 95). Yuki, she tells Hideki, is secretive and "unruly" (101). In *One Bird*, Mori comments defiantly that she is her mother's daughter and that "no one is going to keep" them "apart for seven years" (220). With the help of Dr. Mitzutani, the bird doctor (who has her own story to tell about being trapped in an unhappy marriage), Megumi defies her father's injunctions that she is not to see her mother and demands that she live with her mother during the summers. At the heart of Mori's daughter–mother narratives lies the emotional bond between daughters and mothers.

A Maternal Text

In *Shizuko's Daughter*, Shizuko is never really absent from the text. She is at the center of Yuki's thoughts and feelings. In extensive flashbacks, Yuki's memories of time shared with her mother are continually folded within the temporal time and events of story. Through the frequency of these scenes, it seems, indeed, that the presence of Shizuko is never absent from narrative but continues to be re-represented as an empowering presence for her daughter. "Yuki could still see her mother running up the stairway in her white dress, the roses a blur of pink and green" (26). Mori presences Shizuko throughout by constantly associating her with treasured objects. After Yuki's stepmother has destroyed her mother's "pottery" that "should be passed down as heirlooms"—from mother to daughter—and has thrown out the clothes that Yuki's mother had made for her, Yuki keeps a sketchbook in which she makes drawings of treasured objects associated with her mother—the clothes, the pottery, a "tea set." She had been afraid that her mother's memory would be erased (114). The sketchbook motif is used to double the representations of daughter and mother. More so than in other novels, despite a mother's death, a daughter is focalized and represented through the vision of a loving mother. In a sketchbook kept by her mother:

There she was, page after page, stacking up the wooden blocks into a tower so that she could smash them down and hear the crash, trying to feed her peaches to her pink teddy bear, sticking her nose against the curved bowl of the fishbowl. . . . She could hear the way her mother used to laugh at her. Yuki, you are simply too much, she would say between gasps of laughter; you take everything so to heart (203).

This passage would seem to be analogous to Margaret Homans's description of "a literal language: a language of presence" that is shared between mothers and daughters that represents the value of the bonds between them.[14]

The final sketch of Yuki with "white daisies in her hands painted with bright yellow centers" has a "background" that "looked like a wash of bright light" (203). The images are described by Yuki so as to recall the literal "crash" of blocks, the feel of a "curved" surface (203). Similarly, the memories of Yuki's mother that she draws into her sketchbook recall with a vividness the colors and texture of the "ruby red sleeves" of her mother's dress, the "row of buttons shining down the front," the "glazed plates, the white goblets" she had used (115).

Mori's maternal text is characterized by the language used to mediate loving connections between a daughter and her mother. For example, imagery and metaphors from art and nature are used to mediate identification and loving connections between daughters and mothers. In *One Bird*, Megumi describes the embroidery stitches on the mandala that her mother is making. The embroidered rose in the center of the cloth and the same delicate color seems to appear "out of nothing but air . . ." (220). As she and her mother hold on to each other, Megumi comments that: "The mandala is like the two of us. I cannot tell which is the flower, which is the air" (121). In *Shizuko's Daughter*, Yuki tells of the day she and her mother tasted maple leaves. Shizuko had said: "'It's like eating air, delicious mountain air,' 'Or maybe a wind,' said Yuki. 'I'm eating a south wind'" (113).

A Legacy of Beauty

Mori, who grew up in a Westernized family and moved to the United States at the age of twenty-one, writes in *The Dream of Water* about being both an insider and outsider in relation to the country where she was born. In her article about Japanese writers writing about the daughter–mother relationship, Yoshida Junko writes that a daughter's rebellion frequently was against the traditional Japanese culture that was "embodied" in her mother.

To reconcile with a mother meant also reconciling with Japanese culture (11). In Mori's daughter–mother narratives, while daughters are represented as rebelling, they defy a gender culture that requires their subordination as females and the subordination of matrilinear bonds. However, they are shown to cherish the gift that their mothers have handed down to them—a sensitivity to the beauty around them—a sense of aesthetics that allow them to appreciate the vibrant hues of flowers and the luminous stitch in a work of embroidery. The mothers of Yuki and Megumi are associated with artistry and nature: embroidery, the planting of seeds, and the growing of flowers. "'Whatever did your mother teach you?' Yuki's stepmother, Hanae, had asked her once. 'She taught me things you wouldn't know about,' Yuki had said. 'She taught me to draw and paint. She taught me the names of flowers and stories to tell from memory. She knew things no one else knew'" (95).

The representation of Hanae, associated with barrenness and the breaking and burning of Shizuki's beautiful things, contrasts starkly with the beauty and creativity associated with the mothers of Yuki and Megumi and also with Mori's own mother. Mori writes in *The Dream of Water* how her mother had always wanted "some form of beauty" and had taken Mori as a child to art exhibits. Her mother had surrounded her family with beautiful things whether garden plants, sketches, or embroidery (98–99). This sense of the aesthetic seeps through the permeable borders of Mori's fiction and autobiography—warming and filling her daughter–mother narratives with a vivid sense of color: the reds, yellows, blues, purples, and pinks of columbines, irises, violas; the "branches of cherries, pansies, and jasmine" and peacock feathers used by Megumi's mother in her flower arrangements for the church (71). Even some of Mori's chapter headings in *Shizuko's Daughter* resonate with colors and flowers: "Irises," "Pink Trumpets," "Yellow Mittens and Early Violets." In an episode in which Yuki collects leaves for decorations in a homemaking class, she uses her first-gathered collection to replace the contents of a jar holding frogs preserved in formaldehyde in the school lab. Yuki, thereby, banishes the memory of her mother's death with its accompanying smells of gas and the crematorium and replaces them with memories of her mother that are associated with the beauty of the blazing red leaves of Japanese maples and with pine leaves smelling of mountain air (115–18).

Love, Losses, and Moving Onward

"Though she and her mother would never be old together, Yuki would still remember her and their time together when she was an old woman"

(*Shizuko's Daughter* 156). What is so deeply etched in Mori's daughter–mother narratives is the depth of everlasting love that daughters and mothers share with each other. One of the most poignant scenes in *One Bird* is Megumi's reunion with her mother. As Megumi enters her mother's room, she sees the photos of her that her mother has positioned so that she could see them from every point in the room. She realizes that her mother had really missed her and had treasured their years together (217). As Megumi holds her mother and rocks her in her arms, she describes how physically alike they are:

> My broad palms and long fingers look just like hers. Our thin wrists have sharp knobs of bone sticking out from the side. All four hands and wrists are the same. My mother's eyes are scrunched up behind her tears. When she is done crying, when she opens her eyes, she will look right into my eyes, which are hers, passed on to me (220).

Through her use of metaphor and imagery, Mori encodes a continuity of connections between daughters and mothers. "My mother and I, Yuki thought, we are moving on. We leave behind nothing but empty spaces— empty spaces turning green as we move away from here" (156). Mori writes of the pain, anger, and loss that daughters experience when their mothers make the deliberate decision to leave their daughters. In *The Dream of Water,* Mori writes: "I am the daughter my mother had meant to set free into the larger world through her losses. . . . My mother wanted me to move on, not to be afraid of uncertainty, not to be bound to old obligations" (275). Heard through Mori's voice are echoes from the voices of Yuki and Megumi. At the closure of *Shizuko's Daughter*, Yuki takes a photograph of a heron which shows up as a white blur on a gray background. Her mother, she thinks, "wanted to be that blurred heron at the center of my mind, almost swallowed up by the light around it but always there" (204). In contrast, the background of Shizuko's last sketch of Yuki is described as awash with bright light (203). Her mother, Mori writes in *The Dream of Water,* had "loved the impressionists, who blinded you with their light" (98).

Masa and Matrilinear Bonds

Mori's story of Shizuko and her daughter is literally framed between the voices of a mother and a grandmother. The novel beginning Shizuko's dream concludes with an "Epilogue" in which Yuki's grandmother, on her seventy-fifth birthday, lies thinking of her dead husband and Shizuko, praying that she can soon be with them both (217). Kept apart from her grandparents when her mother dies, Yuki visits the maternal grandparents she loves when she leaves her father's house and is free to visit as she pleases. It is, for Yuki, a going back home. Mori builds connections between Shizuko, Yuki, and her grandmother through images of flowers, clothes, and colors—doubling images so that they are revisioned in the text. Masa, for example, remembers back to when Shizuko had driven to see her on her birthday bringing her "pink and white peonies and a kimono of silver gray that she had sewn for her. The peonies, larger than her face and so pale, kept nodding, brushing against her cheeks" (217). Shizuko's last drawing of Yuki in her sketchbook is "a portrait of Yuki, with her long hair in two braids, red ribbons tied around each. She was smiling, holding a bunch of daisies to her face" (171). Yuki's grandmother makes a "quilted cover" for her futon stitched from the kimonos her daughters had worn as children; and Yuki makes herself a "quilted vest" from her grandmother's old kimonos; they are literal matrilinear bonds joining a generation of women (208–09).

In *Double Stitch*, a collection of writings by black women about the mother–daughter relationship, Patricia Bell-Scott and Beverly Guy-Sheftall describe how quilting has been an essential element of African American women's culture and of the mother–daughter relationship since it has embodied "the transmission of skills" and "a value system handed down from grandmother to mother to granddaughter. In the context of slavery, this bonding was, for example, an essential part of family and community survival" (2). Chapter ten discusses the African American daughter–mother narratives in young adult novels.

NOTES

1. See Orenstein; Taylor, Gilligan, and Sullivan.
2. See, for example, Joseph and Lewis *Common*.
3. For discussion on the changing images and constructions of the Virgin Mary in the context of Western Civilization, see Kristeva *Stabat* 160–86; Thurer 106–14. For an explanation of how the worship of the Virgin Mary—"marianismo"—is associated with the values of virtue and "proper behavior" and with the covering over of an adolescent girl's sexuality in Latin-American cultures, see Taylor, Gilligan, and Sullivan 61.
4. For explanations and descriptions of how bicultural tensions are experienced by mothers and daughters in the United States, see Taylor, Gilligan, and Sullivan 70–94.
5. See "The Fantasy of the Perfect Mother," Chodorow "Feminism" 79–96.

6. For discussion of how the rhetoric and ideologies of perfect mothering in a dominant culture works on mothers from different ethnic and racial cultures who experience the "harsh social and economic realities" of life in North American culture, see Taylor, Gilligan, and Sullivan 73.

7. For the story of Stacey's mother's childhood, see Yep *Child of the Owl.*

8. For Staples's defense of criticism of her novels, *Shabanu* and *Haveli*, see Staples "Writing" and "A Question."

9. For explanation of the historical position of women in Pakistan, see Hussain 202.

10. For discussions and explanations of the veiling of Muslim women, see Hussain.

11. This opposition is also used to describe how North American girls are socialized into gender appropriate roles. Girls are taken "out of the tree house" of their girlhood and "expected to cultivate social graces" as the divisions between male and female divides girls' worlds, and girls are subjected to dominant images of being female; see Hancock 18–21.

12. Education and economic security, writes Hussain, is seen as women's "only safeguard" from "male dependency." See Hussain 204.

13. This interpretation of Mori's work is in contrast to a review of *Shizuko's Daughter* in which the reviewer stated that the novel is "often sad and sometimes grim . . . a tad grizzly in plot." See Philbrook 132.

14. Homans has criticized androcentric Freudian and Lacanian theories that posit that language is predicated on the absence of the mother. In theories that posit that women (because of their devalued status in a sex–gender system that values the patrilinear) do not have as full an access to the symbolic (language as power and culture) as fathers and sons, the relationship between a mother and daughter is argued to be positioned negatively to language (and culture). Daughters are said to have to free themselves—repress their continued relationship with their mother—in order to identify with the cultural values of patriarchy. See Homans; Kristeva *Desire* 136–37; Kristeva *About* 148–57; Mitchell and Rose.

Ten

African American
Daughter–Mother Narratives

Muh Vy, spoken M'Vy, with the softest sighing to mean, Miss you, Mama;
Love you, Mama.

—Hamilton *Sweet Whispers*

Patricia Collins has referred to the mother–daughter relationship as "one fundamental relationship among Black women" (*Black* 96). Available research studies also suggest that the connections between African American girls and their mothers tend to be strong (Debold, Wilson, and Malave 56).[1] Black feminist writers argue that racial, social, and cultural differences should be taken into account when studying and discussing the relationships between mothers and daughters. They have particularly drawn attention to the inappropriateness of using white psychoanalytic approaches to analyzing the mother–daughter relationship without regard to race and culture and without regard to Black women's own experiences and explanations of the subject.[2] Issues that have been stated as important to the study and analysis of the Black mother–daughter relationship include the double jeopardy of growing up Black and female, social realities of mothering, and the sharing of the collective history of slavery.[3]

Many of the themes and concerns found in writings about Black motherhood and female adolescence are reproduced in African American daughter–mother narratives in young adult novels. This chapter addresses how the above issues continue to inform stories about daughters and mothers in Hamilton's *Plain City* and *Sweet Whispers, Brother Rush*, Johnson's *Toning the Sweep*, Williams-Garcia's *Like Sisters on the Homefront* and Woodson's *I Hadn't Meant to Tell You This* and *The Dear One*.[4] Also iden-

215

tified are some of the themes and ways of telling stories that are characteristic of African American feminist representations of the daughter–mother relationship. The chapter concludes with a discussion of Farmer's feminist daughter–mother narrative in *A Girl Named Disaster,* set in Africa.

PLAIN CITY AND SWEET WHISPERS, BROTHER RUSH

The daughter–mother narratives in Hamilton's novels (and in other African American novels) share characteristics with other writings on African American daughter–mother relationships in that they are produced through discourses of mothering that emphasize the social realities of mothering for Black women. These include the sociohistorical contexts of mothering in which Black women have mothered under oppressive systems of race and gender; the understanding of mothering undertaken within systems of extended family and community networks; and the social structure of the African American family. Hamilton's stories in *Plain City* and *Sweet Whispers, Brother Rush*, for example, speak to the way African American mothers have frequently had to provide both economic and nurturing support for their families. In *Plain City*, twelve-year-old Bulaire, whose mother, Carmen Bluezette Sims, is a blues singer, voices her need for more personal attention from her working mother: "Mom is . . . busy being Mom!" She does not blame her mother, she says, but she still wishes that her mother was with her. "How can she be both places?" (191). In *Sweet Whispers, Brother Rush*, fifteen-year-old Tree, whose mother works as a nurse who lives in other people's homes, also longs for her mother but acknowledges the necessity of her mother working away from home in order to provide for her family: "M'Vy had to be somewhere else so she and Dab and M'Vy, too, could have all the things they had to have" (17). Growing-up for Black daughters, writes Collins, "means developing a better understanding that offering physical care and protection is an act of maternal love" (*The Meaning* 55). Woodson, particularly, draws attention to this aspect of the African American daughter–mother relationship in *The Dear One* discussed later in this chapter.

A practice of mothering in which other-mothers, as opposed to biological mothers, work together to care for children (in the absence or presence of fathers) has also been a central characteristic of African American family and community structures (Collins *Black* 119). Looked after in her mother's absence by her Aunt Digna, Aunt Babe, and Uncle Sam, Buhlaire's relationship with her mother in *Plain City* is placed in the context of such an extended family support system.[5] In *Sweet Whispers, Brother Rush*, however, there are no relatives left alive to help (50). Except for sixty-seven-year-old Miss Pricherd who comes to clean on a Saturday, Tree is left alone to take responsibility for her sick brother, seventeen-year-old Dab who does not have all his mental faculties and who, unknown to Tree, is taking drugs to ease the pain of porphyria. Older than Buhlaire, Tree is representative of teenage-daughter protagonists who are shown to be independent and responsible in their mothers' absences or breakdowns.[6] Vy tells her that she has been a good girl for taking care of her brother so that she could work (184).

Tree, her mother comments, has seen the *"mystery"* that she has been unable to see (129–30). In *Sweet Whispers, Brother Rush*, Tree is able to uncover the mysteries of her family's past history through the mediation of the ghost of Brother Rush, her mother's brother, who had committed suicide rather than suffer any longer from the deadly combination of alcohol and porphyria. Entering through the mirror of light that Brother Rush holds up to her, Tree, who has taken her mother's place in caring for Dab, experiences the shifting double consciousness of both *being* her mother as she whips her young son Dab across the legs until red welts appear and *being* her mother's small daughter who also focalizes her mother: "Tree was there, seeing, but felt herself fading. She was the woman, her gorge rising. She was the girl child, seeing pictures, shapes" (69). This is a powerful example of a daughter switching from her subject position as daughter to identify with the subject position of her mother in order to fully comprehend what it was like for her mother to beat the son who "turned her stomach" (120).

Tree, as an observing child, focalizes her mother clearly as her mother "struck the boy's legs back and forth, whipping, back and forth" and was "forced to see his toes curl as they were struck and struck" (69). Child-daughter Tree is next shown how easy it is to shift subject positions and be the mother who beats her brother. Going into the front bedroom, she tells Dab that she knows where the rope is hidden that is used to tie him to the bedpost. "You want me to tie you to the post? I can do it. I can be the woman, see?" After Tree has threatened her brother with the rope and he reacts with tears, Tree put the rope back and did not touch it again (75). When Dab dies, Tree tells her mother that she hates her. She would put a "kitchen knife" through her mother or herself to "bleed out the hate and the love" (173). Hamilton's story makes visible how "blood and sickness" caused by "a white man's disease," poverty, and a young mother's fear travel down family lines to affect the relationship between a daughter and her mother.

Through the representation of Buhlaire in *Plain City*, Hamilton shows how a daughter is subjected to oppressions of color and social class. Buhlaire is sensitive to the fact that she is regarded as an outsider at school and in the community. She and her family live in one of the Water Houses on the river away from the respectable areas of town. With her "straw-colored" hair in Rasta twists (1) and her "skin with its orangish glow" Buhlaire knows that she stands outside the crowd (15). Buhlaire is also ambivalent about her mother's work as a singer and a fan-dancer. Her mother "had *publicity*" in the form of "embarrassing show bills" (18). Buhlaire had always "thought a fan-dance was a bad kinda dance" (85). Through inviting Buhlaire to see her perform, Bluezy literally invites her daughter to share and take pride in her professional work.

Bluezy's practice of mothering is analogous to that described in a discourse of mothering in which African American mothers are said to both protect their daughters from race and gender oppression while also trying to help their daughters resist by being assertive and by attaining a sense of their own worth (Collins *Black* 124–27). By including Buhlaire's name in one of her songs and by inviting Buhlaire on stage to harmonize with her in a blues rendering of the Beatles' song, "Let It Be," Buhlaire is able to take pride in her own name and voice. More than this, however, Bluezy empowers Buhlaire by inviting her to share in the power and meaning that the blues has had for Black women as a site of expression, self-definition, and resistance for those who are labeled as "other" (Collins *Black* 100).[7] Bluezy partly erodes for Buhlaire the divisions between her private home life and her work in the public sphere except, as Buhlaire later points out to her mother, for the fan-dancing.[8] If she could see her mother dance, Buhlaire explains, she could parry the taunts of other kids. In the face of her mother's silence, Buhlaire has to trust in what her mother has already shown her: *"It's my mom and what she does. It's like singing. Called an art. So there"* (85). Hamilton makes frequent use of interior monologue in which Buhlaire takes up the position of first-person narrator in the text in order to express directly, without mediation, what she feels and experiences. Bluezy and Buhlaire's family are, thus, not always aware of Buhlaire's deepest fears and desires that are shared with a reader.

Bluezy is represented as not being open with her daughter regarding another mystery in Buhlaire's life—the identity of her father. Buhlaire had been told that her father was missing in action in Vietnam. When Buhlaire confronts her mother and family with the knowledge that she has met the father she thought was dead, she is told that her mother had tried to protect Buhlaire from the kind of man that he was and the kind of life he led (160). Described as mentally ill, spending his time on the road, in the Shelter or sometimes in jail, Junior Sims is "rot and pain," Buhlaire's mother tells her (167). Bluezy's mistake, she tells her daughter, was to marry Junior knowing it was a mistake beforehand (159). Hamilton's story makes visible, as do so many of the stories discussed in this chapter, the way racism affects the daughter–mother relationship. Buhlaire believes she was not told the truth about her father because, as tells her family, they were "ashamed" of her vanilla coloring. Her mother may not have wanted her, she tells them. To herself, Buhlaire says: *"Because I was so light, like him and his—"* Bluezy tells her daughter that she was afraid that kids would use Buhlaire's color against her (160). Hamilton's daughter–mother narratives in *Plain City* and *Sweet Whispers, Brother Rush* are both set in socioeconomic contexts in which working mothers bring up their daughters in the absence of fathers. However, in contrast to the oppressed voices of single mothers of daughters in Childress's *Rainbow Jordan,* Sharon Mathis's *Listen for the Fig Tree* and Walter Dean Myers's *Motown and Didi,* the voices of Bluezy Sims and M'Vy in Hamilton's novels remain resilient and strong for their daughters—despite the mistakes they have made in their lives. [9]

In *Sweet Whispers, Brother Rush,* after she had bled the hate and anger against her mother out of her system, Tree is able to appreciate how "strong" her mother could be (214). M'Vy's voice takes on strength at the closure of the novel as she faces up to the truth about her son's illness and her abuse and neglect of Dab. She will "have to live with it" she tells Tree. She tells her daughter that she means to be a "good mother" and that she loves her very much (214). At the closure of *Plain City,* Buhlaire expresses through her inner voice, a desire to be like her mother: *"Maybe when I'm sixteen— will we sing together? Oh, I hope. I'll study real hard. Maybe we'll become Bluezy and Little Blue! Ha! Wonder if she'll dance the fans for me, ever . . ."* (191). The positive representation of Bluezy is reinforced by the principal of Buhlaire's school who is a friend to Bluezy's daughter. Her mother is "smart" and "independent" he tells Buhlaire. "Bluezy Sims does what she does, very well" (24).

One of the strongest characteristics of Hamilton's daughter–mother narratives in *Plain City* and *Sweet Whispers, Brother Rush* is the strong love that is described between teen daughters and mothers despite the anger and divisions that come between them. Buhlaire is described as enjoying the memory of snuggling up to her mother enjoying their intimacy and private daughter–mother talk (86). Hamilton employs language in both novels that emphasizes the literal physical bond between daughter and mother. When Buhlaire is on stage with her mother: "Buhlaire and Bluezy sang together, with Buhlaire's voice way on top of her mom's, and as tight as a silken coat covering Bluezy . . ." (80). In the following passage from *Sweet Whispers, Brother Rush*, Hamilton uses language in a similar way to show the love and harmony between Tree and her mother as they play out together the rhythmic motions of an old nursery game. M'Vy "had Tree's hands in hers. She patted them; took the wrists and patty-caked Tree's hands. Not saying any words, Vy went through the motions of the rhyme of infants."

> Tree giggled. 'Makin me a baby!'
> They sat there, hand in hand (91).

Hamilton's use of language in these passages would seem to be analogous to descriptions by feminist theorists of shared language experiences—dialogic moments—between mothers and daughters. The passage from *Sweet Whispers, Brother Rush* is a particularly good example of a rhythmic and poetic preverbal language shared between mother and child. This "literal language" is an attribute of a maternal text.[10] The emphases placed on the way mothers can be strong for their daughters and on the close, loving relationships between adolescent girls and their mothers in Hamilton's novels are analogous to the new feminist discourses on daughter–mother relationships in adolescence and to Black feminist writings.

LIKE SISTERS ON THE HOMEFRONT

In Williams-Garcia's *Like Sisters on the Homefront*, Ruth Bell is represented as a no-nonsense, single, hard-working, loving mother bringing up her daughter, Gayle, and her elder son, Junie, in New York. When she finds out that fourteen-year-old Gayle, already the mother of seven-month-old José (whose father is married) is pregnant for the second time, she marches her daughter straight down to the abortion clinic. Ruth Bell makes it clear to Gayle and the clinic staff that no arguments can be made that will persuade her daughter to have the baby. When Gayle emerges from the clinic: "Mama wouldn't give Gayle room to vent her feelings about her ordeal and Gayle wasn't about to volunteer the details of her pains" (9). Using the same no-nonsense approach, Ruth Bell strips Gayle's room, packs up her things, and despite Gayle's protests, sends her daughter "down Souf" to stay with her brother Luther, her sister-in-law (Miss Auntie) and Constance—otherwise known as "Cookie."

By sending her daughter to stay with her brother, Luther Gates and his family, Ruth Bell disconnects Gayle from the environment and relationships that have contributed to Gayle's becoming a Black teenage mother. She takes steps to protect her daughter by connecting her to relationships and an environment that will provide Gayle with an alternative value system to that which her daughter has internalized from the streets of New York. Once at her Uncle Luther's, Gayle finds herself under the supervision of Miss Auntie who, despite her "sweetie pies" talk, is tough on spelling out the values and expectations that she expects Gayle to abide by in her home. Describing herself as the "house slave," Gayle learns to fit in with Uncle Luther's family's disciplined lifestyle that is based on the ethics of hard work and responsibility and on the value of community.

When Gayle asks who will care for her son while she has some fun, her aunt's reply is that José is Gayle's "little bundle of fun" and Gayle will take José with her wherever she goes (38). Emphasis is placed in William-Garcia's text on the educating of a teen mother so that she understands that sexual maturity involves responsibility to oneself, to one's child and to one's family. Reproduced in Williams-Garcia's story and in Woodson's *The Dear One* are approaches to teenage pregnancy found in feminist discourses. Avoiding blame and recriminations, these discourses emphasize the empowerment of teen mothers through care and nurturance and through relationships with other women who value and understand them (Taylor, Gilligan, and Sullivan 200–201).

Miss Auntie and Gayle's cousin, Cookie, present Gayle with a model of how a daughter–mother relationship can be other than the conflict-ridden relationship Gayle shares with Ruth Bell. Gayle sees Cookie giggling with her mother as well as asking her for advice. She watches Cookie and Miss Auntie walking together "bumping hips" and play-acting as they walk— taking "their daughter–mother talk with them" (127). Miss Auntie is instrumental in helping Gayle to understand her mother's life so that Gayle can better understand her mother. Ruthie, she tells Gayle, despite two "gospel scholarships," quarreled with her brother, Luther, and left home to marry Gayle's father who tried, unsuccessfully, to promote her career with a record company before he died. At the closure of the novel, Gayle's mother comes back home (with Gayle's brother) for Great's funeral to stay—a circling back home for Ruthie. Miss Auntie had told a disbelieving Gayle that her mother belonged in the family home, that she and Luther miss Ruth Bell. She would bring Ruth Bell "home piece by piece" (120). Written from a feminist perspective, Williams-Garcia's daughter–mother narrative takes the form of a circular rather than a linear form. There is an emphasis on connections and sisterhood in women's and girls' lives. Miss Auntie and Ruth Bell have been "like sisters all our lives." Williams-Garcia writes, too, of continuity and connections between daughters and mothers by showing how Gayle and her mother are related to the collective history of the Gates family.

At the center of Williams-Garcia's daughter–mother narrative is the character of Great—Gayle's great grandmother—and her special relationship with Gayle. As with many other grandmother–granddaughter narratives, the bonding between Great and Gayle is shown to empower an adolescent daughter. Streetwise Gayle finds that she has met her match and more so when she hears the outrageous remarks of Great. She knows about Gayle, Great tells her when they first meet. "You the one like to taste the breeze high up 'cross the crease your backside" (42). One of the delights of Williams-Garcia's text is the sassy humor of Gayle and her open interchanges with Great to whom Gayle goes when she wants comfort or advice. It is through the agency of Great that Gayle regains her self-esteem. She is a "devil" Great tells her but when she has laid aside her "deviling" she will be "stronger than those who lived by the rule all their lives" (92). Along with their bantering talk, Gayle receives the wisdom that Great wishes to hand down to her with the family peach recipe that she asks Gayle to make for her: "Better get this wisdom while I got it to give. It's handed down like the recipe" (50).

Williams-Garcia makes the family collective history of slavery integral to the daughter–mother narrative. Great not only shares her personal history with Gayle but hands down to Gayle "The Telling" when she dies—a history of Gayle's family in the form of an oral slave narrative. By entrusting Gayle with the valuable family history that belongs as much to the matrilineal line of the family as well as to the patrilineal line of male preachers in the family, Gayle's voice is empowered and she gains standing in her mother's family. She was so entrusted, Miss Auntie tells her, because Gayle, like Great, has "good sense" (158). In Great's "Telling," Gayle with her mother and son are made integral to the family history: "Ruth Bell . . . baby girl . . . Gayle Ann . . . blessed . . . with Emanuel . . ." (154). Gayle's baby thus is formally given the name that is decided on by Gayle's mother and family rather than the name, José, which was chosen for him by Gayle because it was the name of his father. The "Telling" also works to give meaning to objects that are a part of the family's collective history—family treasures to which Gayle had previously felt no connection. Gayle now sees that the design on the quilt that Great designed and that her mother helped stitch, which she had called "this old thing," represents the family's history. Now she knows the significance of the bill of sale and of the cowrie shell that she had found in Great's wardrobe (86–87). Williams-Garcia, thus, incorporates into her daughter–mother narrative the importance of quilts in keeping alive, through work and art, the history of women's experiences during slavery and the way that this tradition was passed down from mothers to daughters (Bell-Scott, Guy-Sheftall 1–3).

The "Telling" records the story of Gayle's family from slavery to freedom and begins with the enslavement of Mkebe and her sister who were torn from their homeland as they were gathering cowrie shells by the shore and then torn from each other when they were sold as slaves. "It came from Mbeke, torn from her sister, Who told her child Mahalia. . . ." Great's oral telling bears analogy to a female slave narrative since its origins lie in the "Cotton Song" (the "Calling Up Song") sung by women as they picked cotton and remembered their lost relatives (152–53). In contrast to male slave narratives, female-centered narratives gave voice to women's slave work and especially to their abuse.[11] The "Telling" records how seven of Mkebe's children were sold away from their mother leaving her with only her baby daughter, Mahalia (152–53).

The daughter–mother narrative in *Like Sisters on the Homefront* is thus linked to those female slave narratives that tell how children, including daughters, were forcibly taken from their mothers during slavery.[12] Williams-Garcia's novel can also be linked to other daughter–mother fictional slave narratives in young adult novels. Mary Lyons's *Letters from a Slave Girl*, for example, is a fictionalized version of the female slave narrative, *Incidents in the Life of a Slave Girl* by Harriet Jacobs. In *Tancy*, Belinda Hurmence presents a daughter–mother slave narrative in which she describes a Black mulatto slave girl's emancipation from the white woman, Miss Puddin, who has been her surrogate mother.[13] *Tancy*'s search for her Black mother, from whom she was separated as a baby, is a female coming-of-age story set in the context of Emancipation—a word that has multiple meanings in Hurmence's text.[14] In *Toning the Sweep*, Johnson tells a story in which racism causes divisions between a mother and daughter and shows how the personal history of mothers and daughters is integral to the collective history of African Americans.

TONING THE SWEEP:
A GRANDMOTHER DAUGHTER–MOTHER NARRATIVE

Johnson's story begins with fourteen-year-old Emily narrating how her grandmother Ola has always loved the color yellow. Emily has come with her mother, Diane, from Cleveland, Ohio, to Little Rock, California, to help her grandmother pack up and leave the desert she loves so much—because Ola has cancer. During the few days of packing and visiting with friends, the interrelationships between daughters and mothers are constructed by Johnson—not only from Emily's voice and focalization—but also from the voices and focalization of Diane and Ola who speak as narrating subjects in separate chapters introduced by Emily: "Mama talks . . . ," and "Ola Remembers." The camera, used by Emily to videorecord Ola and her grandmother's friends (a memento for Ola of her life in the desert) also serves as an additional viewpoint and narrating agent in the text—a visual "I." Johnson makes visible in *Toning the Sweep* how family history is constructed—from photographs and videorecordings—as well as through the oral narratives of Ola, Diane, and Ola's friends. Johnson's daughter–mother narrative is characterized by its shifting viewpoints that construct multiple positions from which to see the different relationships between mothers and daughters. Ola's relationship with Emily, and Emily's with Ola, for example, are viewed from all three subject positions of Ola, Emily, and Diane.

Emily and Ola

Ola's close relationship with Emily is an example of the bond between grandmothers and granddaughters found in daughter–mother narratives across different racial and ethnic contexts. The first image of Ola in the text is one from Emily's memory in which Ola is described as wearing a yellow and orange scarf standing by her yellow house in the desert—the kind of woman, Emily thinks, who would know about plants (9). Emily later sees a mirror image of the one she has stored in her memory in a painting of Ola executed by her grandmother's artist friend, Roger—an example of the emphasis on visual imagery in Johnson's text. Ola in her "yellow-flowered" dress and bare feet and laughing is the woman Emily remembers when she was a small child (74). Her grandmother's yellow scarf is used throughout Johnson's text to link Emily to her grandmother. For example, Emily and Ola spend an afternoon playing with Ola's collection of hats and scarves and Emily fixes her grandmother's hair in a ponytail with a yellow scarf just as she had done as a child (45–46).

Johnson constructs differing perceptions of mothers and daughters through visual imagery and a constant shifting of the visual "eye" in the text. The camera enables Emily to see her grandmother's glowing beauty for the first time through the filtering lens of the camera that captures the "blue" light that surrounds her (32). Through the constant textual movement of viewpoint in Johnson's text, Emily's focalization and narrative are decentered as she sees her grandmother from the different perspective of others. She learns from her friend David, as she tapes him, that her grandmother, who has a reputation for her dangerously fast driving, narrowly missed running him over when he was a small boy (27). Emily who has always defended her grandmother in the arguments between Ola and her mother now understands that her mother was not always wrong and her grandmother right (28–29).

The loving relationship between Emily and Ola is heard from Ola's side of story in her chapter. She tells how Emily had followed her everywhere once her mother had brought her to the desert (89). Ola's focalization provides for a reader another perspective of Emily as Ola tells how sad and worried her granddaughter appears during the days they prepare to leave for Ohio (89). The relationship between Emily and her grandmother is also focalized from the subject position of Emily's mother. Diane reinforces the views that Emily and Ola have of their closer relationship. She tells about Emily's crying fits when it was time to leave Ola and the desert (50–53). Diane compares Emily's closeness with her grandmother to her own relationship with Ola:

> I sit outside the kitchen now, watching my daughter and her grandmama cook beans and rice for dinner. They move together and are easy with each other in close quarters. I know that after I was fourteen I was never easy with Ola. She was easy with me, though, when she let me go looking for something that I have long since forgotten (53).

Ola and Diane

On the day that she and her mother travel to the desert, Emily recounts Diane's story about the time Ola had driven from Alabama with Diane, then fourteen years old, to the desert in California. She remembers, Diane tells Emily, that her large feet hung out of the window of the Buick and that she listened to the Supremes (3–4). In the story of Diane's relationship with Ola, Johnson emphasizes the way racism has affected the relationship between mothers and daughters. By driving away from Alabama, Ola had taken her daughter away from the home and relatives she had loved and was ripped from the pain of her father's death (98). He had been shot in 1964 as he stood by the side of the new Buick convertible on which the words "UPPITY NIGGER" were painted (35). She had not forgiven Ola, Diane tells Emily, for taking her away (98).

From her first-person subject position in her chapter of the text, Diane tells of the form her anger took as she left Ola and the desert at the age of seventeen to go to San Francisco. She narrates how Ola had followed the Greyhound bus for five miles in case she changed her mind. Diane had traveled back and forth across the country for ten years only going back home twice although Ola had continued sending her essentials such as money and food. Diane speaks of Emily's liking for the desert that Diane could not wait to get away from (52–53). Johnson uses the different ways the three female voices relate to the desert setting to reveal differences and similarities between Ola, Diane, and Emily.

Ola's side of her relationship with Diane is recounted to Emily. She tells Emily of her happiness with her husband and daughter in Alabama until the husband she had loved was shot. She had run away from the place she had thought was safe, away to the desert. Diane had never forgiven her, she thinks (32–33). Diane, she tells Emily, "rages silently and bleeds inside" (35). In the chapter in which Ola is narrating agent, emphasis is placed, however, on the continuing and loving connections, rather than differences, that are maintained between herself and Diane. Ola tells how Diane and Emily came to stay with her in the summers for two months after Emily was two years old (89). Ola narrates that: "As she got older, Emmie looked more and more like her mother, and sometimes I called her Diane" (89). Emily's likeness to her mother is seen from more than one perspective.

Emily and Diane

Visual imagery is used to build connections between Emily and her mother as Miss Sally, at the store, tells Emily that she is so like her mother, it is "almost a mirage." Through Miss Sally's eyes, Emily sees the difference between Ola and Diane when they moved to Little Rock. Her mother had looked tired out while Ola seemed "refreshed" (78). It is while taping Miss Sally that Emily finds out that it was her mother who had found her murdered father. "Now I know where Mama's anger comes from," Emily narrates (79). A daughter's understanding of her mother brings them closer. As they get ready to tone the sweep that will put her grandfather's soul at rest, Emily narrates:

> I look into her eyes, and they are mine. I think of the ancestors and feel for my mother for the first time. Really the first time. I understand her loss. I feel what it must have been like finding your father dead near a field of kudzu, hot and steamy. I feel for her 'cause she carries the pain and won't forgive her mother for ripping her away from it (98).

Emily, described by her mother as looking like her grandmother in her hat and scarf, joins her mother in holding the hammer that they strike against the metal of the water tower until: "The wind stops and it's just Mama and I, toning the sweep" (99).

The connections and continuities that are built between the generations in *Toning the Sweep* speak to the lineage of grandmothers, mothers and daughters that is celebrated in the poetry, autobiographical writings, and essays of African American women.[15] The narrative strategies used by Johnson in *Toning the Sweep* allow daughters and mothers to speak within the same space. Johnson's plural text with multiple viewpoints is characteristic of feminist texts. As in Williams-Garcia's novel, there is an emphasis on feminist themes of connections and defining self in relationship with others as a means of empowerment—a form of "connected knowing." [16] Johnson writes about Ola's membership in a sistership of aunts—women friends who form a community in the desert and others of the desert community who come to the farewell picnic. These themes correspond to Collins's assertion in *Black Feminist Thought* that: "the conceptualization of self that is part of Black women's self-definitions is distinctive. Self is not defined as the increased autonomy gained by separating self from others. Instead self is found in the context of family and community . . ." (105).

AFENI (*THE DEAR ONE*) AND FEMALE BONDS

Joanne M. Braxton, in her analyses of Black women's autobiographies, writes that in these texts Black women "speak of a perilously intensified adolescence, accompanied by perception of gender as well as racial difference" (205). Woodson particularly addresses how the daughter–mother relationship is produced through race, class, and gender. In *The Dear One*, the double jeopardy of growing up female and Black is heard through the voice of twelve-year-old Afeni: "There's always going to be someone deciding what I can and can't do. If it's not because I am a kid, it'll be because I'm a woman. If it's not because I'm a woman, it'll be because I'm black." Her mother tells her with "something like fear" in her voice to never "feel like you don't have power, Feni" (Woodson 31). Afeni's voice is strengthened by her mother and her friends in a female coming-of-age story in which value is placed on an ethics of care and the defining of self in relationship with others.

The relationship between Afeni (The Dear One) and her mother, an attorney, is set in the context of a story in which fifteen-year-old Rebecca, a teen mother like her mother and grandmother before her, stays with Afeni and her mother until her baby is born. In *The Dear One*, Woodson gives voice to the concept of family and community that has characterized African American approaches to mothering and childcare. Despite Afeni's initial resentment, Rebecca and her baby become part of a loving circle. As Afeni stares at her teenage friend's newly born baby, she narrates:

> In that moment I knew that she, like me and Mama and Rebecca and Marion and Clair and Bernadette and especially my grandmother, was as another part of a long line of dear ones. No one knew yet if she'd be light or dark, gap toothed or dimpled; if her hair would be kinky, curly, or straight; no one knew if she'd find her roots back to Harlem or settle in Seton . . . ; but we were certain of one thing—through the toughest, the saddest, the hardest, and the best of times, all of us would be around somewhere, pulling for her and pulling her through (145).

The grandmother–granddaughter bond is another important element of the daughter–mother narrative. Afeni refers constantly to her loving relationship with her grandmother and to her grief when her grandmother was killed. From her grandmother, Afeni learns that women are strong and are "survivors" (35). Woodson, as do Hamilton, Johnson, and Williams-Garcia, avoids controlling representations of African American women and mothers.[17] There are many kinds of women in the world, Afeni's grandmother tells Afeni, some of whom are weak and some of whom are strong. She tells Afeni that her mother is a "strong" woman who sometimes makes "mistakes" (36). Afeni's mother, a recovering alcoholic, admits her mistakes to her daughter. In *The Dear One*, Woodson writes of an honest and open relationship between Afeni and her mother in which they express their anger and their love to one another.

There is a wonderful passage in which Afeni tests her mother's openness about sex and sexuality: "Would you still love me if I grew up to be gay?" Receiving her mother's affirmative answer, Afeni goes on to ask whether her mother would still love her if she "came home pregnant like Rebecca?" After her mother has delivered a little homily about birth control, Afeni persists: "What if I came home with a baby *and* a girlfriend?" (41). It is through her mother's openness that Afeni has learnt what she must know in order not to grow up "narrow-minded" (123). Afeni's mother is represented as passing on to her a connected knowing that will empower her daughter. This openness between mothers and daughters is noted in conversations with some of the adolescent daughters reported in *Between Voice and Silence*. Black mothers feel obligated to teach their daughters "the realities about racial discrimination and limited resources" (Taylor, Gilligan, and Sullivan 79).

Woodson also exposes the stratifications of social class that divide Black women. Much of the conflict between Afeni, living in a small, wealthy Black suburb in Pennsylvania, and Rebecca from Harlem is centered around socioeconomic difference. This includes the differences between Afeni's mother and Rebecca's mother, Clair—a mother bringing up six children on her own and who has recently lost her teaching position. When Rebecca tells Afeni that her mother is "cold" and does not give Afeni all her attention, she opens up for Afeni the fact that her mother is a career woman and a mother (80). Afeni's mother responds to Afeni's subsequent accusation that she does not "have time for a daughter" by telling her that her love is in "every meal" she eats, "every piece of clothing" she wears and "every clean sheet" she sleeps on (84). Through Afeni's acceptance and growing understanding what it is like to grow up Black and female in Harlem, and through Rebecca's acceptance of the lesbian relationship between Marion and Bernadette, Woodson constructs connections across differences between friends as well as between a daughter and her mother.

I HADN'T MEANT TO TELL YOU THIS: MARIE AND LENA

Through the different stories she tells about daughters and mothers in *The Dear One* and in *I Hadn't Meant to Tell You This*, Woodson makes visible the different ways that the daughter–mother relationship are experienced. There are different emphases and nuances in *I Hadn't Meant to Tell You This*, a much bleaker story, in which Woodson writes about the absence of mothers from girls' lives. Twelve-year-old Marie narrates how she watched her mother, when she was ten years old, walk away without looking back or waving good-bye (23–24). Her mother, she narrates, was constantly sobbing and her medicine cupboard was filled with antidepressants. Her father tells Marie that her mother could only find happiness by leaving. She needed "air" (46–47). For two years, all that Marie has received from her mother are postcards sent from all over the world (no return address) on which she sketches herself "having meals in outdoor cafes, sitting alone by streams, buying oranges from sidewalk vendors" (24). Marie's mother also writes free verse on her postcards—short verses—which would seem to offer explanations why she has chosen to travel away from her family and roots: "If I dare to blink I'll miss the moment in my life" and "I want to catch life, hold on, swing with it" (71).

Through this narrative strategy of telling story, Woodson grants a mother subjectivity and empowerment through telling story in a way that does not allow her daughter or husband to completely speak for her—despite her absence. Her usual signature on the postcards—"Love, Me"—can be read, as Marie's friend Lena says, as if Marie's mother was asking for Marie's love (72). However, it can also be read as the signature of a Black woman—"Me"—who is free from a subjectivity constructed for her by others. Marie's mother, Diane, defines and expresses her subjectivity through her creative use of language and through the representation of self in her sketches. Diane had wanted to be an artist, Marie's father tells his daughter (24). Remembering Alice Walker's well-known question: "What did it mean for a Black woman to be an artist in our grandmother's time?" is it a coincidence that Woodson chooses to represent a Black mother's search for self-definition through art and poetry? (*In Search* 198). Woodson writes a story in which a Black mother has the economic freedom to leave her family and travel in contrast to fictional journeys of Black women that have typically been geographically bound because of ties to children and community (Collins *Black* 105).

> Marie tells Lena that she will search for her mother.
> My first stop will be Paris. I'll drink wine and eat bread and cheese at a sidewalk cafe. I'll look at the faces of the black women who pass, and search for my mother. When I find her, I'll send for my father, and even though it's years and years and years away we'll be a family again (24).

Woodson especially confronts racism, sexism, and class in *I Hadn't Meant to Tell You This* through the story of Lena that is unfolded within Marie's narrative. Stigmatized by the label "white trash" by the girls in the Black community of Chauncey, Ohio, Lena, who lives with her father and younger sister, is subjected to sexual abuse by her father. Her mother, Lena tells Marie, had died from breast cancer. She must have had to grit her teeth, Lena surmises, since they had had no money for doctors (75). Woodson cuts across differences of race and social class through the friendship of Marie and Lena whose hands and hearts are intertwined through the "secrets" that they share. They can be friends, Lena explains, because of the stories about their mothers. "There's stuff we can talk about. . . . About what it's like. White, black—it shouldn't make no difference. We all just people here" (59).

Marie is exposed to how awful the reality of Lena's life is without the protection of her mother. Lena looks "raggedy" because she is afraid to look nice (52–53). Lena makes clear that she submits to her father in order that she and her sister may stay together as a family. Marie, meanwhile, is living with her father who is afraid to barely touch her cheek and who hides in the kitchen when the mother of one of Marie's friends comes to show her how to cope with her period (56). From two sides of story, black and white, Woodson presents the physical and emotional pain of women who are also mothers. From two sides of story, it is shown how the absence of these mothers impact the gendered relationships within a family. Through the stories of daughters, Marie and Lena, a mother's absence is shown to matter. In this African American daughter–mother narrative, there is a lack of empowerment that results from the connected knowing that is passed on to daughters from mothers. Woodson contests the controlling image that all Black daughters grow up within networks of extended families and communities.[18] Woodson refuses to compromise by making things right in this novel. Marie understands why her mother had to leave but that does not make her hurt any less; she just has to be strong enough to go on with her life. Lena's disappearance at closure of the novel when she runs from her father to protect her sister (also at risk) is a gap—an absence—in Marie's life that will perhaps, be covered over: "in three weeks it could be like Lena never was" (116).

THE DAUGHTER–MOTHER RELATIONSHIP
AND CROSS-CULTURAL SCHOLARSHIP

As Lena suggests, there is stuff that can be talked about across differences. As a white woman, I have listened to the voices of daughters and mothers in stories set in different racial and cultural contexts and have found that, cross-culturally, there are similar ways of thinking and talking about this fundamental relationship. Described in Johnson's *Toning the Sweep,* for example, are personal dynamics of the daughter–mother relationship that bears resonance with some of the descriptions used in white daughter–mother relationships. These include the differences between an adult daughter and her mother, the closer relationship between a granddaughter and her grandmother, the dialogues of love and anger, the emotional bonds between daughters and mothers, and the coming-to-terms with the daughter–mother relationship. Heard in Woodson's *I Hadn't Meant to Tell You This* is a daughter voicing her longing for her mother and her feelings of anguish now that her mother is physically absent from her—a voice that reverberates through many daughter–mother narratives no matter differences of race,

ethnicity, and place. However, personal dynamics of the relationship are
shown to be shaped by specific racial, ethnic, and sociohistorical contexts.
The African American fictional daughter–mother narratives discussed in this
chapter contribute to a Black feminist discourse on daughter–mother relationships by addressing issues of race and gender. Identified in these novels are other themes and narrative strategies characteristic of feminist representations of the daughter–mother relationship: the value placed on
connections and relationships; the empowerment of daughter's voices attained through the strong and valued voices of mothers; the connected
knowing that is handed down from mother to daughter.

bell hooks writes of a "cross-ethnic feminist scholarship" (*Talking* 48).
There *are* points of connection between white and black feminist approaches to the daughter–mother relationship. Both emphasize the developing of self in relationship with others, the connections and continuity
between mothers and daughters and the need to contest gender power relationships and sexism. While white feminist scholars have often placed
more emphasis on psychoanalytical frameworks, black feminists have used
social constructivist approaches examining the daughter–mother relationship in the context of race, class, and gender. The new discourse on daughter–mother relationships in adolescence is also beginning to make connections across differences as they make visible the power relationships that
daughters are subjected to in different cultural contexts. The African American concept of other-mothers is being used by Debold, Wilson, and Malave
who visualize a "revolution of mothers" who will "share the power and responsibility of mothering by becoming other-mothers" (246).

As mentioned in chapter nine, young people also have the opportunity
to make connections across differences through the increased availability
of stories set in different racial and ethnic contexts that work to present a
more plural representation of the daughter–mother relationship. Nancy
Farmer's daughter–mother narrative, set in Mozambique and Zimbabwe,
has many of the characteristics that have been used to identify feminist
coming-of-age novels and feminist representations of the daughter–mother
relationship.

TRAVELLING WITH A MOTHER'S SPIRIT:
A GIRL NAMED DISASTER

Farmer tells the story of Nhamo, a Shona girl, who sets out alone to travel
by boat from Mozambique to Zimbabwe on a quest to find her father. Dur-

ing her long journey, she encounters dangerous river hippotomi, near starvation, a damaged boat, and other tests that challenge her ingenuity and endurance. Farmer writes this female *Bildungsroman* from a feminist perspective. What makes Nhamo's journey so different from survival stories that are modeled on the male *Bildungsroman* is that Nhamo takes with her the spirit of her mother and the empowering legacies handed down to her by her grandmother. While Nhamo's journey is set in the context of a patrilineal culture, Farmer writes an African girl's coming-of-age story in which matrilinear bonds are celebrated.

Nhamo has lived with her grandmother, Ambuya, and other members of her mother's family in a Mozambique village since her mother, Runako, was killed by a leopard when Nhamo was three years old. Her father, Proud Jongwe, had come from a wealthy African family but was an alcoholic. He had murdered a man in a neighboring village and had run away leaving his wife and child. Unpopular, because in normal circumstances she would have been claimed by her father's family, Nhamo is treated almost as a slave by her mother's sister, Aunt Chico, and other family members. As Nhamo learns, a girl's value in her community is calculated by her bride-price that is usually arranged by a young woman's father's family. Her *roora* would pay for her father's son's wives and so insure that a father would become an ancestor (24). As the daughter of a father who was a murderer and who had abandoned her, Nhamo knows that she is worthless as an object of exchange (58).

Ambuya

On another continent in a different cultural context, Farmer's story also gives voice to the special bond between a grandmother and granddaughter. Nhamo's existence is made tolerable by the affection and favor shown to her by her grandmother who addresses Nhamo as her "Little Pumpkin" and "My beloved child." Farmer's representation of Ambuya can be read in context of the culture of the Shona people who, writes Farmer, treat the elderly with great respect for the power they accrue from being close to the spirit world (303). [19] Farmer uses Ambuya's voice to encode a feminist consciousness in her text. In a community in which men make the decisions, Ambuya possesses the power and independence to enter the men's public meeting place—the "dare." Ambuya is said to maintain "far more control of her wealth and affairs than any woman Nhamo knew" (55). She also claims her right to drink and smoke a pipe. The Portuguese trader's wife tells Nhamo that she was "a remarkable woman, intelligent and independent" who had, moreover, seen that Nhamo's mother had been educated (70).

It is through the agency, courage, and quick-wittedness of her grandmother that Nhamo is able to escape being trapped in a marriage that would have been no more than enslavement. Ambuya challenges the political and religious power of the *muraki*. She speaks out against sexist practices when the *muraki* decrees that Nhamo must marry the old man, Zororo Mtoko, brother to the man Nhamo's father had murdered in order to appease the *ngozi*—the avenging spirit of the murdered man. Through Ambuya, Farmer gives voice in her story to the way women are accomplices to patriarchal practices through their silence, and to the way women have been labeled as sick or even mad when they speak out. Despite being held by other anxious women, who attempt to hush her words and calm her as if she were "an angry infant," Ambuya shouts that there is nothing wrong with her: "We live in modern times, and girls don't have to be given away as slaves" (63). Ambuya's powers are, however, limited in the public power politics that govern the region. In private, she strips the mystery from witchcraft for Nhamo and exposes the fakery and lies that were employed by dishonest *ngangas* (healers). Ambuyo enables her granddaughter's escape by providing through her memory a visual map of the journey Nhamo is to undertake and a warning about some of the obstacles that Nhamo will encounter (78–79).

Ambuya empowers her granddaughter by passing on to her a courageous spirit and nuggets of gold that will enable Nhamo to become really free in that she will be economically independent of her father's family at the end of her journey. Equally significant, Ambuya passes on the gift of storytelling. This latter gift gives Nhamo a form of connected knowing akin to the "Telling" in Williams-Garcia's *Like Sisters on the Homefront*. Ambuya has been the person in the village who has transmitted, through story, the culture and traditions of her people. Nhamo has already learned the art of storytelling from her grandmother. Even before her journey begins, she tells her cousin that she had listened to her grandmother's stories enough times in order to tell them. They help to make things better, she tells Masvita (30).

Through Farmer's integration of Ambuya's tales and Nhamo's songs, the oral narrative tradition becomes part of Nhamo's story. It serves as a lifeline to keep her grounded in the memories of her people and to transport her from her loneliness during the months of solitude: "It had been all right when she was telling the story. Somehow, she was transported away. Mother had been there; even the *njuzu girls* [water spirits] *had listened from their watery houses*" (115). Nhamo creates her own songs using the words that boys used in boasting about their feats—boasts that girls were not supposed to use. *"I am she who lifts mountains / When she goes to hunt . . ."* (101). Crossing the lake, she sings, *"I am Nhamo, a mighty woman / For whom crossing a measly river was not enough!"* (142). Nhamo thus appropriates the language reserved for males to celebrate self and constructs herself through song into what, in North American literary tradition, is called a tall-tale heroine.

Mother

Abuyo tells Nhamo that her mother's spirit will be "watching over" her. Her mother will "warn her of any danger" (86). In her feminist approach to the representation of the daughter–mother relationship, Farmer builds connections and continuity between Nhamo and the spirit of her mother, Runako, making this emotional bond central to her life. Before Nhamo sets out on her journey she fetches "Mother"—represented by a beautiful woman with braids and wearing a flowered dress on the cover of a magazine. Mother is engaged in cutting a slice of white bread with yellow margarine for her small daughter, and Nhamo, when possible, had visited Mother where she had hidden her and had talked and had tea with her.

Throughout her journey (until baboons destroy her picture), Nhamo communicates with her mother whose voice alternately comforts her, warns her, and gives her advice. When Nhamo lingers too long on an island thus delaying working on her leaky boat, her mother tells her that she has *"to stop following baboons around and work on the boat"* and that she belongs *"with people"* (194). Embedded within the belief system of the Shona is the understanding that personal family spirits have the power to contact family members to give advice or warnings (303). Therefore, Nhamo's conversations with her mother occur as naturally as Nhamo's conversations with the spirit of Crocodile Guts and other spirits that help her on her way. They blend in as natural elements of Nhamo's world—a world that is perceived through Shona eyes.

Matrilinear Bonds

Farmer continues to make a mother figure and the daughter–mother relationship central to Nhamo's life through the character of Dr. Everchoice Masuko, a woman scientist who works at a Zimbabwe experimental tsetse fly station where, wracked by fever, starving, and exhausted after fighting off a pack of dogs, Nhamo had collapsed. Confusing Dr. Masuko with the picture she had had of "Mother," she is told that she had "*imprinted*" on the woman scientist because she was the first "thing" she saw after regaining consciousness—it was as if she were reborn (291). Dr. Masuko is another feminist presence and voice in the text. She tells Nhamo that she should open a bank account with her grandmother's nuggets because once her great-grandfather—the nganga—who favors her dies, Nhamo's future at her father's family home will be uncertain. Nhamo, she tells her, is "far too intelligent to be turned into a family drudge or forced into a bad marriage. Women are never free until they can control their own money" (290). Nhamo will spend her summers at the station with Dr. Everchoice Masuku and her colleagues. Farmer's feminist *Bildungsroman* concludes as Nhamo communicates with the spirits of her grandmother and mother. "*You've done well, Little Pumpkin*," said Grandmother. "*A bank account at your age!*" (292). In return to her unspoken question of whether their spirits will return, her mother replies that: "*The paths of the body are long, but the paths of the spirit are short*" (293).

In this feminist coming-of-age story, the voices of Ambuya and Dr. Masuko, who are mother figures for Nhamo, are strong and empower a daughter. Nhamo empowers self through her own voice during her journey. The nonlinear pattern of Nhamo's meandering voyage is characteristic of journeys that have been identified as representing female rather than male journeys of self-discovery.[20] Nhamo travels with the spirits of others, and during her journey, she integrates self with her environment—fighting and hunting only to preserve self.

The African American daughter narratives of Hamilton, Williams-Garcia, Johnson, and Woodson are also distinguished by feminist themes as they give voice to the racism and sexism that daughters encounter as they come of age and to the strong loving connections between daughters and mothers. Intertextually, their narratives show the diversity and plurality of African American daughter–mother relationships—quilting together many of the themes set out at the beginning of this chapter. Chapter eleven brings together themes and narrative strategies used in feminist daughter–mother narratives.

NOTES

1. See, for example, Ward.

2. See Joseph "Black Mothers and Daughters: Their Roles and Function in American Society" 76–81; Collins *Black* 116.

3. See Cole xiii–xv; Ward 220.

4. For an analysis of the mother–daughter relationship in African American literature for young adults, see also Crew "Feminist."

5. For other young adult novels that set a teen daughter's relationship with her mother in the context of a network of other-mothers, see Hunter and Mathis.

6. See, for example, novels by Mathis and Myers.

7. The blues are also important to the daughter–mother narrative in *Lou in the Limelight*. See Hunter.

8. Collins explains that the divisions that have been set up equating the public outside world with work and the private inside home with family and childcare in white nuclear families do not "fit" the history of socioeconomic circumstances of Black women and African American families. See *Black* 46–47.

9. See Crew "Feminist."

10. In her concept of the semiotic, Kristeva posits a signifying function of language that, accessing the rhythmic communication of mother and child, disrupts the patriarchal symbolic order. Kristeva's theorization of the semiotic is predicated on the repression of the child's unity with the mother and on women's negative position in relation to language. See Kristeva *Desire* 134. Homans, from a different theoretical position, employs Chodorow's theory in positing a "literal language shared between mother and daughter: a language of presence." See Homans 13 and 15.

11. For the differences between male and female slave narratives, see Valerie Smith.

12. For oral histories of North Carolina slave women, see Hurmence *My Folks.*

13. For further discussion of this novel, see Crew "Feminist."

14. See, for example, *Once on This River,* which tells of an eleven-year-old daughter who finds that she was separated from her slave mother as a baby. See young adult novel by Wyeth.

15. For example, see Bell-Scott et al., eds.

16. Connected knowing is a way of knowing that places emphasis on an empathetic sharing of another's experiences and knowledge. See Belenky et al. 112–30.

17. For a discussion about the "controlling images" of African American mothers, see Collins *Black* 117.

18. Daughters are also represented as growing up without these support systems in Childress's *Rainbow Jordan* and Myers's *Motown and Didi.* See Crew "Feminist."

19. For a discussion of the grandmother's function in the family in the continent of Africa and for her representation in literature, see Hill-Lubin.

20 For "A Model of Female Voices in Youth Literature," see Vandergrift "Journey" 17–46.

Eleven

Celebrating Daughters and Mothers

'I thought all along you were *his* daughter,' said Jaive. 'Obsessed with things, mechanical gadgets. But you're mine. Tanaquil, you're a sorceress.'

—Lee

Feminist research on female adolescence has demonstrated the woeful inadequacy of traditional models of adolescent development in accounting for the experiences of growing up female. The work of Apter, Gilligan, and others has demonstrated how girls' experiences have been either devalued or not represented in cultures in which theories of adolescent development have been dominated by male patterns of development and a masculinist discourse.[1] Feminist research has unmasked the ideologies and gender bias in Freudian discourses that devalue a girl's relationship with her mother, devalue the voices and presence of mothers, and have failed to affirm the valuable role that mothers can continue to have in their daughters' lives.

This chapter uses the following novels to bring together and discuss narrative strategies of telling story about daughters, mothers, and their relationships that reverse, subvert, or contradict Freudian narrative plots of the daughter–mother relationship: Creech's *Walk Two Moons*, Hall's *The Leaving*, Kimberley Holt's *My Louisiana Sky*, Lee's *Black Unicorn*, Rodowsky's *Julie's Daughter*, and Susan Terris's *Author! Author!* These writers re-vision traditional Freudian daughter–mother narratives by employing one or more of the following narrative practices: disrupting or subverting Freudian paradigmatic plots of the daughter–mother relationship; decentering a daughter's voice by recognizing plural voices and subjectivities of daughters and

239

mothers; subverting stereotypes of mothers; and avoiding narratives of mother-blame. In view of the plurality of discourses from which daughter–mother narratives are composed, a feminist representation of the daughter–mother narrative is broadly defined as one that, in addition to employing narrative strategies outlined above, is composed from discourses that work to liberate rather than to essentialize and constrain the representations of daughters and mothers. The chapter concludes with suggestions for discussions with teens that will be useful for those who work with young people and literature.

Because their theoretical work engages with the mother–daughter relationship and maternity, the writings of Helene Cixous and Irigaray have been used by feminist literary critics to demonstrate the inadequacy of linear narratives and of male discursive practices in representing female development.[2] Feminist writers have used alternative conventions and plot patterns in order to place value on what has been marginalized. One narrative practice feminist writers have used in order to disrupt a dominant narrative, for example, is to "break the sequence" and create a "rupture" in an expected "narrative order" (DuPlessis 34). Circular and cyclical forms of plotting are also used to encode connections and bonding between mothers and daughters.[3]

THE LEAVING: A STORY OF BONDING

In *The Leaving*, Hall tells the story of eighteen-year-old Roxanne, who reluctantly leaves her mother's farm to travel to the "testing ground" and "ultimate arena" of Des Moines (24). It is made clear that Roxanne leaves because she feels she is expected to conform to societal expectations that she leave home, get a job, and acquire a boyfriend in order to show her independence (17). After three months, all these tasks accomplished, Roxanne returns home to the farm and to her mother. Roxanne has decided against continuing the relationship with her boyfriend since she wishes to avoid limiting her choices to marriage and babies (110 and 115). Hall's text thus avoids the closed ending of the romance plot at the point when, according to Freudian versions of female development, the heterosexual plot of romance and marriage might have been expected to be the outcome of Roxanne's departure to Des Moines.

In Hall's female *Bildungsroman*, Roxanne's circling home encodes an understanding of the relationship between a daughter and her mother as a bond. Hall's narrative plot bears resonance with the Demeter and

Persephone story that has been employed by feminist critics as a paradigmatic story of female development.[4] Roxanne leaves her mother in late Fall after Thanksgiving and returns in the Spring. Roxanne's mother, Thora, moreover, is associated with agriculture. The daughter–mother narrative comes full circle as a segment of the last chapter mirrors the opening chapter showing Roxanne undertaking the daily task of collecting the eggs and delivering them to her mother. The final sentence encodes the plenitude of the daughter–mother bond: "The two women ate their meal wordlessly, but with pleasure" (116). A daughter is imagined as fully replicating her mother. Thora focalizes Roxanne as "herself reborn" (40). Cletus, Roxanne's father, describes his daughter as "Thora's offspring, one hundred percent" (82). Celebrated in this text is the return of the adolescent girl to her mother, which, however, is constructed in the psychoanalytic discourse of adolescence and in psychoanalytic feminist writing as regressive.

The closed-in female world constructed in Hall's text excludes the father, who signifies lack and absence. Cletus's exclusion from the bond of mother and daughter is emphasized through his focalization of his position as outside the "closed pair, a complete entity." They had no "need for him prying in between them" (84). He was a "stranger" to Roxanne for most of her childhood, and when older she "had no curiosity about her father, no desire to get to know him" (84). Hall's valorization of the matrilineal over the patrilineal is described through Cletus's exclusion from ownership of the farm that is to be passed down "directly" to Thora's daughter "excluding" Cletus (83).

Hall substitutes a story of daughter–mother bonding for a Freudian story of separation. There has been criticism of closed-circle narrative forms in that they can be viewed as "vicious circles" from which there is no liberation (Greene 16). Hirsch has criticized the substitution of a "female vision of plenitude, shared knowledge, connection and continuity for male narrative models based on lack and dissatisfaction" (*Mother* 103). Hall's daughter–mother narrative is certainly interesting to discuss with young people in terms of to what extent Hall essentializes or liberates the representation of the daughter–mother relationship in adolescence.

BLACK UNICORN: SUBVERTING THE FREUDIAN LINEAR PLOT OF FEMALE ADOLESCENCE

In *Black Unicorn* and *Author! Author!*, respectively, Lee and Terris employ narrative strategies used in feminist revisions of generic fiction. Feminist fiction is identified by Cranny-Francis in *Feminist Fiction* as making "visible" narrative practices by which conservative discourses are stitched in to a text (2 and 205). Both Lee and Terris make visible Oedipal plots and the ideologies of gender encoded in them in order to challenge and contradict these "myths" and "fantasies" of female development. Their daughter–mother narratives construct alternative models for daughters to live by. Lee especially has appropriated the genre of fantasy as a means to challenge patriarchal discourses.[5]

The daughter–mother narrative plot in *Black Unicorn* begins by following a traditional pattern. Tanaquil, soon to be sixteen, is angry with her sorceress mother, Jaive, when her mother's magic spells invade her life. Tanaquil's wary suggestion that she leave her mother's "fortress" to go to her father is angrily rejected by Jaive who tells her daughter that she has "renounced" Tanaquil's father and that Tanaquil must forget him. Besides that, she tells her daughter, only a sorceress could manage the journey across the desert. Tanaquil is her daughter, she tells her, and she wishes Tanaquil to "remain" with her (8). Through the agency of a unicorn that Tanaquil has skillfully put together from bones found in the desert by her pet peeve (a desert animal), Tanaquil gets her wish. Magically coming to life, the unicorn defies the magic of Jaive and Tanaquil is propelled into the desert— away from her mother.

With her peeve, Tanaquil travels to the patriarchal city where she discovers she has a half-sister, Lizra. Through Lizra, Tanaquil learns that the ruler of the city, Prince Zorander, is her father. The Freudian linear plot of female adolescence is fractured by Lee at the point at which she would be expected to turn to her father and be claimed by him as his daughter. Instead, Tanaquil finds that she does not "like" him. She is neither recognized nor acknowledged as his daughter. He is "nothing to her," she tells Lizra. Tanaquil, in turn, is told by Lizra that she is "only another unnecessary daughter" to her father (90).

The ideology of power and gender, stitched so seamlessly in Freudian discourse, is unmasked in Lee's text. The setting of the secondary world in *Black Unicorn* is used to provide a perspective from which to critically view the gender ideology to which girls and women are subjected in contemporary cultures. It is in the desert that lies between the bounds of the walls of her mother's fortress and protection and the city that Tanaquil is first exposed to sexist discourse. When she joins a caravan of merchants in whose company she travels partway to the city, Tanaquil becomes aware of "how most of the men of the world looked at females. It irritated her, but she concealed this" (62). She also is quickly made aware of how men's fear of women as "other" causes them to construct women as witches. Because she is seen with and associated with the unicorn—the "Sacred Beast" of the city— whose fearsome image fills men with terror, Tanaquil is threatened with death as a sorceress and witch in the desert and in her father's city. In one legend, Lizra explains to Tanaquil, the unicorn who had founded the city would return and endow the Prince of the City with "mighty powers—make him immortal, impervious to harm, that sort of thing. And then the city will flourish as never before" (115). The unicorn, however, becomes the means by which the city's other legend is fulfilled. The patriarchal order of the city is destroyed and the Prince maimed by the Sacred Beast whom the city had angered.

Lee demolishes myths of patriarchy and substitutes alternative myths based on the power of women. Tanaquil is rescued from her father's soldiers when they first attempt to seize her—through the agency of her mother who sends her personal demon to snatch Tanaquil away from certain death. Tanaquil, her mother tells her, is a sorceress. Her magical arts lie in her gift for mending things—"not some cold artisan's knack but a true magic" (150). The unicorn had come to Tanaquil because of her magic, Jaive assures her daughter, and there is one more task for Tanaquil to perform. She must repair the broken archway in the rock so that the unicorn may return to the "perfect" world from which it came (152).

Through her mother, Tanaquil learns of another side to the legend—a side that has been suppressed through its retelling by the patriarchal fathers: the "crime" that was "worked against the unicorn bringing it from its perfect home, shutting the door on it," committed by "the first ruler of the city" (151). The false stories of patriarchy and the corrupt order upon which the city was built are thus revealed to a daughter through a woman's (a mother's) retelling. It is Tanaquil, rather than her father, who is granted the gift of "invulnerability" by the unicorn as a reward for her repair of the gateway; the gift protects Tanaquil from a spear aimed at her by one of her father's soldiers (177). Tanaquil's sister, Lizra, described by Tanaquil as "Like me. Just like me" stays to help the disgraced Prince Zorander—"a woman who would rule" (185). Lee thus makes Lizra and Tanaquil central to the city's governance and history.

In Lee's re-visioning of the Freudian linear narrative plot of female adolescence, a daughter's relationship with her mother is reimagined as an empowering one. Her mother, Tanaquil comments when her mother rescues her, is "beautiful, the awful woman" (150). Jaive, however, while awe inspiring does not dominate Tanaquil's life. Tanaquil has "her own map" for her journeys (137). Tanaquil has grown equal in stature to her mother—

perhaps more so since she, and not her mother, had gained entry to the "perfect world." Lee does employ some of the conventions used in the personal dynamics of the representation of the daughter–mother relationship in young adult novels. The wit and humor in the repartee between Tanaquil and her mother serve to foreground the conventionality of their dialogue. Lee imagines the relationship between a young woman and her mother as one of separations and reconnections—a familiar daughter–mother pattern. Tanaquil writes:

> Mother, I must see this world. Later, one day, I'll come back. I promise that I'm not my father, not Zorander. I won't leave you . . . that is, I won't let you *renounce* me. When we meet again, we'll have things to talk about. It will be exciting and new. You'll have to trust me, please (187).

The alterity of Lee's daughter–mother narrative lies not so much in changing the personal dynamics of the relationship but in showing how it can successfully confront and unmask the gender ideologies of patriarchy.

AUTHOR! AUTHOR!: MARGINALIZING A FREUDIAN "FAMILY ROMANCE"

"Sometimes," narrates twelve-year-old Valerie Meyerson, "I think I'm a changeling or adopted" (17). In *Author! Author!* twelve-year-old Valerie, who aspires to be a writer, fantasizes that her parents' former friend, Tekla Reiss, "had been a surrogate mother and her father, through artificial insemination, was Stan Meyerson" (37). Gathering the principal actors in her fantasy together, including her mother, Claire Meyerson, she tells them that she has worked it all out: "I know, Mom, why we don't look anything alike. You don't have to pretend that I have Aunt De-De's chin anymore. And, T. J., I know why I look so much like you" (69). Smiling at her mother, she tells her that she still loves her "and always will. You've raised me and you're my mom. It's just that I know now that Tekla is my biological mother, that you asked her to do this after all those miscarriages when you thought you'd never . . ." (70).

The story of the interrelationships between Val, her mother and father, and Tekla is framed by a metafiction—Val's version of the Freud's "Family Romances"—a "foundling fantasy." This fantasy is commonly found used in psychoanalytic texts to explain how, in fantasizing that they are adopted and that their real parents are from the nobility or very famous or wealthy, teenagers view their parents as less than ideal.[6] Valerie's melo-drama of lost twin girls brought up by a peasants, who are searching for their royal mother, is written out on the top margins of the first pages of each chapter except for the final one. It thus literally borders the text of Val's own fantasy of replacing her mother, Claire, a banker, by Tekla Reiss, a poet. Val, of course, is interested in Tekla as a mentor who will "mother" her own development as a writer.

Terris subverts Freudian fantasies by using Val's metanarrative as parody in order to draw attention to the fictive nature of Val's (Freud's) foundling fantasy and to Val's fantastic claims about her origins. Written on the top of the page of each opening chapter, Val's metanarrative about Sarolinda (who, raised by peasants, is now searching for her twin sister and real parents) is literally marginalized, and then interrupted by the down-to-earth realism of Val's everyday life. This is done with a playfulness and wit that serves to emphasizes the absurdity of Val's fantasies. Val's father (tellingly) says to his daughter: "There's not a shred of truth to this theory of yours. It simply isn't true. Val, this is all fantasy. Total fantasy" (70). Val finally immolates her manuscript (her Freudian romances) on a "ceremonial funeral pyre" (148).

In *Author! Author!*, Terris brings a conscious awareness to the artifice and ideological practices of fiction. The daughter–mother narrative in Terris's text is shown to be, itself, in process as Valerie both works through her fantasies about her relationship to her mother and the creative process of writing. In this self-reflexive text, Terris draws attention to ideological practices of telling story. The "question of voice—who's speaking, whose point of view a book takes—," Val's cousin states, "is so complicated" (83). Although Val's focalization dominates the telling of story in *Author! Author!*, Val's viewpoint is constantly decentered by her parents and Tekla. Terris uses an anonymous narrator to distance Val by subjecting her to the gaze and critique of others. Claire Meyerson's commentary on her daughter's fantasies, for example, is placed in the context in which Val had asked E. L. Doctorow (at a public lecture) about how Billy in *Billy Bathgate* had known "all those wonderful words? He talks in the *most* incredible way. Why? How come?" (81). "You're twelve years old," her mother tells her shortly after. "Just twelve." Turning to Claire's cousin, she continues:

> I mean, how does this all strike you? She's only twelve and already preoc-cupied by the idea of fame, unable to tell imaginary things from real ones. Adoptive mothers. Surrogate mothers. Writers. . . . Tonight Val thinks she's a meteor, because she asked an important question. She didn't even know

what was significant about it. Now she's sitting here acting pretentious, yet she can't even do her algebra assignments and hand them in on time (86).

Val's voice is frequently decentered through this kind of distancing. While she causes mayhem in raking over the complicated relationships between her parents and Tekla, it is made clear that she does not comprehend the history of these relationships. Nor, as her father points out, is it appropriate that a teenage daughter should know everything about her parents' private lives (161). The voices of Val's father and the voices and views of Claire and Tekla are all validated in Terris's daughter–mother narrative. The strong and honest voice of Tekla especially serves as a reality check for Valerie. Tekla cuts right through Val's illusions.

Reality for Valerie is the close and loving relationship that she has with her mother. At the closure of Terris's novel, Val and her mother are sitting at the edge of the pool—literally in touch as Val kneads "the soft flesh of her mother's thigh" and listens to her mother's stories about when she was a competitive ice skater (165–66). Terris, as does Lee, constructs similarities between teen daughters and their mothers but also inserts differences between them. She has tried to find some way in which they are alike, Val says to her mother, and now she has found it. Her "baby toes curve up and over just like yours" (164).

Terris's daughter–mother narrative, in contrast to Freudian discourses, is constructed through a gyno-centered discourse. Terris foregrounds a woman's body with references to menopause, to childbirth and miscarriages, and to a teenage daughter's "body raging with hormones." While a mother's body is frequently desexualized and hidden in young adult novels just as a daughter is represented as becoming sexually mature, Terris strips a woman's body for a daughter's gaze. Constructed from the position of Val's angled gaze is a view of a woman's body that certainly differs from descriptions of mothers as sexless, diminutive teenagers: "Even from an angle, [Val] was aware that Tekla's body, although slim, had flesh that was dimpled, rippled, and ribbed with stretch marks like Claire's body" (20).

Terris uses this gyno-centered discourse to construct differences between Tekla and Claire. Valerie meets with Tekla at the swimming pool and tells her that she wishes to be friends with her. She even wishes, Val continues, that Tekla was her mother. Tekla compares swimming in the pool to returning "to the womb—all that whooshing in warm liquid" (18). Tekla, however, is represented as the antithesis of a figure of maternity. The womb of the pool is the place in which Tekla is described as feeling "dizzy." Valerie finds Tekla's body exhausted—"curved into a jellyfish position somewhere just above the drain" (19). Approaching menopause, Tekla's body is marked with a long scar signifying the loss of a baby (21). Later in story, Valerie floating in the "warm, comforting, supportive water" of the swimming pool, remembers the "round face" of her mother—"shining and soothing" in the operating room where she was having her tonsils removed (162). The chlorine in the pool, in contrast to the poisonous associations it arouses in Tekla—a "telltale, poisonous green tinge"—is described differently by Val's mother: "Oh, it smells wonderful in here and brings back all kinds of memories. Just like your laundry when you were a baby—so clean and so new . . ." (164). While the use of such imagery has been criticized for encoding a biological essentialism, Terris inscribes into a young adult novel a refreshing look at women's bodies that is constructed from the oblique gaze of the female rather than from the full gaze of the male. As Hirsch points out, "Nothing entangles women more firmly in their bodies than pregnancy, birth, lactation, miscarriage, or the inability to conceive" (*Mother* 166).

Through the representations of Val's mother, Tekla, and the other women characters in the novel, Terris represents for a reader the differences and pluralities of being gendered as a woman. Val is a "young woman of infinite possibilities," her mother tells her (165). Chodorow argues that granting a mother her own selfhood apart from her role as mother is essential to a feminist perspective of development (*Feminism* 104–5). In daughter–mother narratives in young adult novels, a daughter's ability to recognize a mother's subjectivity and that her mother has a life of her own other than attending to a daughter's needs is frequently used as a marker of a daughter's maturity. In one of Nixon's daughter–mother narratives, for example, Cassie feels "like Alice on the wrong side of the looking glass" when she steps "into her mother's world" and realizes that she "hadn't given her mother the right to love what she wanted and did so well" (*Overnight* 172).

WALK TWO MOONS:
WALKING IN A MOTHER'S MOCCASINS

In Creech's *Walk Two Moons*, Salamanca Tree Hiddle, accompanied by her grandparents, goes on a two-thousand-mile trip from Ohio to Lewiston, Idaho. The real reason for their journey, Salamanca narrates, lies buried underneath things left unsaid but it is to do with Salamanca's mother who had gone on a journey of her own and had not returned. Salamanca's grandparents and father wish Salamanca to see her mother, Chanassen Hiddle Pickford "resting peacefully in Lewiston, Idaho" (5). Creech uses a narrative form associated with feminist texts by constructing the story of Chanhassen as a palimpsest. Just as Salamanca's father had scraped away at a plaster wall to reveal a hidden fireplace, so does Sal's story of her mother and their relationship lie under the surface story of Phoebe Winterbottom and her mother—the story that Salamanca tells her grandparents to entertain them during the long hours of their journey.

As Salamanca's first-person narrative weaves back and forth from the present to the past and from Phoebe's story to her own, the knowledge that her mother had died in a bus that fell off the side of a mountain in Lewiston, Idaho, lies buried beneath the surface details of the trip just as Salamanca has tried to hide the truth of her mother's death from herself. She had needed, Salamanca later narrates, time in which she could still believe that her mother would return in order to be able to finally accept her death. Creech creates that space for Salamanca (and a reader) by retaining the mystery of Salamanca's mother's disappearance—spinning it out slowly with foreshadowing and other clues—until Salamanca finally sees with her own eyes the site of the crashed bus and her mother's grave. As Salamanca realizes later, her grandmother and grandfather Hiddle wanted to give her the chance "to walk in her mother's moccasins—to see what she had seen and feel what she might have felt on her last trip" (276). Salamanca's growing ability to understand things from her mother's point-of-view is shown at the closure of the novel. Although she is jealous that her mother had wanted other children, Salamanca can put herself in her mother's moccasins: "If I were my mother, I might want more children—not because I don't love my Salamanca, but because I love her so much. I want more of these" (278–79).

Before leaving on her journey, Chanassen had told Salamanca and her father that her going away was something she has to do on her own. "She *had* to" (110). It was important to tell Salamanca this. Chanhassen had had a stillborn baby after Salamanca had fallen out of a tree and Chanhassen, pregnant, had carried her home. Her mother could have no more babies (149). Two things that Salamanca learns about her mother's leaving and her death is that she, Salamanca, had nothing to do with her mother's decision to leave and that she nor anyone else owns their mother (176). When Sal complains to her father that her mother should never have gone, her father replies that you "cannot cage a person." Her mother, he was sure, had meant to return (141). Chanhassen's reason for leaving is a personal one—to find out from her cousin what she was really like *"underneath"*—as Chanhassen—before she became a wife and mother (143). She wanted to be called by her real Indian name (meaning "tree sweet juice"), Chanhassen had told her husband before she left—not Sugar. Salamanca's father shows his respect for his wife's wish by writing "Chanhassen" on the newly exposed fireplace (110–11). Chanhassen is thus accorded an individual subjectivity, separate from her role as a mother, which is recognized by her husband and daughter.

Made visible in Creech's daughter–mother narratives in *Walk Two Moons* are mothers' pasts and important sides to their lives that are buried under their surface roles of wives and mothers. Phoebe's mother leaves home because of a buried past that she has hidden from her family. She leaves a distraught Phoebe who believes her mother must have been kidnapped because, Phoebe tells Salamanca, her mother would never have left her. In her wildest imaginings about the "lunatic" who visits Phoebe's home and the neighborhood and who is seen in the company of her mother, Phoebe had not guessed the real truth—that he was the illegitimate son of her mother before her marriage. Salamanca comments that she thinks the different problems of Phoebe's family and the disappearance of Phoebe's mother helped her with understanding her own mother (277). Mothers, with their infinitely different lives and possibilities, are shown to be valued by their families in Creech's text: Phoebe's mother, the conscientious housewife who feels she lives a "tiny life"; Chanhassan Hiddle, associated with the beauty and joy of nature; Salamanca's grandmother Hiddle with her joyful spirit and the refrain, "Huzza, huzza"; and Salamanca's friend Ben's mother, who reminds Salamanca of her own mother when she was depressed after losing the baby. There is an emphasis on relationships and attachments in Creech's novel that extends beyond the value that is also placed on daughter–mother connections.

The subjectivities of Salamanca's mother and other characters in Creech's text are constructed through Salamanca's ability to switch positions so that she can see from other viewpoints—by wearing their moccasins. In other daughter–mother narratives, multiple subject positions are constructed by granting mothers ability to narrate their own stories.

JULIE'S DAUGHTER:
MOTHERS' VOICES AND PAINFUL CHOICES

Mentioned briefly in chapter one, Rodowsky's *Julie's Daughter* is a good example of how a plural daughter–mother narrative gives voice and agency to two mothers and a daughter. When seventeen-year-old Slug's grandmother, Gussie, dies, Slug meets her mother, Julie, who, as a teenage

mother, had abandoned Slug shortly after she was born. Slug has not seen
her mother since her mother left her in a red wagon at the bus depot. After
Gus's funeral, Julie offers to take her daughter home with her. She could
not take care of her before, she explains, but now she can (58). Slug, therefore, finds herself "in a strange house, in a strange city, with a woman" she
"didn't know" (35).

Described as treading warily around each other, Slug and Julie, a nurse,
become involved in taking care of the elderly artist, Harper Tegges, who
has suddenly collapsed because of a malignant brain tumor. As Julie and
Slug take care of Harper so that she may die in peace at home, the stories
that the three women tell each other about their lives are woven together
into a plural daughter–mother narrative that spans three generations. Their
names, Slug, Julie, and Harper appear as titles on alternate chapter headings, each speaking from a different subject position in the text. Slug's
narrative opens and closes the novel so her voice frames the story, but her
narrative does not dominate story so as to marginalize the voices of Julie
and Harper.

The compelling voice of Harper Tegges narrates how she rebelled as a
young woman against the strictures and limited opportunities of growing
up "fettered" in an affluent white family in North Carolina. "The trouble
was that everybody's cocoon was my straitjacket. It was as though I were
fettered there" (76). Harper tells how she fought to be an artist: "I knew
that I had to go to art school—or to go to no school, and just paint. And I
fought my parents as if my life depended on it. And my life *did* depend on
it" (77). Harper's story reproduces the split that almost haunts the daughter–mother narratives in novels in this study: procreation versus creativity,
artistic career versus the responsibilities of mothering.[7] In Rodowsky's text,
the childbirth metaphor is appropriated, through the voice of Harper, in a
way that splits it wide open in terms of showing the pain and joy of creativity as an artist and the joy and pain of childbirth and motherhood. The
day she and Richard had "learned about the baby," Harper had not known
"that one kind of creativity would rob another" (27). Harper had danced
with "abandonment"—but this "abandonment" takes on a double valence
when she later abandons her daughter, Suzanne.

> Good baby—good hand. Good hand. I traded my baby for—No, not that. I
> took all of me—all that was left—and went away. I told Richard and then I
> left. Mama's grandchild and she never knew. I couldn't not go. And I would
> go again. And oh, my God, it hurt. It hurts (196).

On one occasion, Julie, Slug's mother, watches Harper stroking "her right hand, cradling it, crooning to it" (164). Harper's hand signifying the pain of the schism between creative art and motherhood is yet another example of how a gyno-centered language is employed by a woman writer in a daughter–mother narrative. Focalized by Slug, Harper:

> stopped rocking and hit her hands against her chest, clawing at her breasts through her nightgown. 'Pretty baby sucked and sucked—and I was—soon there wouldn't be any more—I knew that I was all being used up. The paintings and the things I had to do' (194).

In these unmediated passages of interior monologue, a reader has direct access to a mother's pain, thoughts, and emotions so readers can potentially identify directly with Harper's voice as well as with the voice of a teenage daughter. If readers do identify with Harper, they are positioned to experience the contradictions that are raised in the text between issues of career, ambition, and responsibility to self and to motherhood. There is a constant shifting viewpoint between the differing subject positions. The doubling of the maternal voices of Harper and Julie works to set up identification and connections between these two women. They speak as daughters as they tell about their lives as adolescents and also as mothers who have experienced the pain of abandoning their daughters.

Julie's experience of abandoning Slug enables her to identify with the subjectivity of Harper. Listening to Harper's story of her need to leave her family and home, Julie "felt all Harper's mother's words scolding against my lips. All at once I was her father, and her brothers leaving her sitting on her suitcase in the middle of the station. But more than any of them, I was Harper. Knowing that she had to go, and going" (161). The doubling of mothers' voices in Rodowsky's daughter–mother narrative has the effect of decentering the voice of a daughter's voice. Julie also explains why she, too, abandoned her baby daughter: "there had been little enough of me to begin with—and now it was as if what was left was in danger of being thrown away with the afterbirth" (156). "My leaving had nothing to do with you," Julie tells her daughter. "I didn't even know you. I couldn't know you. Because at that time I didn't have enough self to know anyone" (171). Slug angrily faces Julie; she had not forgiven her for being abandoned. Julie was her mother and should not have abandoned her. "How about you," Julie asks Slug. "Could you have done any better?" Slug stops and thinks that she "could have. That I would have. And suddenly not sure" (224).

Harper, in her confusion during her last days, mistakenly identifies Slug as her daughter, Suzanne, and explains to her why she had left Suzanne with her father, Richard (192–93). Julie listens as Harper tells her that her daughter had come to visit her earlier. "Suzanne. My daughter. I thought she never would—told Richard never to tell—but she did and I did. Told her why—how I had left her there because—and I would again. She was here and gone. In and out. But she came—I knew she would—." Realizing that Harper had told Slug the story of how she had abandoned Suzanne so that Slug had had to live through the story of another daughter's abandonment, Julie thinks about Slug knowing what Harper had done to Slug and knowing what she had also done to her daughter (218).

Rodowsky's *Julie's Daughter* is one of the best examples in this book of how a plural narrative can create positions from which both a teenage daughter and a mother speak as narrating subjects. Through the shifting positions of focalization and the doubling of identity, a daughter-centered narrative that colludes with mother-blame is avoided. Censorious scripts of mothering are interrogated in Rodowsky's daughter–mother narrative as Slug is asked to understand and forgive her mother as Harper wishes her daughter to forgive her. "Should. Should. Should," Harper Tegges says to Slug. "Who's to say what someone should and shouldn't do. Can do or can't" (75).

MY LOUISIANA SKY: REVERSING STEREOTYPES

Value is placed on a daughter's mother, and thereby on the relationship between a young teen daughter and her mother in Holt's *My Louisiana Sky*, by subverting stereotypes. Holt tells the story of twelve-year-old Tiger Ann Parker, who lives with her capable and energetic grandmother, her mentally disabled mother, Corinna, and her father, Lonnie, who is "slow." Tiger, however, to the surprise of the community where her family has always lived, is smart—a straight A student and a winner of school spelling bees (4). Tiger feels that she is "growing up past" her mother. She had realized at six years old that her mother was different from other mothers. She wonders, too, why her grandmother could have two daughters who are so different—Dorrie Kay who is "fancy" and has a job and apartment in Baton Rouge and her mother who is happy "just being plain and simple" (30).

Although Tiger has shared a loving relationship with her mother, adolescence is constructed in Holt's daughter–mother narrative (as in others) as a time when a daughter questions her relationship with her mother and sees her mother from a more objective viewpoint. Tiger begins to feel ashamed of her mother after the incident in which she had left her mother and grandmother in the bookmobile to go into the school gym. Corinna had come looking for her daughter and had entered the gym sobbing because she had thought her daughter lost. Tiger, not wanting to acknowledge her mother in front of the peer group of girls to which she wishes to belong, wished she could be "invisible" (56). Tiger's attitude toward her mother changes as Tiger now disparages her mother: "How many other mothers watched a stupid puppet show? Abby Lynn and the other girls would laugh if they caught sight of Momma on her pillow, engrossed in a kiddie program" (63). She comments to her grandmother that she doesn't know why anyone would like the "dumb show" (64). When Tiger's grandmother suddenly dies from a heart attack, Tiger is only too willing to accompany her aunt, Dorrie, for a short stay in Baton Rouge—just to see if she likes it enough to live there on a permanent basis. Tiger believes that she will have a better life in Baton Rouge than if she remains in the country with a mother and father incapable of looking after her.

Holt, however, shows that Tiger's focalization of her mother (and father) is mistaken by placing value on alternative viewpoints in the text and by deconstructing stereotypes and images associated with the mentally disabled. When Tiger complains to her grandmother about her mother, her grandmother tells her that "People are afraid of what's different. That don't mean different is bad. Just means different is different" (65). During Tiger's brief stay in Baton Rouge, she learns from her aunt why her mother is different. At the age of six years, Corinna had climbed up a ladder leaning against a tree after her young sister (Dorrie Kay) who had reached one of the branches. Attempting to rescue her sister, Corinna had fallen and landed on her head. She had never recovered, and intellectually, remained the bright, six-year-old child she was then.

In Holt's feminist daughter–mother narrative, a physically disabled mother is shown to possess qualities that are of value to her daughter. Using the skills she retains from her early childhood, for example, she had taught Tiger to read. Tiger also hears from her grandmother how much her mother loves her. "Your mother may have a simple mind, Tiger," she tells her, "but her love is simple too. It flows from her like a quick, easy river" (81). When a hurricane strikes, Tiger sees for herself the power of her mother's protective love. As the wind begins to blow, Corinna goes out to search for Tiger who, because she has stopped to rescue a calf stuck in the mud, fails to reach home before the storm begins. Tiger, who had arrived home without meeting her mother, goes out and finds her mother still searching for her in the woods. As they hold on to each other, Tiger tells how "for the first time in a long time," she feels "safe" in her mother's arms (196). Her mother had wanted to protect her in the same way she had rescued the calf (186–87).

In Holt's daughter–mother narrative, the strength and independence of a daughter protagonist is not created in opposition to a weak, dependent mother despite Corinna's disability. Magnolia, Dorrie Kay's maid, who comes to help the family after Tiger's grandmother's death, tells Tiger that she is of an age when she is old enough to take care of herself (158). When she was Tiger's age, Magnolia continues, her mother had died and she had taken care of her younger brothers and sisters. Her family "needs her" Magnolia tells Tiger (159). In reference to Dorrie Kay's plans to have Tiger stay with her in Baton Rouge, Magnolia tells Tiger that her parents are "good people." It seems, she says, that "a girl has everything she want here. A momma and daddy that love her. A fine home . . ." (158). Tiger's grandmother has shown Tiger how to be strong and responsible. She shows Tiger how to make her special chicken-and-dumplings recipe the night before she dies. However, in contrast to those grandmother daughter–mother narratives in which a teenager's mother is shown to be either absent from her daughter's life or to have a less powerful presence in her daughter's life than that of a grandmother's, Tiger's mother is represented as a significant maternal figure. Corinna is described as a person who has abundant love, joy, and beauty. Tiger comments that her mother "looked like a pretty sunflower in the yellow dress she had made" at the Thompson's party (196). Through descriptions of her loving relationship with Lonnie, Tiger's father, she is shown to be a warm, vibrant, sexually alive woman.

Holt's female coming-of-age story is composed of other themes that are characteristic of feminist novels: an ethics of care and nurturing, and an emphasis on different ways of knowing. Tiger's father, labeled by some as "simple" and "retarded," has difficulty with letters and numbers. He does, however, possess other intelligences—other ways of knowing—through his affinity with nature. He possesses the ability to listen for and read the signs of the earth, including the weather, and has a special way with plants.[8] There is in Holt's daughter–mother narrative, as in other feminist texts, an emphasis on growing up in relation to and interdependence with others.

YOUNG ADULTS, LITERATURE, AND
THE DAUGHTER–MOTHER RELATIONSHIP

The new discourses on female adolescence and on the daughter–mother relationship in adolescence have given us different ways of thinking and talking about girls' experiences, including their relationships with their mothers. It is important that young people are also exposed to other sides of story—stories that tell about the value of mutual relationships between parents and teens. As Vandergrift writes: "Literature as culture and ideology organizes and presents dominant world views to young readers that aid them in their social construction of reality" ("A Feminist" 26).

Freudian discourses have been naturalized into our culture, particularly in regard to the representation in story of family relationships. Given the gender biases embedded in discourses of traditional adolescent psychology, one might ask how alienating this construction of development might be to male or female adolescent readers. Narratives that give voice only to aspects of conflict and separation, especially those that speak about young people having to achieve emotional independence from their parents, do so at the cost of placing less or no value on relational aspects of human development for boys as well as girls.[9] It is important, too, that teen boys and girls encounter the empowering voices of mothers. Young people, like all of us, need to learn, like Salamanca, to walk in their mothers' (and other people's) moccasins. The way a gendered discourse shapes the daughter–mother relationship usually lies buried under the surface story of plot. Just as Salamanca's father discovers the fireplace behind the plaster wall in *Walk Two Moons*, we often have to chip away at this surface level in order to reveal what is hidden. Girls need, like Nhamo in Farmer's *A Girl Named Disaster*, to know that they can empower themselves through language and story.

The theoretical lenses through which we see do affect how we review and discuss literature with young people. Understanding the daughter–mother relationship through parameters of separation or connection can place emphasis and value on different sides of story. A succinct example of how different theoretical approaches lead to different interpretations is found in critical appraisals of Jamaica Kincaid's novel *Annie John*, which is frequently on recommended reading lists for young adults. Donelson and Nilsen describe the novel as "a daughter's painful gaining of emotional independence from her mother" (90). Natov, using feminist theory to frame her analysis, writes that Kincaid "emphasizes the pain of connection between mother and daughter" and the "continuous and primary nature of the pre-oedipal bond" (13). The theoretical positions we adopt make the difference between reading Creech's *Walk Two Moons* as a story that fits into the archetypal story of the hero as read Donelson and Nilsen (57) and interpreting it as a feminist coming-of-age story about loving relationships—a story in which Salamanca learns to accept the truth that her beloved mother is really dead.

The daughter–mother relationship is frequently not seen as either a central theme, nor a part of the text at all, for purposes of indexing. Many texts included in this book, for example, are not assigned the subject heading: "Mothers and daughters—Fiction" including Cannon's *Begin the World Again*, Creech's *Walk Two Moons*, Johnson's *Toning the Sweep*, Hathorn's *Thunderwith*, and Honeycutt's *Ask Me Something Easy*. Similar experiences have been reported by others writing on this topic. There are a number of questions that can be raised. Is this because the daughter–mother relationship is simply not perceived as significant in relation to other elements of the text? Is the conception of the daughter–mother relationship in adolescence problematic—a perception problem—because narratives of adolescent development and cultural narratives have, until recently, discursively constructed the relationship as one of nonrelationship?

Irigaray has argued that the relationship between a mother and a daughter, "heavily invested with the meanings and values of patriarchy, needs another 'syntax', another 'grammar' of culture through which to articulate the relationship" (*This Sex* 143). While only a beginning, Gilligan and other feminists, who are engaged in re-visioning female adolescence, including the daughter–mother relationship, are indeed constructing a different "syntax" in which to articulate the relationship. This language is heard, for example, in the title of *Mother–Daughter Revolution* by Debold, Wilson, and Malave. It is heard in the words of Brown and Gilligan:

> We are acutely aware of the need to listen to girls and explore relationships between women and girls in different settings. . . . When women and girls meet at the crossroads of adolescence, the intergenerational seam of a patriarchal culture opens. If women and girls together resist giving up relationship for the sake of 'relationships', then this meeting holds the potential for societal and cultural change (232).

It is through social and cultural change that conventional ways of understanding our everyday life and relationships also change. It is through cultural changes in society and belief systems that conventions used in genre literature also are modified since the ideologies and discourses they encode also change (Cranny-Francis 206). There are now available an increasing number of daughter–mother narratives in young adult novels written from a feminist perspective. Feminist narrative strategies of telling story are increasingly being used in order to subvert and contradict ideologies of gender embedded in Freudian discourses of female adolescence. As professionals working with young people and literature, we can:

- ensure that professional collections and parent collections in public libraries and collections in school media centers reflect the new research and writings about female adolescence.
- incorporate a knowledge of feminist research on adolescence and literature in workshops for teachers and parents in public libraries and schools.
- incorporate, when appropriate, recent research on female adolescence and feminist approaches to young adult literature in book discussions for young people.

Daughter–mother narratives in young adult novels and adult books can be especially useful for discussing some of the topics outlined below:

i) issues of gender and the representation of family relationships in story.

ii) to what extent societal expectations shape teens' relationships with parents.

iii) the diversity of daughter–mother relationships in various racial, ethnic, and cultural contexts. Casey's *Over the Water*, Mori's *Shizuko's Daughter*, Kim's *The Long Season of Rain*, Staples's *Shabanu*, Farmer's *A Girl Named Disaster*, Hamilton's *Plain City*, Woodson's *The Dear One*, and various stories in *Stay True: Short Stories for Strong Girls* edited by Marilyn Singer are some suggested titles.

Appropriate adult books about mothers and daughters in different cultural contexts can also be used with older teens. Some suggested titles are: Michael Dorris's *Yellow Raft in Blue Water*; Jo Ann Yolanda Hernandez's *White Bread Competition*; Barbara Kingsolver's *The Bean Trees*; Dori Sanders's *Clover*; Ntozake Shange's *Betsey Brown*; Amy Tan's *The Joy Luck Club*; and *My Mother's Daughter: Stories By Women*, edited by Irene Zaheva that includes stories by Audre Lourde and Ntozake Shange.

iv) issues raised in daughter–mother narratives about mothers and mothering. The contradictions, for example, that young women face between marriage and family and personal wishes for self-development remain pertinent today. Bridgers's *Notes for Another Life*, Brooks's *Midnight Hour Encores*, Rodowsky's *Julie's Daughter*, and Woodson's *I Hadn't Meant to Tell You This* are some titles that address these issues. Some of the short stories in Singer's *Stay True: Short Stories for Strong Girls* are also relevant.

v) the representation of the daughter–mother relationship in traditional fairy tales including comparisons with retellings of the tales in young adult novels or with contemporary stories of daughters and mothers. Napoli's *Zel*, Galloway's *Truly Grim Tales*, and the Geras trilogy of *The Tower Room, Pictures of the Night*, and *Watching the Roses* are suggested titles but there are now available a number of collections of feminist fairy tales for young adults and adults. This topic could be expanded to a general discussion on gender ideologies in fairy tale.[10]

vi) female oral slave narratives using daughter–mother narratives in Hurmence's *Tancy*, Lyons's *Letters from a Slave Girl*, Williams-Garcia's *Like Sisters on the Homefront*, and Sharon Wyeth's *Once on This River*. Other sources include Hurmence's *My Folks Don't Want Me to Talk About Slavery* and Harriet Jacobs' *Incidents in the Life of a Slave Girl*. These can supplement discussions and units in the classroom on oral narratives and slavery.

vii) links can be made across the curriculum to other autobiographies and informational books that highlight the relationship between girls and their mothers. In *Thanks to My Mother* by Schoschana Rabinovici, winner of the 1998 Mildred L. Batchelder Award, for example, a daughter's voice is a testament to the spirit and endurance of the mother who kept her alive during the Holocaust.

The emphasis in this last chapter has been on celebrating teen daughters, their mothers, and the daughter–mother relationship in adolescence. We all have different stories and our own different personal experiences of this relationship. We all have our own "daughter–mother talk" that we use and which we hear in everyday dialogues between mothers and their adolescent daughters. We need, however, to unmask for ourselves and for sons and daughters the scripts and dialogues that we use, so as to foster different ways of knowing about relationships between teen daughters and their mothers.

It is important for teachers and librarians working with young people and literature to give voice to the diversity and plurality of the mother–daughter relationship in adolescence. I hope that, together, we can emulate in classrooms and in libraries the story telling that takes place in Greyling's grandmother's home in Thesman's *The Rain Catchers* and in the circles of daughters and mothers formed through daughter–mother discussion book clubs. In these environments, girls' voices are empowered and their voices validated so that they, in turn, will empower the voices of their own daughters and sons.

NOTES

1. See Goldberger et al.; Taylor, Gilligan, and Sullivan.
2. See, for example, DuPlessis 36–37; Hirsch 130–38.
3. For an analysis of the cyclical narrative plot of Katherine Lasky's *Beyond the Divide*, see Erol.
4. The myth of Demeter and Persephone has been used as an alternative myth to the Oedipal myth for descriptions and explanations of the daughter–mother relationship. See Hirsch 5–6; for criticism, see Walters 19–20.
5. For an analysis of Lee's fantasy fiction, see Cranny-Francis 87–90, 93–94.
6. See Elkind 28. For examples of how the "foundling fantasy" has been used to interpret and explain narrative plots, see Hirsch and Griswold. For an example of how Freud's explanation of a child's "fantasy" of being a "foundling in a family of provisional parents" is used to interpret fairy tale, see Kaplan 295–98.
7. For a discussion on creativity and the childbirth metaphor, see Friedman.
8. The concept of different ways of knowing is from *Women's Ways of Knowing*. See Belenky. For the concept of multiple intelligences, see Gardner.
9. An example is Robert Havighurst's developmental tasks quoted in a major textbook on adolescent literature. See Donelson and Nilsen 34; Havighurst.
10. See, for example, Crew "Feminist."

Young Adult Novels

Adler, C. S. *The Shell Lady's Daughter*. New York: Coward-McCann, 1983.

Anderson, Mary. *Step on a Crack*. New York: Atheneum, 1978. New York: Bantam, 1985.

Bridgers, Sue Ellen. *Notes for Another Life*. New York: Knopf, 1981. New York: Bantam, 1982.

Brooks, Bruce. *Midnight Hour Encores*. New York: Harper, 1986. Harper: Keypoint, 1988.

Brooks, Martha. *Two Moons in August*. Boston, Mass.: Little, Brown, 1992.

Calvert, Patricia. *Yesterday's Daughter*. New York: Charles Scribner's Sons, 1986.

Cannon, A. E. *Amazing Gracie*. New York: Delacorte, 1991. New York: Laurel-Leaf, 1991.

Cannon, Bettie. *Begin the World Again*. New York: Charles Scribner's Sons, 1991.

Casey, Maude. *Over the Water*. New York: Holt, 1994. New York: Puffin, 1996.

Childress, Alice. *Rainbow Jordan*. New York: Coward, McCann and Geoghegan, 1981.

Choi, Sook Nyul. *Echoes of the White Giraffe*. Boston, Mass.: Houghton Mifflin, 1993. New York: Yearling-Dell, 1993.

Colman, Hila. *Claudia, Where Are You?* New York: Morrow, 1969.

———. *Forgotten Girl*. New York: Crown, 1990.

———. *Rich and Famous Like My Mom*. New York: Crown, 1988.

———. *Sometimes I Don't Love My Mother*. New York: Vagabond-Scholastic, 1977.

Creech, Sharon. *Walk Two Moons*. New York: HarperCollins, 1994.

Culin, Charlotte. *Cages of Glass, Flowers of Time*. Scarsdale, N.Y.: Bradbury, 1979.

Deaver, Julie Reece. *You Bet Your Life*. New York: Charlotte Zolotow, 1993.

Elfman, Blossom. *A House for Jonnie O*. Boston, Mass.: Houghton Mifflin, 1977. New York: Bantam, 1978.

Ellis, Sarah. *Pick-Up Sticks*. New York: McElderry Books, 1992.

Farmer, Nancy. *A Girl Named Disaster*. New York: Orchard, 1996. New York: Puffin, 1998.

First, Julie. *Look Who's Beautiful!* New York: Franklin Watts, 1980.

Fosburgh, Linda. *The Wrong Way Home*. New York: Bantam, 1990.

Freeman, Suzanne. *The Cuckoo's Child*. New York: Greenwillow, 1996.

Geras, Adele. *Pictures of the Night*. London, England: Hamilton, 1992. New York: Harcourt Brace, 1993.

———. *The Tower Room*. London, England: Hamilton, 1990. New York: Harcourt Brace, 1992.

———. *Watching the Roses*. London, England: Hamilton, 1991. New York: Harcourt Brace, 1992.

Gerber, Merrill Joan. *Please Don't Kiss Me Now*. New York: Dial, 1981.

Gerson, Corinne. *How I Put My Mother Through College*. New York: Atheneum, 1981.

Greenberg, Jan. *Exercises of the Heart*. New York: Farrar, Straus and Giroux, 1986.

———. *The Pig-Out Blues*. New York: Farrar, Straus and Giroux, 1982.

Greene, Bette. *Summer of My German Soldier*. New York: Dial, 1973.

Hall, Lynn. *The Leaving*. New York: Charles Scribner's Sons, 1980.

———. *Letting Go*. New York: Charles Scribner's Sons, 1987.

Hamilton, Virginia. *Plain City*. New York: Blue Sky Press, 1993.

———. *Sweet Whispers, Brother Rush*. New York: Philomel, 1982.

Hathorn, Libby. *Thunderwith*. Boston, Mass.: Little, Brown, 1991

Hautzig, Deborah. *Second Star to the Right*. New York: Greenwillow, 1981.

Holl, Kristi D. *Patchwork Summer*. New York: Atheneum, 1987.

Holland, Isabelle. *Of Love and Death and Other Journeys*. New York: Lippincott, 1975. New York: Dell, 1987.

Holt, Kimberly Willis. *My Louisiana Sky*. New York: Holt, 1998.

Honeycutt, Natalie. *Ask Me Something Easy*. New York: Orchard, 1991.

Hunter, Kristin. *Lou in the Limelight*. New York: Charles Scribner's Sons, 1981.

Hurmence, Belinda. *Tancy*. New York: Clarion, 1984.

Ingold, Jeanette. *The Window*. New York: Harcourt Brace, 1996.

Irwin, Hadley. *What about Grandma?* New York: Macmillan, 1982. New York: Avon, 1991.

Johnson, Angela. *Toning the Sweep*. New York: Orchard, 1993.

Kim, Helen. *The Long Season of Rain*. New York: Holt, 1996.

Klass, Sheila S. *To See My Mother Dance*. New York: Charles Scribner's Sons, 1988.

Klause, Annette Curtis. *Blood and Chocolate*. New York: Delacorte Press, 1997.

———. *The Silver Kiss*. New York: Delacorte Press, 1990.

Lee, Tanith. *Black Unicorn*. New York: Tor-Tom Doherty, 1993.

L'Engle, Madeleine. *Camilla*. 1965. New York: Laurel-Leaf-Dell, 1982.

Levitin, Sonia. *Beyond Another Door*. New York: Atheneum, 1977. New York: Fawcett Juniper-Ballantine, 1994.

Lifton, Betty Jean. *I'm Still Me*. New York: Knopf, 1981.

Lowry, Lois. *Find a Stranger, Say Goodbye*. Boston, Mass.: Houghton Mifflin, 1978. New York: Pocket, 1979.

Lyons, Mary E. *Letters from a Slave Girl: The Story of Harriet Jacobs*. New York: Charles Scribner's Sons, 1992.

Macdonald, Caroline. *Speaking to Miranda*. New York: Perlman, 1992.

Mathis, Sharon Bell. *Listen for the Fig Tree*. New York: Viking, 1974.

Mazer, Harry. *Someone's Mother Is Missing*. New York: Delacorte, 1990.

Mori, Kyoko. *One Bird*. New York: Holt, 1995.

——. *Shizuko's Daughter*. New York: Holt, 1993.

Myers, Walter Dean. *Motown and Didi: A Love Story*. New York: Viking, 1984.

Napoli, Donna Jo. *Zel*. New York: Dutton, 1996.

Nixon, Joan Lowerty. *Encore*. New York: Bantam, 1990.

——. *Overnight Sensation*. New York: Bantam, 1990.

——. *Star Baby*. New York: Bantam, 1989.

Okimoto, Jean Davies. *Molly by Any Other Name*. New York: Scholastic, 1990.

Oneal, Zibby. *A Formal Feeling*. New York: Viking, 1982. New York: Puffin, 1990.

Pascal, Francine. *Hangin' Out with Cici*. New York: Viking, 1977.

Peck, Richard. *Representing Superdoll*. New York: Viking, 1974.

Pearson, Kit. *A Handful of Time*. Markham, Canada: Viking, 1987.

Perkins, Mitali. *The Sunita Experiment*. Boston, Mass.: Little, Brown, 1993.

Pfeffer, Susan. *The Beauty Queen*. New York: Doubleday, 1974.

Rabinovici, Schoschana. *Thanks to My Mother*. New York: Dial, 1998.

Riley, Jocelyn. *Crazy Quilt*. New York: Morrow, 1984.

——. *Only My Mouth Is Smiling*. New York: Morrow, 1982.

Rodowsky, Colby. *H. My Name Is Henley*. New York: Farrar, Straus and Giroux, 1982.

——. *Hannah in Between*. New York: Farrar, Straus and Giroux, 1994.

——. *Julie's Daughter*. New York: Farrar, Straus and Giroux, 1985.

Rostkowski, Margaret I. *After the Dancing Days*. New York: Harper, 1986.

Sachs, Marilyn. *Just Like a Friend*. New York: Dutton, 1989.

Schwartz, Sheila. *Like Mother, Like Me*. New York: Pantheon, 1978.

Shreve, Susan. *The Revolution of Mary Leary*. New York: Knopf, 1982.

Smith, Stephanie. *Snow-Eyes*. New York: Daw, 1985.

Snyder, Carol. *Leave Me Alone, Ma!* New York: Bantam, 1987.

Staples, Suzanne Fisher. *Shabanu: Daughter of the Wind*. New York: Knopf, 1989.

——. *Haveli*. New York: Knopf, 1993.

Terris, Susan. *Author! Author!* New York: Farrar, Straus and Giroux, 1990.

Thesman, Jean. *Cattail Moon*. Boston, Mass.: Houghton Mifflin, 1994.

——. *The Rain Catchers*. Boston, Mass.: Houghton Mifflin, 1991.

Tolan, Stephanie. *The Liberation of Tansy Warner*. New York: Charles Scribner's Sons, 1980.

Voigt, Cynthia. *Dicey's Song*. New York: Atheneum, 1982. New York: Fawcett, 1984.

Williams-Garcia, Rita. *Like Sisters on the Homefront.* New York: Lodestar, 1995.
Wood, June Rae. *A Share of Freedom.* New York: Putnam, 1994.
Woodson, Jacqueline. *The Dear One.* New York: Delacorte, 1991. New York: Dell, 1993.
———. *I Hadn't Meant to Tell You This.* New York: Delacorte, 1994.
Wyeth, Sharon Dennis. *Once on This River.* New York: Knopf, 1998.
Yep, Laurence. *The Star Fisher.* New York: Morrow, 1991. New York: Puffin, 1992.
———. *Thief of Hearts.* New York: HarperCollins, 1995.
Zindel, Bonnie, and Paul Zindel. *A Star for the Latecomer.* New York: Harper, 1980.

SHORT STORIES

Bray, Marian Flandrick. "The Pale Mare." *Stay True: Short Stories for Strong Girls.* Comp. and Ed. Marilyn Singer. New York: Scholastic, 1998, 99-108.
Galloway, Priscilla. "A Bed of Peas." *Truly Grim Tales.* New York: Delacorte Press, 1995, 36-59.
———. "A Taste of Beauty." *Truly Grim Tales.* New York: Delacorte Press, 1995, 97-106.

COLLECTIONS

Galloway, Patricia. *Truly Grim Tales.* New York: Delacorte Press, 1995.
Singer, Marilyn, comp. and ed. *Stay True: Short Stories for Girls.* New York: Scholastic, 1998.

Bibliography

Abel, Elizabeth. "Narrative Structure(s) and Female Development: The Case of Mrs. Dalloway." Abel, Hirsch, and Langland, 161–185.

Abel, Elizabeth, Marianne Hirsch, and Elizabeth Langland, eds. *The Voyage In: Fictions of Development.* Hanover, N.H.: University Press of New England, 1983.

Adelson, Joseph, and Margery J. Doehrman. "The Psychodynamic Approach to Adolescence." *Handbook of Adolescent Psychology.* Ed. Joseph Adelson. New York: Wiley, 1980.

Agee, Jane M. "Mothers and Daughters: Gender-Role Socialization in Two Newbery Award Books." *Children's Literature in Education* 24 (1993): 165–183.

American Association of University Women. *The AAUW Report: How Schools Shortchange Girls.* Washington, D.C.: AAUW, 1992.

Apter, Terri. *Altered Loves: Mothers and Daughters During Adolescence.* New York: St. Martin's Press, 1990.

Ashliman, D. L. *Snow White and Other Tales of Aarne Thompson Type 709.* 9 October 1999 <http://www.pitt.edu~dash/type 0709.html>.

Atkinson, Joan. "Portrayal of Parents." *Journal of Youth Services in Libraries* 1, no. 3 (1988): 310–322.

Bal, Mieke. *Narratology: Introduction to the Theory of Narrative.* Trans. Christine van Boheemen. 1985. Toronto, Canada: University of Toronto Press, 1992.

Bank, Barbara J., and Peter M. Hall. *Gender, Equity, and Schooling Policy and Practice.* New York: Garland, 1997.

Basile, Giambattista. *The Pentamerone of Giambattista Basile.* Trans. Benedetto Croce. Ed. N. M. Penzer. Vol.1. New York: Dutton; London: John Lane: The Bodley Head, 1932.

Baym, Nina. "The Madwoman and Her Languages: Why I Don't Do Feminist Literary Theory." Warhol and Herndl, 154–167.

Belenky, Mary Field, et al. *Women's Ways of Knowing: The Development of Self, Voice, and Mind.* New York: Basic, 1986.

Bell-Scott, Patricia, and Beverly Guy-Sheftall. Introduction. Bell-Scott et al., 1–3.

Bell-Scott, Patricia, et al., eds. *Double Stitch: Black Women Write About Mothers and Daughters.* New York: Harper, 1991.

Benjamin, Jessica. *The Bonds of Love: Psychoanalysis, Feminism, and the Problem of Domination.* New York: Pantheon, 1988.

Bettelheim, Bruno. *The Uses of Enchantment: The Meaning and Importance of Fairy Tales.* New York: Vintage, 1977.

Blos, Peter. "Modifications in the Traditional Psychoanalytic Theory of Female Adolescent Development." *Adolescent Psychiatry* 8. Chicago, Ill.: University of Chicago Press, 1980, 8–24.

————. *On Adolescence.* New York: Free Press, 1962.

————. "The Second Individuation Process of Adolescence." *The Psychoanalytic Study of the Child* 22 (1967): 162–186. Rpt. in *The Psychology of Adolescence: Essential Readings.* Ed. Aaron H. Esman. New York: International University Press, 1975, 156–176.

Bowlby, John. *Attachment.* Vol.1 of *Attachment and Loss.* 2nd ed. New York: Basic Books, 1982.

Braxton, Joanne M. *Black Women Writing Autobiography: A Tradition within a Tradition.* Philadelphia, Pa.: Temple University Press, 1989.

Brooks, Peter. *Reading for the Plot: Design and Invention in Narrative.* New York: Knopf, 1984.

Brown, Lyn Mikel, and Carol Gilligan. *Meeting at the Crossroads: Women's Psychology and Girls' Development.* Cambridge, Mass.: Harvard University Press, 1992.

Brown, Margaret E. "Whose Eyes Are These, Whose Nose?" *Newsweek*, 7 March 1994, 12.

Bruggen, Peter, and Charles O'Brian. *Surviving Adolescence: A Handbook for Adolescents and Their Parents.* London: Faber, 1986.

Caplan, Paula J. *Don't Blame Mother: Mending the Mother–Daughter Relationship.* New York: Harper, 1989.

Chatman, Seymour. *Coming to Terms: The Rhetoric of Narrative in Fiction and Film.* Ithaca, N.Y.: Cornell University Press, 1990.

Chernin, Kim. *The Hungry Self: Women, Eating, and Identity.* New York: Times Books, 1985.

Chira, Susan. "The Good Mother: New Realities in Conflict With Old Images." *The New York Times.* 4 October 1992, 32 (L).

Chodorow, Nancy J. *Feminism and Psychoanalytic Theory.* New Haven, Conn.: Yale University Press, 1989.

————. *The Reproduction of Mothering: Psychoanalysis and the Sociology of Gender.* Berkeley, Calif.: University of California Press, 1978.

Chodorow, Nancy J., with Susan Contratto. "The Fantasy of the Perfect Mother." Chodorow, *Feminism*, 79–96.

Christian-Smith, Linda K. *Becoming a Woman through Romance*. New York: Routledge, 1990.

Cixous, Helene. "The Laugh of the Medusa." *Signs* 1.4 (1975). Rpt. Warhol and Herndl, 334–349.

Claffey, Anne, et al. "Rapunzel's Revenge." *Rapunzel's Revenge: Fairy Tales for Feminists*. Dublin, Ireland: Attic, 1995, 36–41.

Cohan, Steven, and Linda M. Shires. *Telling Stories: A Theoretical Analysis of Narrative Fiction*. New York: Routledge, 1988.

Cole, Johnetta. "Preface." Bell-Scott et al., xiii–xiv.

Coleman, James S. *The Adolescent Society: The Social Life of the Teenager and Its Impact on Education*. New York: Free Press, 1961.

Collins, Patricia Hill. *Black Feminist Thought: Knowledge, Consciousness, and the Politics of Empowerment*. 1990. New York: Routledge, 1991.

————. "The Meaning of Motherhood in Black Culture and Black Mother–Daughter Relationships." Bell-Scott et al., 42–60.

Coward, Rosalind. *Female Desires: How They Are Sought, Bought and Packaged*. New York: Grove, 1985.

Cranny-Francis, Anne. *Feminist Fiction: Feminist Uses of Generic Fiction*. New York: St. Martin's Press, 1990.

Crew, Hilary S. "A Narrative Analysis of the Daughter–Mother Relationship in Selected Young Adult Novels." Diss. Rutgers, The State University of New Jersey. 1996.

————. "Feminist Theories and the Voices of Mothers and Daughters in Selected African-American Literature." *African-American Voices: Tradition, Transition, Transformation*. Ed. Karen Patricia Smith. Metuchan, N.J.: Scarecrow, 1994, 79–114.

————. "Making Connections across Differences: Multicultural Stories of the Daughter–Mother Relationship in Young Adult Novels." *VOYA* 20.3 (1997): 173–176.

Dally, Ann. *Inventing Motherhood: The Consequences of an Ideal*. New York: Schocken, 1983.

Dalsimer, Katherine. *Female Adolescence: Psychoanalytic Reflections on Works of Literature*. New Haven, Conn.: Yale University Press, 1986.

Davidson, Cathy N., and E. M. Broner, eds. *The Lost Tradition: Mothers and Daughters in Literature*. New York: Ungar, 1980.

Davis, Flora. *Moving the Mountain: The Women's Movement in America since 1960*. New York: Simon and Schuster, 1991.

DeBold, Elizabeth, Marie Wilson, and Idelisse Malave. *Mother Daughter Revolution: From Betrayal to Power*. New York: Addison-Wesley, 1993.

De La Force, Mlle. *Persinette*. "Der Herkunft des Grimmschen Rapunzel-marchens." By Max Luthi. *Fabula: Journal of Folktale Studies*. 3 Band, Heft 1/2. Walter De Gruyter: Berlin, 1959: 96–100.

DeMarr, Mary Jean, and Jane S. Bakerman. *The Adolescent in the American Novel since 1960.* New York: Ungar, 1986.

Deutsch, Helene. *The Psychology of Women: A Psychoanalytic Interpretation.* Vol.1. New York: Grune, 1944.

————. *Selected Problems of Adolescence: With Special Emphasis on Group Formation.* The Psychoanalytic Study of the Child 5. New York: International University Press, 1967.

Dodson, Shireen, with Teresa Barker. *The Mother–Daughter Book Club: How Ten Busy Mothers and Daughters Came Together to Talk, Laugh, and Learn Through Their Love of Reading.* New York: Perennial, 1997.

Donelson, Kenneth L., and Alleen Pace Nilsen. *Literature for Today's Young Adults.* 5th ed. New York: Longman, 1997.

Dorris, Michael. *A Yellow Raft in Blue Water.* New York: Holt, 1987.

Douglas, Susan J. *Where the Girls Are: Growing Up Female with the Mass Media.* New York: Times Books, 1994.

DuPlessis, Rachel Blau. *Writing Beyond the Ending: Narrative Strategies of Twentieth-Century Women Writers.* Bloomington: Indiana University Press, 1985.

Eagle, Carole J., and Carol Colman. *All That She Can Be: Helping Your Daughter Achieve Her Full Potential and Maintain Her Self-Esteem during the Critical Years of Adolescence.* New York: Simon and Schuster, 1993.

Elchoness, Monte. *Why Can't Anyone Hear Me?: A Guide For Surviving Adolescence.* 2nd ed. Selpulveda, Calif.: Monroe, 1989.

Elkind, David. *All Grown Up and No Place to Go: Teenagers in Crisis.* New York: Addison-Wesley, 1984.

Erikson, Erik. *Identity, Youth, and Crisis.* New York: Norton, 1968.

Erol, Sibel. "*Beyond the Divide*: Lasky's Feminist Revision of the Westward Journey." *Children's Literature Association Quarterly* 17 (1992): 5–8.

Eyer, Diane E. *MotherGuilt: How Our Culture Blames Mothers for What's Wrong with Society.* New York: Times Books, 1996.

————. *Mother–Infant Bonding: A Scientific Fiction.* New Haven, Conn.: Yale University Press, 1992.

Faludi, Susan. *Backlash: The Undeclared War against American Women.* 1991. New York: Anchor, 1992.

Farnham, Marynia. *Modern Women: The Lost Sex.* New York: Harper, 1947.

Ferguson, Mary Anne. "The Female Novel of Development and the Myth of Psyche." Abel, Hirsch, and Langland, 228–243.

Flax, Jane. "Mother–Daughter Relationships: Psychodynamics, Politics, and Philosophy." *The Future of Difference.* Ed. Hester Eisenstein and Alice Jardine. New Brunswick, N.J.: Rutgers University Press, 1985, 20–40.

————. *Thinking Fragments: Psychoanalysis, Feminism, and Postmodernism in the Contemporary West.* Berkeley, Calif.: University of California Press, 1990.

Forman, Jack. Rev. of *A Star for the Latecomer,* by Bonnie Zindel and Paul Zindel. *School Library Journal* 26.4 (1980): 129.

French, Fiona. *Snow White in New York*. Oxford, England: Oxford University Press, 1986.

Freud, Anna. "Adolescence." *The Psychoanalytic Study of the Child*. Vol. XIII. New York: International University Press, 1958, 255–278.

Freud, Sigmund. *Beyond the Pleasure Principle*. Trans. and ed. James Strachey. Rev. ed. New York: Liveright, 1961.

————. "Family Romances" (1909) [1908]." *The Standard Edition of the Complete Psychological Works of Sigmund Freud*. Vol. IX. London, England: Hogarth and The Institute of Psychoanalysis, 1959: 235–241.

————. "Femininity." *Introductory Lectures on Psychoanalysis*. Ed. and trans. James Strachey. New York: Norton, 1965, 112–135.

Friday, Nancy. *My Mother/My Self: The Daughter's Search for Identity*. New York: Dell, 1981.

Friedan, Betty. *The Second Stage*. New York: Summit, 1981.

Friedman, Susan Stanford. "Creativity and the Childbirth Metaphor: Gender Difference in Literary Discourse." *Feminist Studies* 13.1 (1975): 49–82. Rpt. Warhol and Herndl, 371–396.

Gardiner, Judith. "A Wake for Mother: The Maternal Deathbed in Women's Fiction." *Feminist Studies* 4 (1978): 146–165.

Gardner, James E. *The Turbulent Teens: Understanding, Helping, Surviving*. San Diego, Calif.: Oak, 1982.

Gerlach, Jeanne. "Mother Daughter Relationships in Lois Duncan's *Daughters of Eve*." *The ALAN Review* 19.1 (Fall 1991): 36–38.

Gilbert, Lucy, and Paula Webster. *Bound by Love: The Sweet Trap of Daughterhood*. Boston, Mass.: Beacon, 1982.

Gilligan, Carol. "Exit-Voice Dilemma in Adolescent Development." Gilligan et al., *Mapping*, 141–158.

————. *In a Different Voice: Psychological Theory and Women's Development*. Cambridge, Mass.: Harvard University Press, 1982.

————. "Preface." Gilligan, Lyons, and Hanmer, 6–29.

————. "Prologue." Gilligan, Lyons, and Hanmer, 1–5.

————. "Remapping the Moral Domain: New Images of Self in Relationship." Gilligan et al., *Mapping*, 3–19.

Gilligan, Carol, Annie Rogers, and Lyn Mikel Brown. "Epilogue: Soundings into Development." Gilligan, Lyons, and Hanmer, 314–334.

Gilligan, Carol, Nona P. Lyons, and Trudy J. Hanmer, eds. *Making Connections: The Relational Worlds of Adolescent Girls at Emma Willard School*. Cambridge, Mass.: Harvard University Press, 1990.

Gilligan, Carol, et al., eds. *Mapping the Moral Domain: A Contribution of Women's Thinking to Psychological Theory and Education*. Cambridge, Mass.: Harvard University Press, 1988.

Glickman, Rose L. *Daughters of Feminists*. New York: St. Martin's Press, 1993.

Goldberger, Nancy, et al., eds. *Knowledge, Difference, and Power: Essays Inspired by Women's Ways of Knowing*. New York: Basic Books, 1996.

Greenberg, Mark T., Judith M. Siegel, and Cynthia J. Leitch. "The Nature and Importance of Attachment Relationships to Parents and Peers during Adolescence." *Journal of Youth and Adolescence* 12.5 (1983): 373–385.

Greene, Gayle. *Changing the Story: Feminist Fiction and the Tradition.* Bloomington: Indiana University Press, 1991.

Grimm, Jacob Ludwig Karl. "Rapunzel." *Kinder und Hausmarchen Gesammelt Durch Die Bruder Grimm.* Berlin, Germany: Wilhelm Hertz, 1899.

Grimm, Jacob, and Wilhelm Grimm. *The Complete Fairy Tales of the Brothers Grimm.* Trans. with an Intro. by Jack Zipes. New York: Bantam, 1992.

———. *Grimm's Tales for Young and Old.* Trans. Ralph Manheim. New York: Doubleday, 1997.

———. *The Juniper Tree and Other Tales from Grimm.* Trans. Lore Segal and Randall Jarrett. New York: Farrar, Straus and Giroux, 1973.

Griswold, Jerry. *Audacious Kids: Coming of Age in America's Children's Classic Children's Books.* New York: Oxford University Press, 1992.

Hall, G. Stanley. *Adolescence.* 1904. 2 Vols. Reprint ed. New York: Arno, 1969.

Hammer, Signe. *Daughters and Mothers, Mothers and Daughters.* New York: Quadrangle, 1975.

Hancock, Emily. *The Girl Within.* New York: Fawcett, 1989.

Havighurst, Robert. *Developmental Tasks and Education.* New York: D. McKay, 1972.

Haviland, Virginia. *Favorite Fairy Tales Told in Germany: Retold from the Brothers Grimm.* Boston, Mass.: Little, Brown, 1959.

Havris, Kathryn. Rev. of *Someone's Mother Is Missing,* by Harry Mazer. *School Library Journal* 36.9 (1990): 255–256.

Hernandez, Jo Ann Yolanda. *White Bread Competition.* Houston, Tex.: Pinata, 1997.

Hill-Lubin, Mildred. "'Tell Me, Nana:' The Image of the Grandmother in the Works of Ama Ata Aido." *Sage* V.1 (1988): 37–42.

Hirsch, Marianne. *The Mother/Daughter Plot: Narrative, Psychoanalysis, Feminism.* Bloomington: Indiana University Press, 1989.

Hite, Molly. *The Other Side of the Story: Structures and Strategies of Contemporary Feminist Narrative.* Ithaca, N.Y.: Cornell University Press, 1989.

Hite, Shere. "The Secrets Mothers Keep." *New Woman.* June 1995, 96–99.

Homans, Margaret. *Bearing the Word: Language and Female Experience in Nineteenth-Century Women's Writing.* Chicago: University of Chicago Press, 1986.

hooks, bell. *Talking Back: Thinking Feminist, Thinking Black.* Boston, Mass.: South End Press, 1989.

Hurmence, Belinda, ed. *My Folks Don't Want Me to Talk about Slavery: Twenty-One Oral Histories of Former North Carolina Slaves.* New York: Cornell University Press, 1985.

Hussain, Freda, ed. *Muslim Women.* New York: St. Martin's Press, 1984.

Irigaray, Luce. "And the One Doesn't Stir Without the Other," *Signs: Journal of Women in Culture and Society* 7.1 (1981): 63.

———. *The Irigaray Reader*. Ed. and with an Intro. by Margaret Whitford. Cambridge, Mass.: Blackwell, 1991.

———. *This Sex Which Is Not One*. Trans. by Catherine Porter with Carolyn Burke. Ithaca, N.Y.: Cornell University Press, 1985.

Jacobs, Harriet. *Incidents in the Life of a Slave Girl*. New York: Oxford University Press, 1988.

Jones, Ann Rosalind. "Writing the Body: Toward an Understanding of l'Écriture féminine." *The New Feminist Criticism: Essays on Women, Literature, and Theory*. Ed. Elaine Showalter. New York: Pantheon, 1985, 361–377.

Joseph, Gloria I. "Black Mothers and Daughters: Their Roles and Function in American Society." Joseph and Lewis, 75–126.

———. "Black Mothers and Daughters: Traditional and New Perspectives." Bell-Scott et al., 94–106.

Joseph, Gloria I., and Jill Lewis. *Common Differences: Conflicts in Black and White Feminist Perspectives*. Boston, Mass.: South End Press, 1986.

Josselson, Ruthellen. "Ego Development in Adolescence." *Handbook of Adolescent Psychology*. Ed. Joseph Adelson. New York: Wiley, 1980, 188–210.

Junko, Yoshida. "Mother–Daughter Stories in Japan." *Bookbird* 35.2 (1997): 6–11.

Kaplan, Louise J. *Adolescence: The Farewell to Childhood*. New York: Simon and Schuster, 1984.

Kerber, Linda K., et al. "On *In A Different Voice*: An Interdisciplinary Forum." *Signs: Journal of Women in Culture and Society* 11 (1986): 304–333.

Kertzer, Adrienne. "Reclaiming Her Maternal Pre-text: Little Red Riding Hood's Mother and Three Young Adult Novels." *Children's Literature Association Quarterly* 21 (Spring 1996): 20–27.

Kertzer, Adrienne. "This Quiet Lady: Maternal Voices and the Picture Book." *Children's Literature Association Quarterly* 18.4 (1993-1994): 159–164.

Kiell, Norman. *The Universal Experience of Adolescence*. New York: International University Press, 1964.

Kincaid, Jamaica. *Annie John*. New York: Farrar, Straus and Giroux, 1983.

Kingsolver, Barbara. *The Bean Trees*. New York: Harper Perennial, 1989.

Klein, David, and Marymae E. Klein. *Your Parents and Yourself*. New York: Charles Scribner's Sons, 1986.

Kolodny, Robert C., et al. *How to Survive Your Adolescents' Adolescence*. Boston, Mass.: Little, Brown, 1984.

Kristeva, Julia. "About Chinese Women." *The Kristeva Reader*, 138–159.

———. *Desire in Language: A Semiotic Approach to Literature and Art*. New York: Columbia University Press, 1980.

———. *The Kristeva Reader*. Ed. Toril Moi. New York: Columbia University Press, 1986.

———. "Stabat Mater." *The Kristeva Reader*, 160–186.

———. "Women's Time." *The Kristeva Reader*, 186–213.

Kroger, Jane. *Identity in Adolescence: The Balance between Self and Other.* New York: Routledge, 1989.

Lacan, Jacques. "The Mirror Stage." *Critical Theory Since 1965.* Ed. Hazard Adams and Leroy Searle. Tallahassee: Florida State University Press, 1986, 734–738.

Lanser, Susan S. "Toward a Feminist Narratology." *Style* 20.3 (1986). Rpt. Warhol and Herndl, 610–629.

Lewis, Mary K. "Loss of Voice in Women's Coming of Age Stories." Vandergrift, *Mosaics,* 67–89.

Lorber, Judith, et al. "On the *Reproduction of Mothering*: A Methodological Debate." *Signs* 6.3 (1981): 482–513.

Lowinsky, Naomi Ruth. *Stories from the Motherline: Reclaiming the Mother–Daughter Bind, Finding Our Feminine Souls.* Los Angeles, Calif.: Tarcher, 1992.

Luthi, Max. "Der Herkunft des Grimmschen Rapunzelmarchens." *Fabula: Journal of Folktale Studies.* 3 Band, Heft 1/2. Walter De Gruyter: Berlin, 1959, 95–118.

Mahler, Margaret. "Thoughts About Development and Individuation." *The Psychoanalytic Study of the Child.* Vol. XVIII. New York: International University Press, 1963: 307–324.

Maxwell, Rhoda J. *Images of Mothers in Literature for Young Adults.* New York: Lang, 1994.

Miller, Jean Baker. *Toward a New Psychology of Women.* 2nd ed. Boston, Mass.: Beacon, 1986.

Mitchell, J., and J. Rose, eds. *Feminine Sexuality: Jacques Lacan and the école freudienne.* New York: Norton, 1982.

Mori, Kyoko. *The Dream of Water: A Memoir.* New York: Holt, 1995.

———. "Landscapes." In "A Nation of Immigrants: Are We Us òr Them?" Garza de Cortes, Oralia, et al. *Journal of Youth Services in Libraries* 9.2 (1996): 135–139.

Nadeau, Frances A. "The Mother/Daughter Relationship in Young Adult Fiction." *The ALAN Review* 22.2 (1995): 14–17.

Napoli, Donna Jo. *The Magic Circle.* New York: Dutton, 1993.

Natov, Roni. "Mothers and Daughters: Jamaica Kincaid's Pre-Oedipal Narrative." *Annual of the Modern Language Association Division on Children's and The Children's Literature Association* 18 (1990): 1–16.

Nilsen, Alleen Pace, and Kenneth L. Donelson. *Literature for Today's Young Adults.* 4th ed. New York: HarperCollins, 1993.

"Oh Mom, What Am I Made Of?: A Daughter/Woman." Vandergrift, *Mosaics,* 91–101.

Orenstein, Peggy with The American Association of University Women. *SchoolGirls: Young Women, Self-Esteem, and the Confidence Gap.* 1994. New York: Anchor, 1995.

Palmer, Paulina. *Contemporary Women's Fiction: Narrative Practice and Feminist Theory.* New York: Harvester, 1989.

Payne, Karen. *Letters between Ourselves: Letters Between Mothers and Daughters 1750-1982.* Boston, Mass.: Houghton Mifflin, 1983.

Perlman, Mickey, ed. *Mother Puzzles: Daughters and Mothers in Contemporary American Literature.* New York: Greenwood, 1989.

Philbrook, John. Rev. of *Shizuko's Daughter*, by Kyoto Mori. *School Library Journal* 39. 6 (1993): 132.

Pipher, Mary. *Reviving Orphelia: Saving the Selves of Adolescent Girls.* New York: Ballantine, 1995.

Polster, Miriam F. *Eve's Daughters: The Forbidden Heroism of Women.* San Francisco, Calif.: Jossey-Bass, 1992.

Rabinovici, Schoschana. *Thanks to My Mother.* New York: Dial, 1998.

Rabinowitz, Peter J. *Before Reading: Narrative Conventions and the Politics of Interpretation.* Ithaca, N.Y.: Cornell University Press, 1987.

Rich, Adrienne. *Of Woman Born: Motherhood as Experience and Institution.* 1976. New York: Norton, 1986.

Rich, Sharon. "Daughters' Views of their Relationships with Their Mothers." Gilligan, Lyons, and Hanmer, 258–273.

Ross, Catherine, "Young Adult Realism: Conventions, Narrators, and Readers." *Library Quarterly* 55. 2 (1985): 174–191.

Rothchild, Ellen. "Female Power: Lines to Development of Autonomy in Adolescent Girls." *Female Adolescent Development.* Ed. Max Sugar. New York: Brunner, 1979, 274–29.

Ruddick, Sara. *Maternal Thinking: Toward a Politics of Peace.* New York: Ballantine, 1990.

Sadker, Myra, and David Sadker. *Failing at Fairness: How America's Schools Cheat Girls.* New York: Charles Scribner's Sons, 1994.

Sanders, Dori. *Clover.* New York: Fawcett Columbine, 1991.

Scheper-Hughes, Nancy. *Death without Weeping: The Violence of Everyday Life in Brazil.* Berkeley, Calif.: University of California Press, 1992.

Schulz, Friedrich. *Rapunzel.* "Der Herkunft des Grimmschen Rapunzelmarchens." By Max Luthi. *Fabula: Journal of Folktale Studies.* 3 Band, Heft 1/2. Walter De Gruyter: Berlin, 1959, 100–103.

Secunda, Victoria. *When You and Your Mother Can't Be Friends: Resolving The Most Complicated Relationship of Your Life.* New York: Delta, 1990.

Shange, Ntozake. *Betsey Brown.* New York: St. Martin's Press, 1985.

Showalter, Elaine. "Feminist Criticism in the Wilderness." *The New Feminist Criticism: Essays on Women, Literature and Theory.* Ed. by Elaine Showalter. New York: Pantheon, 1985, 243–270.

Small, Robert C. "The Literary Value of the Young Adult Novel." *Journal of Youth Services in Libraries* 5 (1992): 277–285.

Smith, Sidonie. *A Poetics of Women's Autobiography: Marginality and the Fictions of Self-Representation.* Bloomington: Indiana University Press, 1987.

Smith, Valerie. "Introduction." *Incidents in the Life of a Slave Girl: Harriet Jacobs.* By Harriet Jacobs. New York: Oxford University Press, 1988, xxvii–xl.

Sommers, Christina Hoff. *Who Stole Feminism: How Women Have Betrayed Women.* New York: Simon and Schuster, 1994.

Sprengnether, Madelon. *The Spectral Mother: Freud, Feminism, and Psychoanalysis.* Ithaca, N.Y.: Cornell University Press, 1990.

Stanek, Lou Willett. "Growing Up Female: The Literary Gaps." *Media and Methods* 13 (Sept. 1976): 46–48. Rpt. in *Young Adult Literature: Background and Criticism.* Comp. by Millicent Lenz and Ramona Mahood. Chicago: American Library Association, 1980. 232–237.

Staples, Suzanne Fisher. "A Question of Culture." *Signal* XX . 3 (Summer 1996): 27–30.

———. "Writing About the Islamic World: An American Author's Thoughts on Authenticity." *Bookbird* 35.3 (Fall 1997): 17–20.

Stephens, John. *Language and Ideology in Children's Fiction.* New York: Longman, 1992.

Sutherland, Zena, ed. Rev. of *Claudia, Where Are You?*, by Hila Colman. *The Best in Children's Books: The University of Chicago Guide to Children's Literature, 1966-1972.* Chicago: University of Chicago Press, 1973, 84.

———. Rev. of *Second Star to the Right,* by Deborah Hautzig. *The Best in Children's Books: The University of Chicago Guide to Children's Literature, 1979-1984.* Chicago: University of Chicago Press, 1986, 182.

Tan, Amy. *The Joy Luck Club.* New York: Putnam, 1989.

Tatar, Maria. *The Hard Facts of the Grimm's Fairy Tales.* Princeton, N.J.: Princeton University Press, 1987.

Taylor, Jill McLean, Carol Gilligan, and Amy M. Sullivan. *Between Voice and Silence: Women and Girls, Race, and Relationship.* Cambridge, Mass.: Harvard University Press, 1995.

Thurer, Shari L. *The Myths of Motherhood: How Culture Reinvents the Good Mother.* Boston, Mass.: Houghton Mifflin, 1994.

Trites, Roberta Seelinger. *Waking Sleeping Beauty: Feminist Voices in Children's Novels.* Iowa City: University of Iowa Press, 1997.

Turk, Blossom M. *Living with Teens and Enjoying Them Too!* Boise, Idaho: Legendary, 1990.

Tyler, Lisa. "Food, Femininity, and Achievement: The Mother–Daughter Relationship in *National Velvet.*" *Children's Literature Association Quarterly* 18.4 (1993-1994): 154–158.

Vandergrift, Kay E. *Child and Story: The Literary Connection.* New York: Neal-Schuman, 1986.

———. Exploring the Concept of Contextual Void: A Preliminary Analysis." *Library Education and Leadership: Essays in Honor of Jane Anne Hannigan.* Eds. Sheila S. Intner and Kay E. Vandergrift. Metuchen, N.J.: Scarecrow Press, 1990, 349–363.

———. "A Feminist Perspective on Multicultural Children's Literature in the Middle Years of the Twentieth Century." *Library Trends* 41 (1993): 354–377.

————. "A Feminist Research Agenda in Children's Literature." *Wilson Library Bulletin* 68.2 (1993): 23–27.

————. "Journey or Destination: Female Voices in Youth Literature." Vandergrift, *Mosaics,* 17–46.

————. *Snow White.* 9 Oct. 1999 <http:www.scils.rutgers.edu/special/kay/snowwhite.html>

Vandergrift, Kay E., ed. *Mosaics Of Meaning: Enhancing the Intellectual Life of Young Adults Through Story.* Lanham, Md.: Scarecrow Press, 1996.

Velde, Vivian Vande. *Tales from the Brothers Grimm and the Sisters Weird.* New York: Harcourt, 1995.

Walker, Alice. *In Search of Our Mothers' Gardens.* San Diego, Calif.: Harcourt, 1983.

Walters, Suzanne Danuta. *Lives Together/Worlds Apart: Mothers and Daughters in Popular Culture.* Berkeley, Calif.: University of California Press, 1992.

Ward, Janie. "Racial Identity Formation and Transformation." Gilligan, Lyons, and Hanmer, 215–232.

Warhol, Robyn R., and Diane Price Herndl, eds. *Feminisms: An Anthology of Literary Theory and Criticism.* New Brunswick, N.J.: Rutgers University Press, 1991.

Warner, Mariner. *From the Beast to the Blonde: On Fairy Tales and Their Tellers.* New York: Farrar, Straus and Giroux, 1994.

White, Barbara. *Growing Up Female: Adolescent Girlhood in American Fiction.* Westport, Conn.: Greenwood, 1985.

Willard, Ann. "Cultural Scripts for Mothering." Gilligan et al., *Mapping,* 225–243.

Winnicott, D. W. *Playing and Reality.* New York: Basic Books, 1971.

Witham, W. Tasker. *The Adolescent in the American Novel, 1920-1960.* New York: Ungar, 1964.

Wolf, Naomi. *The Beauty Myth: How Images of Beauty Are Used Against Women.* New York: Morrow, 1991.

Yep, Laurence. *Child of the Owl.* New York: HarperCollins, 1977.

Youniss, James, and Jacqueline Smoller. *Adolescent Relations with Mothers, Fathers, and Friends.* Chicago: University of Chicago Press, 1985.

Zaheva, Irene, ed. *My Mother's Daughter: Stories by Women.* Freedom, Calif.: Crossing, 1991.

Zipes, Jack. "Once There Were Two Brothers Named Grimm." Grimm, Jacob, and Wilhelm Grimm. *The Complete Fairy Tales,* xvii–xxxi.

Index

Freeman, Suzanne, 133
French, Fiona, 48, 53n19
Freud, Anna, 56, 59
Freud, Sigmund, 3, 77, 85, 120n6,
145n13, 188n4, 244
Friday, Nancy, 109
Friedan, Betty, 163

Galloway, Priscilla, 27, 33, 37, 42–43,
48–50, 258
Gardiner, Judith, 97n18
Geras, Adele, 31, 33, 37, 43–48, 50,
53n21, 258
Gerber, Merrill Joan, 110–11, 114,
115, 116
Gerson, Corinne, 152, 155–57, 158
Gilligan, Carol, 1, 3, 4, 62–63, 75n17,
78, 103, 105, 109, 115, 116, 140,
191, 192, 239, 256
Girl Named Disaster, A, 323–36, 257
Girl Within, The, 56
Glickman, Rose L., 8, 159
Goldberger, Nancy, 12n10
grandmother daughter-mother
relationship, 169–89, 252; bonds,
182–88, 224, 233; conflict, 175–
77; cross-cultural, 196–97, 211–
12, 233–35; scripts of, 171–73,
181–82. *See also* mother-
daughter relationship
Greenberg, Jan, 99, 112–13, 115, 151
Greene, Bette, 106, 107–8, 109
Grimm Brothers, 31, 32, 33, 36
Grimm, Jacob Ludwig Karl and
Wilhelm, 37
Griswold, Jerry, 97n16
Guy-Sheftall, Beverly, 212

H. My Name Is Henley, 84, 86, 149,
151
Hall, G. Stanley, 74n10
Hall, Lynn, 58–59, 127–28, 170, 239,
240–41
Hamilton, Virginia, 7, 215, 216–20,
228, 236, 257

Hammer, Signe, 75n27
Hancock, Emily, 56, 172, 213n11
Handful of Time, A, 179–80
Hangin' Out with Cici, 171–72
Hannah in Between, 23, 150
*Hard Facts of the Grimm's Fairy
Tales, The*, 37
Harvard Project on Women's
Psychology and Girls' Develop-
ment, The, 3, 9
Hathorn, Libby, 94, 134, 137–38
Hautzig, Deborah, 61–62
Haveli, 199, 205
Havighurst, Robert, 259n9
Hernandez, Jo Ann Yolanda, 257
Hill-Lubin, Mildred, 237n19
Hirsch, Marianne, 6, 24, 28, 87,
97n21, 106, 131, 241, 247
Hite, Molly, 23–24, 124
Hite, Shere, 111
Holl, Kristi D., 152, 155–56, 157, 158
Holland, Isabelle, 80, 94, 135–36
Holt, Kimberly Willis, 239, 252–54
Homans, Margaret, 209, 213n14,
237n10
Honeycutt, Natalie, 22–23, 165–66
hooks, bell, 232
House for Jonnie O, A, 102, 103, 131–
32, 142
*How I Put My Mother Through
College*, 152
Hunter, Kristin, 237n5n7
Hurmence, Belinda, 223, 258

I Hadn't Meant to Tell You This, 7,
27, 215, 231, 257
I'm Still Me, 132, 142, 144
In a Different Voice, 4
Incidents in the Life of a Slave Girl,
223, 258
Ingold, Jeanette, 183
Irigaray, Luce, 5, 75n25, 86, 160,
182, 240, 256
Irwin, Hadley, 110, 173, 181, 182

About the Author

Hilary S. Crew is an assistant professor, Department of Communication Sciences and Educational Services, Kean University, with an M.L.S. and Ph.D. from the School of Communication, Information, and Library Studies at Rutgers, The State University of New Jersey. She is Graduate Coordinator of the Master of Arts Educational Media Specialist Program. She has a chapter on mother–daughter relationships in *African-American Voices* in *Young Adult Literature: Tradition, Transition, Transformation* (Scarecrow Press, 1994) and a chapter on the representation of heroines in historical novels in *Mosaics of Meaning: Enhancing the Intellectual Life of Young Adults Through Story* (Scarecrow Press, 1996). She has written several articles including "Feminist Scholarship and Theories of Adolescent Development: Implications for Young Adult Services in Libraries" (*Journal of Youth Services in Libraries*, Summer 1997) and "Transforming the Hidden Curriculum: Gender and the Library Media Center" (*Knowledge Quest*, May/June 1998).